Tony Aspler

Vintage Canada

To Bruce :
with best wishes
Tony Aspler.

Prentice-Hall Canada Inc., Scarborough, Ontario

*This book is dedicated to all those who raise a glass
and have found pleasure in Canadian wines . . . and to those
who have yet to discover them.*

Canadian Cataloguing in Publication Data

Aspler, Tony, 1939-
   Vintage Canada

Bibliography: p.
Includes index.
ISBN 0-13-942111-4

1. Wine and wine making—Canada—History.   2. Wine
lists—Canada.   I. Title.

TP559.C3A86   641.2′22′0971   C83-098672-3

Prentice-Hall, Inc., Englewood Cliffs, New Jersey
Prentice-Hall International, Inc., London
Prentice-Hall of Australia, Pty., Ltd., Sydney
Prentice-Hall of India Pvt., Ltd., New Delhi
Prentice-Hall of Japan Inc., Tokyo
Prentice-Hall of Southeast Asia (PTE.) Ltd. Singapore
Editora Prentice–Hall do Brasil Ltda., Rio de Janeiro

ISBN 0-13-942111-4

Production Editor: Linda Findlay
Design: Steven Boyle
Production: Alan Terakawa
Cover Photograph: Ken Bell

Composition: CompuScreen Typesetting Ltd.

1   2   3   4   5   6   88   87   86   85   84   83

Printed and bound in Canada

Contents

Acknowledgments

No one can write a wine book alone. Every author is largely dependent on the collective wisdom of winemakers past and present and the generosity of an industry renowned for its readiness to share its products and its expertise with you. In writing this book and compiling tasting notes on Canadian wines I have travelled from Nova Scotia to British Columbia and everywhere I stopped to visit a winery, a farm, a company or a research facility, I was welcomed with warmth and interest. The list of people in the trade—winemakers, company executives, grape growers, Liquor Board personnel, government researchers, and my fellow wine writers—is too long to acknowledge in full here, but I thank you all for your kindness and cooperation nonetheless.

However, I would like to single out Sheila Kennedy of the Ontario Editorial Bureau who not only gave me my title on one of our many trips down to the Niagara Peninsula, but arranged tastings and coordinated winery visits for me. And also my wife, Brenda, who typed the manuscript, made many insightful suggestions, tasted the wines with me and never grumbled about the growing forest of bottles on the kitchen cabinet; and my children, Annabel and Guy, who watched the mammoth tastings with a mixture of awe, curiosity and amusement.

Vintage Canada

Introduction

*"I find that the public generally prefer native wines after
they have begun to use them."*

*(William Haskins, a Hamilton winemaker, in a report to the
Ontario Agricultural Committee, 1880.)*

In 1965 a group of twenty French officers from the International Police
Association were visiting Toronto. While being shown around a local
station they were much intrigued by a large cell area known as the "drunk
tank". Through an interpreter they asked why there were so many men
inside. The station sergeant replied that they had been found inebriated in a
public place.

The French police went into a huddle and asked the interpreter to inform
their host that they thought it was a terrible thing to lock people up for
drinking. As they left they passed the liquor cabinet where all the confiscated
alcohol was kept. One of the French policemen grabbed half a bottle of 75-
cent Ontario wine and took a sip. He handed it round to his compatriots who
immediately proceeded to huddle again. After an animated discussion they
instructed the interpreter to pass on the message: "Anyone who drinks this
stuff *ought* to be locked up!"*

Apart from a few table wines made from hybrid grapes, Canadian wines
in 1965 were virtually all sherries and ports, sweet as candy and highly
alcoholic. They attracted the trade of people—to use George Bain's felicitous
phrase—"who did much of their social drinking in doorways". In the late
1960s the table wine boom happened and the nation's wineries switched
gears to satisfy the taste for drier, less heady products. The Canadian wine
industry—or, to be more precise, the Ontario and BC industries—has made
monumental strides since those days but it still has some way to go. Witness
this excerpt from the respected French food and wine magazine, *Gault-
Millau* (July, 1982). Under the headline "Canadian Diplomacy in Danger" the
item reads:

> "Great news! The Canadian government has decided to serve Canadian wines
> at all official receptions in its embassies and diplomatic missions throughout the

---

*I am indebted to Alex Eberspaecher, policeman turned wine writer, for that
eyewitness account.

world, a decision which will not be without consequences for the Canadian economy. In the first place it will provide an excellent opportunity for Ontario's wine producers to unload a few bottles of wine without actually having to consult the consumers. Secondly, the notorious spongers, always abundantly in evidence at diplomatic functions, will not need much persuading to go off and try the festivities of the Italians and the French, which will have a very salutary effect on the Federal government's budget in these times of restriction."°

This kind of satiric posturing by the French is very much in keeping with the chauvinism that motivates all winemakers. The Californians damn the wines of New York State. The Germans have little good to say about the Austrian products. The Italians denigrate the Swiss. The French dismiss everybody and even within that country there are factional rivalries: the Bordelais disparage the Burgundians and they both turn up their noses at the Rhône. Only in Canada is it a national pastime for everyone to dump on all our domestic wines and to drink instead any cheap European import as long as the label looks foreign and the name is unpronounceable.

Today the Canadian wine industry is on the verge of producing products in the blended table wine range that can stand up against those from any wine-producing country in the world. Canada may never produce a Château Lafite, a Richebourg or a Hermitage, but a fine white Chardonnay or Johannisberg Riesling is certainly within reach—as well as wines that have nothing to do with a European taste tradition, like Seyval Blanc, Vidal, Baco Noir and Maréchal Foch. Given our climate and the delicacy of the vines which produce the noble wines of Europe we can only hope that through clonal selection the wineries can find varieties sturdy enough to withstand winter cold and fungal diseases and, equally important, to find the right soil and microclimate in which to plant them.

Ultimately it all comes down to the quality of the raw material. To make good wine you have to start with a good grape. There are 8,000-odd grape varieties grown around the world and currently 45 of these are being commercially grown in Ontario. Bad winemaking technique can spoil good grapes but all the knowhow in the world won't make Château Mouton-Rothschild out of Concord grapes. It is only in the last fifteen years that the industry as a whole has accepted the need for better grape varieties and urged growers to plant them.

The quality of Canadian wines up until the early 1960s was inhibited by the vines in the ground. To understand why the products tasted the way they did

---

°While it is not a regulation that Canadian embassies serve our wine at official functions, the idea was suggested in a letter from the Department of External Affairs (prompted by the Canadian Wine Institute). Minister of Agriculture, Eugene Whalen, tells the story that when the American secretary of Agriculture was dining in Ottawa in 1976 he was served Canadian wines. After three glasses he looked at the bottle and said to Whalen, "You didn't dare!" The Minister replied, "But I did and you didn't know."

for so long, you have to look at the grapes. The first tentative commercial winemaking activity in Canada, during the early years of the nineteenth century, relied upon vines propogated from cuttings of Vitis labrusca. This species, like Vitis riparia, grew wild along the river banks of the eastern United States and Canada. The problem was that labrusca grapes have a heavy "foxy" odour and taste which may be acceptable in grape juice and food flavouring but not in wine. As a wine grape, it may not taste good but very little can be done to stop it from growing or to kill it. Like death and taxes, the Concord grape is still with us. Disease resistant and winter hardy, without doubt it's the farmer's friend—but not the wine lover's.

Also in this category are varieties whose names will no doubt be familiar to those whose wine-drinking days started before the Second World War: Catawba, Delaware, Isabella, Agawam, Niagara and Dutchess. In the 1930s a whole range of bogus, European-sounding products were made from these grapes including "Champagne", "Sauternes", "Burgundy" and "Claret". French hybridizers, many of whose names have been perpetuated in the successful crossings they achieved, created new varieties in the early part of this century by marrying North American non-labrusca cultivars with European viniferas. The object was to create a strain that had the finesse and flavour of European wine grapes and the rugged staying power of the native North American vine. The best known names are Baco, Ravat, Seibel, Landot, Vidal and Seyve-Villard.

These French hybrids were introduced into Canada by Brights in the spring of 1946 along with the first plantings of European vinifera vines, such as Chardonnay, Riesling, Pinot Noir and Perle de Csaba. Vitis vinifera is the generic name for such noble grapes as Chardonnay (from which is made white Burgundy, Chablis and Blanc de Blancs champagne), Pinot Noir (red Burgundy), Riesling (the grape of the Rhine Valley), Gamay (Beaujolais) and Merlot (a Bordeaux grape).

The Canadian wine industry is based on these three grape types: 25% are vinifera, mainly imported from the United States and Europe; 40% are vinifera hybrids; and 25% are labrusca. Ontario imports 15% vinifera; BC over 50%, while non grape-growing provinces buy in practically all vinifera from abroad. The industry as a whole sells approximately 20,000,000 gallons of Canadian wine, 25% of which is based on the labrusca grape.

As Canadian consumers have become more sophisticated in their wine tastes the demand for European products has increased. The first real impact of French, Italian, German and Austrian wines on the marketplace occurred in 1964. The upward curve of these wines over the years—to a point where they now outsell the cheaper domestic products—can be interpreted in two ways. Either the wineries across the country are just not providing wines of a quality to compete with European blends, or the Canadian consumer is drinking the label and not the product. Certainly, there is snob value in serving an imported wine over its Canadian counterpart. The wineries are all too aware of this knee-jerk social reaction and, with the current fad for Rhine-style whites, they have designed their labels with German gothic script, and christened them with such names as Schloss Laderheim, LiebesHeim and Hochtaler in an attempt to garner some cachet (and cash) for themselves.

Ed Arnold, President of Brights House of Wine, sums up the difficulty facing the Canadian industry when he looks at the variety of wines available to consumers on Liquor Board shelves. "We compete with the world. If you bought a different bottle of wine every day, you wouldn't repeat yourself for three years. No other wine-producing country has to compete with so many other countries." That is true; there are over 1,200 different brands of wine available at the Liquor Control Board of Ontario stores, (as opposed to 122 whiskies of all kinds.) And in order to compete with the world the big Canadian companies crush as many as eight or ten different types of grape to make eight times that number of products. In Europe each region grows the grape best suited to its soil and produces one or two wines.

In an effort to make wine drinkers take a second look at the products put out by the domestic industry, Chateau-Gai ran an advertising campaign in 1978 based on the theme, "We can change your mind". The company actively wanted the public to associate its product, Alpenweiss, with German wines. To make the label look more "foreign" the Chateau-Gai name appeared in tiny print on the bottom. The idea was that by creating a wine which resembled Black Tower, and dressing it up in everything but lederhosen, the company could make the consumer feel differently about Canadian products. Chateau-Gai and Calona in BC started that particular ball rolling and now every other commercial winery is running with it. (But at least this is a few steps up from the "come-alive-for-a-dollar-five" image of Canadian wines.)

The truth of the matter is that there is no such thing as a Canadian wine. There are wineries in seven provinces but the only product that tastes the same across the country is Brights President Champagne. What we have is a provincially-dominated industry in which each government sets the regulations as to what wines can be imported for blending and how much can be in any one blend. Ontario's regulations, thanks to a determined lobby by the grape growers of Niagara, are the most stringent. Non grape-growing provinces like New Brunswick and Manitoba have virtually no controls on the importation of juice to make wine. In Quebec there may soon be the extraordinary situation of eleven wineries competing against imports and the Quebec Liquor Board, by bottling finished wines from abroad, if the legislation currently promised is passed. The SAQ (la Société des Alcools du Québec), as it is known in Quebec, is very much part of the wine business as the largest single bottler of French wines in the world. And, meanwhile, British Columbia, behind the Rockies, goes its own way: as long as BC wineries buy up the entire crop of grapes they can bring in as much California juice or wine as they like. The result is that a national brand like Alpenweiss, the semi-dry German-style white wine, has several different taste profiles across the country according to where it is made. In BC the blend contains

Californian Muscat, while Alberta uses more Riesling than Ontario. And if a Vancouverite whose favourite wine was Schloss Laderheim moved to Toronto and ordered the same product he might think the waiter had given him the wrong wine! It is hoped that this state of affairs will be obviated when the newly drafted federal wine standards drawn up by the Canadian Wine Institute are accepted by the industry.

Not only are the regulations about winemaking different across the country, but so, too, are the mark-up policies by which governments create vast revenues and can—in grape-growing provinces—protect the local industry against extra-provincial and international competition. Both BC and Ontario have higher mark-ups for each other's wines than their own locally made products. (An Ontario wine entering BC is marked up at 110%, the same as a French or German wine would be; a BC wine coming to Ontario carries an 85% mark-up and a 25-cent per bottle handling charge.) So much for federalism. At the time of writing, this levying of tax on products sold between provinces was the subject of a legal action in Ontario which challenged the constitutionality of provincial mark-ups. But perhaps the most bizarre situation exists in the Northwest Territories. In every other province foreign imports are marked up higher than wines made in Canada—or at least at the same level—except in NWT. There, imported table wines carry 110% tax and Canadian products 150%. For fortified wines the ratio is 150% to 200%.

Only in the last twenty years has Canada become what could be called a wine-drinking nation. Per capita we consume 9.4 litres a year, slightly more than the United States. But we are well behind the French and the Portuguese who knock back 90 and 88 litres a head respectively, while the Italians drink 74 litres each. (France and Italy lose in evaporation each year more wine than is made by all Canadian wineries.) And if we were to switch our allegiance to domestic products and forego foreign imports the companies could not meet consumer demands. Roughly 60% of all wines made in Canada come from the Niagara Peninsula area of Ontario where most of the country's grapes are grown. The land is for the most part flat and fertile with sufficient rainfall. By contrast, Canada's other major grape area—the Okanagan Valley of British Columbia—is arid sagebrush desert with granite mountains and pine trees encompassing the vineyards. Most of the vines are grown on the steep valley slopes and have to be irrigated with lake water.

From these two provinces come the grapes; the wines themselves can bear the labels of Truro, Nova Scotia, St. Hyacinthe, Quebec or Scoudouc, New Brunswick—wherever a winery can be licenced to set up its operations. And exactly how much water goes into them or how much California blending wine is a secret jealously guarded by the winemaker and the company executives.

But to understand the Canadian wine industry, how it functions and why it produces the wines it does we have to go back to the beginning.

one

In the Beginning

*"A bunch of grapes is beautiful, static and innocent. It is
merely a fruit. But when it is crushed it becomes an animal,
for the crushed grapes become wine and wine has an
animal life."*

(*William Younger*, Gods, Men and Wine)

Winemaking is the world's second oldest profession. According to a
Persian legend it was a woman who first discovered the delights of
the fermented grape. This unnamed heroine was a concubine in
the harem of King Jamsheed. Her royal master had a weakness for grapes and
ordered bunches to be stored in jars so that he could enjoy them at his table all
year round (presumably as raisins).

One of the jars began to ferment and the raisins lost their sweetness. The
king supposed that the juice was poisonous and had the container labelled as
such. One day, our unknown benefactress, who suffered from constant
migraines, decided to put herself out of her misery. Finding the jar marked
"poison" she drank deeply and immediately fell asleep. She awoke feeling on
top of the world and returned to the jar to finish it off. Summoned before the
king to explain her odd, euphoric behaviour she confessed her misdemeanor.
Intrigued, King Jamsheed ordered a quantity of wine to be made for the
delectation of his entire court. The fabled king is said to have lived for 700
years—the earliest testimonial we have to the salutary effects of the
fermented grape.

William Younger, in *Gods, Men and Wine*, argues that winemaking may
date back 10,000 years or more to the Magdalenian rock painters of southern

France. "During the Upper Palaeolithic Age which marks the emergence of 'modern man', some of the conditions existed for the deliberate making of wine, although they did not exist for the deliberate growing of grapes."

It is a pleasing thought that those primordial artists working in the bowels of the earth with their charcoal and vegetable dyes might have stepped back to admire their work by the light of the fire, with a bowl of wine in their hands.

Certainly they would have had grapes to eat, if not to ferment, since wild vines have existed since the Tertiary Period, a million to 60 million years ago. But the first vigneron, who deliberately cultivated grapes, was Noah. According to the Book of Genesis (IX, 20), "Noah began to be an husbandman, and he planted a vineyard: And he drank of the wine, and was drunken; and he was uncovered in his tent." Scholars have placed that first vineyard near Erivan in Armenia, though they have yet to agree on what "uncovered" meant.

The Old Testament is replete with references to vineyards, grapes and wine. Perhaps the best-known has provided the logo for the Israeli Tourist Board—Moses' spies returning from Canaan, the land of milk and honey: "and they came upon the Brook of Eschol and cut down from thence a branch with one cluster of grapes and they bare it between two upon a staff" (Numbers XII, 23). One bunch of grapes requiring two men to carry it! Grape growers through the ages must share this same sense of hyperbole when it comes to describing the quality of their harvest!

The story of Moses' spies has its echo in the first documented discovery of grapes growing in Canada.

In the summer of 1001 A.D., Leif Ericsson set sail from Norway in a Viking longboat. According to the two sagas written from oral sources around 1250, Leif, a newly baptized Christian, was "a big strapping fellow, handsome to look at, thoughtful and temperate in all things." But this did not prevent him from provisioning his crew of 35 with beer and mead to help them survive the rigours of the journey.

The expedition sailed first to Baffin Island which Leif named "The Country of Flat Stones", and then on to Labrador ("Land of Forests"). Historians still argue where the intrepid explorer made his final landfall on the American continent—the place he was to call "Vinland". As Samuel Eliot Morrison says in *The European Discovery of America*, "There are few local histories of seaport towns between Newfoundland and the Virginia capes which do not open with a chapter asserting 'Leif Ericsson was here!'" In the Latin translation of the sagas published by Thormodus Torfaeus at Copenhagen in 1705, the author identified Vinland unequivocably as Newfoundland.

In 1960 Helga Ingstad, a Norwegian archeologist, pinpointed Leif's landfall at L'Anse aux Meadows in northern Newfoundland. Morrison is convinced that this is the spot "where Leif Ericsson spent one winter and where members of his family founded a short-lived colony". The exact

Leif Ericsson's presence in North America is commemorated by this statue by Anne Whitney on Commonwealth Avenue in Boston.
Courtesy: International Portrait Gallery / Gale Research

location is significant because of what the sagas tell us in the narrating of the "history" of the voyage to Vinland. According to a tale in the "Greenlanders Saga", one member of the party—Leif's foster father, a German named Tyrker—wandered off. Search parties were organized but before they could set out Tyrker emerged triumphantly from the woods "rolling his eyes and babbling, first in a German dialect none of his shipmates understood, then in Norse." The crew gathered round him and the excited old man broke the news: "I found grape vines and grapes!" Leif was incredulous and not a little dubious. "Certainly," replied the German. "I was born where there is no lack of either vines or grapes."

Leif ordered his men to harvest the grapes and load them aboard along with the cargo of timber they had cut. When spring allowed the expedition to sail home again, Leif had already named the unknown country Vinland—the land of vines.

Adam of Bremen was the first chronicler of Leif Ericsson's original voyage and around the year 1075 he reported to the King of Denmark that Leif "spoke of an island in that (northern) ocean, discovered by many which is called WINLAND, for the reason that vines yielding the best of wine grows there wild".

Grapes growing in northern Newfoundland? Grapes that produce "the best of wine"? Certainly, today, the finest European grapes as well as hybrids and our native labrusca varieties flourish in the Annapolis Valley above the

Bay of Fundy in Nova Scotia. So perhaps there is a microclimate where the hardy wild grapes might have grown around L'Anse aux Meadows in Newfoundland.

Cynics have suggested that what Leif Ericsson actually found were blueberries, wild red currants, gooseberries or, possibly, the mountain cranberry. Samuel Eliot Morrison dismisses such speculation: "If it be objected that Leif Ericsson, after whooping it up in the court of King Olaf (of Norway), must have known wine and would not have been put off by a poor substitute made from berries, one may reply that, just as his father Eric (the Red) put the "Green" in Greenland to attract settlers, so Leif put the "Vin" in Vinland. And with such success as to throw off all Vinland-seekers for centuries!"

But it was 500 years after Ericsson before we have more evidence of grapes and winemaking in eastern Canada. In 1535 when Jacques Cartier sailed down the St. Lawrence on his second voyage to New France, he anchored off "a great island". Here Cartier found masses of wild grapevines growing up the trees. He named it *Ile de Bacchus* but on reflection—thinking that this might seem too frivolous for his masters in Paris—renamed it *Ile d'Orleans* after the duc d'Orleans, son of his monarch, Francis I.

From this point on the history of the grape is closely bound with the history of Canada.

The Jesuit missionaries who followed in Cartier's footsteps brought sacramental wine with them and when they ran out they tried their hand at winemaking using the native wild grape. They recorded that the grapes were plentiful but the wine they produced (probably from Vitis riparia) was

The Small Coopers (Jean Jacques de Boissieu): French winemaking at the end of the eighteenth century.

Harvest Time (Charles-François Daubigny): gathering the grapes for winemaking in nineteenth-century America.

obviously only tolerable enough to be sipped at Mass, not to be quaffed back to warm the hearts of the settlers during the long winters.

The Jesuits may have been able to supply their own sacramental needs but their congregation required something a little more palatable. In 1648 a certain Jacques Boisdon in Quebec City applied to the Council of New France for a licence to open the first tavern. The Council agreed and even supplied Boisdon with eight barrels of French wine, free of charge, to help him start his business. But in true bureaucratic style they set down stringent regulations: "to prevent any unseemliness, drunkenness, blasphemy or games of chance", the inn had to be located in a public square within sight of the church, allowing the priest to be a one-man Liquor Control Board.

But the Church fathers, far from frowning on the practice of winemaking, actively encouraged it. Father Jacques Bruyas wrote in a letter dated 1668: "If one were to take the trouble to plant some vines and trees they would yield as well as they do in France . . . and (properly pruned) the grapes would be as good as those of France"—a sentiment which would be echoed down the years to our own day by every grape grower who put a plant in the ground.

If the new settlers, accustomed to the wines of France, were less than enthusiastic about the possibility of winemaking from wild grapes, the indigenous peoples of Upper Canada were untroubled by such latent wine snobbery. Indian tribes, such as the Seneca, Tuscarora and Cayuga, are believed to have offered tributes of fermented grape juice to the gods who lived at the foot of Niagara Falls. The ceremony, during which the wine was poured into the churning waters to placate the gods, was known as the

Wischgimi. The bands travelled great distances to make their offering and as Percy Rowe suggests in *The Wines of Canada*, "It is conceivable that the journey would have been a dusty one so that the Indians were sufficiently tempted to slake their throats with a portion of the 'gifts'."

If wild grapes like Vitis riparia and Vitis labrusca flourished in eastern Canada it would not be until the nineteenth century when committed amateurs tried to cultivate vines for the express purpose of producing wines fit to drink. The wild labrusca grapes with their small berries would have produced a wine of poor quality—harsh and acidic, with a decidedly "foxy" flavour.

Father Bruyas' suggestion of planting vines had already been tried by British colonists in Virginia and the Carolinas at the instigation of Lord Delaware who, in 1619, imported French cuttings along with French *vignerons* to oversee their planting. The vines they planted died, unfortunately, before a commercial wine industry, based on French vinifera grapes, could be established in the new colonies. But their presence among the native varieties was enough to create new strains. Through cross-pollination with wild grapes the first North American hybrids were created.

two

The Early Years

*"Canadian wines? You're kidding. Look at any map; it is
white above the border, which means there is snow in
Canada. All they have is beer and whiskey."*

(*William E. Massee*, Wines of America)

In the years to follow, the nascent Canadian wine industry in the east was
to benefit from American grapes which flourished in the more conducive
climate to the south.

The poor performance of imported vines forced the early American
winemakers to re-evaluate the native stock. As early as 1683 William Penn
called for better viticultural practices to improve the quality of the vine in the
hope that "the consequence will be as good wine as any European countries
of the same latitude do yield." Some 90 years later, during the American
Revolution, Governor John Penn's gardener, a certain John Alexander,
discovered the first accidental hybrid growing by a river near Philadelphia.
He had been experimenting unsuccessfully with European varieties, and
some of them survived long enough to cross with nearby wild varieties.
Alexander planted a cutting and happily it took root in Governor Penn's
garden. The Alexander grape became popular around 1800 as the Cape, a
name which suggested South African origins.

With the blessing of President Thomas Jefferson, who had vines growing
in his garden in Virginia, the Alexander enjoyed a brief moment in the sun
before it was eclipsed by two new hybrids—Isabella, introduced in 1816, and
Catawba in 1823.

At the same time, in Ontario, a retired German soldier, Corporal Johann
Schiller, was tending his labrusca vines on 20 acres of ground by the Credit

River. He had built himself a house on North Dundas Street, Cooksville (now Mississauga) on land granted to him for his military service.

By 1811 Schiller, who had previous winemaking experience in the Rhine, was fermenting grapes he had presumably grown from cuttings of wild vines and early American hybrids furnished by settlers from Pennsylvania. He made sufficient quantities to be able to service his own needs and sell to his neighbours. Johann Schiller is generally acknowledged to be the father of the Canadian wine industry.

We have no indication as to how long Schiller's winery lasted. The property was bought in 1864 by Count Justin M. de Courtenay, who formed a company called the Vine Growers Association. He extended the original vineyards to 40 acres of Clinton and Isabella grapes, making his Clair House label the largest in Ontario.

De Courtenay was an aggressive evangelist in the cause of Canadian wine, harrying the government of the day with letters and pamphlets to proselytize its members in support of the infant industry.

The owner of Clair House had begun his wine-producing experiences in Quebec. He was convinced that European grapes could not only grow in Lower Canada but could outperform their Burgundian cousins in terms of the wine they produced: "It will be easily perceived the importance attached in Burgundy to their wines," wrote de Courtenay, "and there is no reason why we should not produce better ones on the borders of the St. Lawrence."

To prove his point de Courtenay sent some bottles to the Premier of Lower Canada, L.V. Sicotta, on January 15th, 1863, with a covering letter:

> "I have now the honour to present you with samples of wine furnished by the cultivated wild grape, and am persuaded that, making allowances for the green taste which it possesses in common with almost all new wines, you will consider it equal to ordinary Burgundy which it resembles not only in flavour but in its qualities and colour ... The fact that a good, sound wine can be produced in this country, I consider has been by me practically demonstrated."

The Hon. L.V. Sicotta was not won over by such confident huckstering and passed the bottles over to a government consultant, a Mr. McDougall, who pronounced the wine sour.

But de Courtenay would not take this criticism of his wine lying down. He shot back a letter to Quebec City full of righteous indignation: "I deny the wine in question being sour, but admit it to be bitter in consequence of containing too much tannin." The age-old cry of the winemaker: "all it needs is bottle-age."

What Justin de Courtenay could not accomplish in Quebec he tried with more success in Ontario. His Clair House wines he considered of sufficient quality to be exhibited in Paris in celebration of Canada's nationhood in 1867. On July 8th the *Toronto Leader* printed the following story:

> "The French exposition has established the character of our Canadian wines. The jury on wines, which would naturally be composed of the best judges to be

found in Europe, speak in very high terms of the wines sent from the Clair House Vineyards, Cooksville. They find in them a resemblance to the Beaujolais wine, which is known to be the best produced in France. They say of those wines that they resemble more the great French table wines than any other foreign wines they have examined, and that the fact of the wine being so *solide* as to bear the sea voyage, and the variations of heat and cold without losing anything of either its quality or limpidity, should be a question of great consideration even to our own producers."

"This authoritative opinion of the quality of Ontario wine will do more than anything else that could possibly occur, at present, to bring this wine into general use. . . . The time will come, we hope and verily believe, when grape-growing and wine-making will be one of the principal employments of our population; and when it does come, the cause of temperance will be advanced to a degree which could be reached by no other process."

De Courtenay had been vindicated. His red wine, at an alcoholic strength of 13%, was the talk of Toronto. But the newspaper's predictions failed to come about. In 1878, no longer able to secure a grant from the Parliament of Upper Canada, de Courtenay was forced to close his winery.

Justin de Courtenay, the flamboyant count who dashed off letters of blistering irony to parliamentarians, quoting Pliny and Virgil, overshadowed the efforts of those stolid Ontario farmers of lesser education who laboured quietly in the background. For example, Porter Adams was shipping grapes to the Toronto market from the Queenston area in the same year that de Courtenay was shipping his wines to France. John Kilborn—as early as 1862—won a prize of $3 at the Provincial Exhibition in Toronto for the "best bottles of wine made from the grape". Kilborn owned 17 acres of land on Ontario Street in Beamsville. In 1860 he reported to *The Canadian Agriculturalist* that his wine was fetching $1.75 a gallon locally "and probably would bring in more if we asked for it. At all events it is worth four times as much as the miserable stuff sold by our merchants under the name of wine."

Winemaking in the late nineteenth century was more of a basement hobby than a business. When it was not sold through the kitchen door it would have been available at the local drug store. Farm wineries such as those owned by John Kilborn and W.W. Kitchen of Grimsby were, however, large enough to advertise their products. Kitchen's broadsheet declared that his wines were "in use by some Hundreds of Churches for sacramental services". In addition, "It is sold by most of the principal Chemists in Canada East and West".

The problem for those early winemakers, whether they made it for their own consumption or profit, was the alcohol strength. The native hybrids like Catawba and Isabella were low in sweetness and high in acidity so sugar had to be added to the fermentation to bring up the alcohol level. The grapes would be pressed a second time after water or sugar syrup had been added to the skins to get every last ounce of juice out of the grape. This practice is still engaged in by the trade today, especially the big companies. They call it euphemistically "amelioration"—its critics call it "stretch".

The first growers along that Niagara Peninsula, like Porter Adams, planted their vines basically to service the fresh fruit trade. One of the best table varieties, as well as an excellent taste for jams and jellies, was the Concord grape whose flavour is unmistakable to us today as the essence of virtually all grape-flavoured products. The grape was named after the Massachusetts town where it was propogated by a man who rejoiced in the splendid name of Ephraim Wales Bull.

As a boy growing up in New York's Hudson River Valley, Bull became interested in grape growing. In 1836 he moved to Concord to pursue his hobby more vigorously. And to make wine. In his quest for a grape which would survive the New England winter better than the Isabella, he planted the seeds of some wild labrusca grapes. The one that succeeded best he named Concord in honour of the town where it was raised.

In 1854 Bull offered his Concord vines to nurseries at a hefty price of $5 a vine. But the nurserymen managed to propogate the vine for themselves and Bull saw little remuneration for his gift to the North American wine industry. He died penniless in Concord's Home for The Aged in 1895. His tombstone bears the forlorn legend: "He sowed, but others reaped".

When the Concord grape was exhibited at the Massachusetts Horticultural Society, it was an instant winner. In his book *American Wines and How to Make Them*, Philip Wagner explains why. "It produces so cheaply and abundantly that it makes a dismal joke of all competition; it is virtually indifferent to climate, growing rankly in both hot and cold regions, and flourishes in practically any soil; it is immune to most of the vine diseases and thrives under neglect; it travels well and withstands storage moderately well; it does not winter kill . . ."

The only problem is that Concord grapes make awful wine. As grape juice it can be enjoyable or when its "foxy" taste is camouflaged as sherry or port, but as wine I'd rather drink the gum they used to stick on the label. Yet the Concord was to become the backbone of the Canadian wine industry up until the 1940s—and as the major constituent in the "Duck" range of pop wines it provided 90% of company profits until the late 1970s.°

Not only did the Americans send their grapes north, they also dispatched their entrepreneurs whose presence would give the youthful industry a nudge toward the twentieth century. In the 1860s most of the operations in Ontario were small-volume businesses, a sideline for farmers who had crops other than grapes to harvest.

In 1866 "a company of gentlemen from Kentucky," according to a letter in the *Canadian Farmer*, "who have been in the grape business for 14 years, have purchased a farm on Pelee Island and planted 30 acres this spring, and intend to plant 20 acres next spring." Pelee Island—the most southerly part of

---

°Ten years after it started its grape-breeding program in 1913, the Horticultural Research Institute of Ontario at Vineland had given up using the Concord as a "parent". In 1942 the Institute stated in its report that the goal of the grape-breeding program was to produce hybrids which no longer had the labrusca taste characteristics and resembled more those of the European viniferas.

Canada, on the same latitude as northern California—stands 12 miles to the north of Kelly's Island in Lake Erie. In 1860 Catawba grapes were successfully planted there to supply the wineries at Sandusky, Ohio, one of the oldest winemaking centres in the United States. (In 1893 Brights bought Catawba from Pelee Island to produce a sweet table wine.)

The southern gentlemen were D.J. Williams, Thomas Williams and Thaddeus Smith, who formed a company called Vin Villa to create the first commercial winery on Pelee Island. Before they had built a house on their land, they excavated a wine cellar, forty feet by sixty feet and twelve feet deep, which showed that this was to be no bathtub operation.

But Vin Villa was not to be without competition. A few months after the Kentuckians acquired land on Pelee Island, two English brothers, Edward and John Wardoper, purchased 15 acres and planted a rival vineyard. Today the Pelee Island Vineyards boast the largest vinifera planting in Canada—Riesling, Gewurztraminer, Chardonnay and Pinot Noir—planted by Walter Strehn in 1980.

An enterprising grocer in Brantford named Major J.S. Hamilton bought the grapes as well as finished wine from the Pelee vineyards. Hamilton had opened his store in 1871 and in the same year was granted a royal charter to sell wine and liquor. Three years later he met Thaddeus Smith and was impressed by the yield of his vineyards (four to five tons per acre of Delaware and Catawba) and the quality of his wine. He asked Smith if he could sell Vin Villa wine for him in the eastern United States.

Hamilton also wanted to market these wines in Canada and to do so he entered into an agreement with the Pelee Island growers to transfer the winemaking operation from the island to the city of Brantford.

The assets of J.S. Hamilton and Company Limited, which absorbed the Pelee Island Wine and Vineyard Company in 1909, would be sold in 1949 to London Winery, giving that company the longest pedigree in the venerable art of Canadian winemaking.

In the same decade that Major Hamilton was shipping casks of wine over from Pelee Island, some 2,000 miles away, the Oblate fathers' tiny vineyard at their mission seven miles south of Kelowna in British Columbia's Okanagan Valley was reaching maturity. In BC, as in Quebec, it was the Church that first fostered and encouraged the cultivation of the grape for winemaking.

If Justin de Courtenay moved from Quebec to Ontario to find more favourable microclimates in which to grow vines to produce better burgundies than those of France, other English-speaking farmers remained to battle the winters. A Mr. Menzies of Pointe Claire, Quebec, created a vineyard "on a larger scale than usual in the province" which he called "The Beaconsfield Vineyard". Two years later he was joined by a partner but the association was brief. After a few months Mr. Menzies was forced to publish a pamphlet warning his clients that his former associate had set up a farm a mile from his own from which the rascal had been selling American wines under the name of The Beaconsfield Vineyard.

But the lustiest child in the nation's vinicultural nursery was Ontario. From the 1860s vineyards flourished in the Beamsville-Vineland-Grimsby area. Grape growers experimented in their own backyards to find a new variety that was disease resistant and winter hardy. The process was long and difficult. It takes four to five years for a vine to produce a commercial crop, let alone the years it takes to develop a successful crossing. So when a new variety was introduced the effect was rather like a coronation or the arrival of a royal baby.

In 1868, in Lockport, New York, two growers created what they were to call the Niagara grape by crossing the Concord with a relatively little known variety called the Cassady. It was to be the white wine equivalent of the unkillable purple Concord. The two growers, mindful of what had happened to Ephraim Bull, sold their vines at $1.25 a piece with a written understanding that the purchaser would return all cuttings to them so the vines could not be pirated.

In 1882 the Niagara grape was introduced to Ontario and, like the Concord, it is still with us.

By 1890 there were 41 commercial wineries across Canada, 35 of which were situated in Ontario. The great majority of these, fully two-thirds, were centred around Essex county, which in 1904 boasted 1784 acres of vines. The pre-eminence of Essex as Canada's grape-growing centre was to last 30 years. By 1921 the grape vines had been torn out in favour of such cash crops as tobacco and soft fruit. A mere 50 acres remained, but this concentration was still greater than anywhere else in Canada.

In 1873, two years after Major James Hamilton had shaken the hand of the gentlemen from the South to confirm their business arrangement, George Barnes, a relative of Porter Adams by marriage, started a winery at St. Catharines. With the literalness of a German wine label, he embraced every function of the company in its name so there could be no mistaking its purpose: the Ontario Grape Growing and Wine Manufacturing Company, Limited. What it lacked in imagination, it made up for in longevity because it still operates today as Barnes Winery.

George Barnes' vines had been in the ground one year when Thomas Bright and his partner, F.A. Shirriff, opened a winery in Toronto. In naming it they must have subconsciously realized they would have to move closer to their grape supply. They called it the Niagara Falls Wine Company and move they did 16 years later, in 1890, to the outskirts of the town. In 1911 they changed the name to T.G. Bright and Company.

Those years at the end of the nineteenth century showed a remarkable growth for Ontario, and for the grape-growing areas south and southwest of the province. At the turn of the century there were some 5,000 acres under vine along the Niagara Peninsula.

But two events were to check the new wine industry and to set it off on a path of incipient self-destruction: World War I and Prohibition.

three

Prohibition

"It is a fight with an enemy more mighty, more merciless, more beastly, more fiendlike, more diabolical than the Teuton."

(The Reverend C.A. Williams preaching prohibition at the Timothy Eaton Memorial Church in Toronto, September 1919.)

In the early days of this century what passed for the Canadian wine industry resided in Ontario. And those companies that survived into the 1900s were targets for the growing number of drum-beating temperance societies in the province, particularly in the rural areas. Some farmers refused to sell their grapes to winemakers, and by 1892 the public outcry against alcoholic beverages had reached such a crescendo that even the idea of planting more vineyards in Niagara came under scrutiny.

When World War I broke out the government's need for industrial alcohol to make explosives synchronized with the popular sentiment for prohibition. Once the Temperance Act had been passed the distilleries could be converted to the production of industrial alcohol for the war effort.

On September 15, 1916 the government of Sir William F. Hearst, himself an active Methodist layman and dedicated temperance advocate, passed the legislation known as the Ontario Temperance Act. Under its statutes all bars, clubs and liquor shops would be closed for the duration of the war. No one could sell any intoxicating liquor unless authorized to do so by the province and no one could "have, keep, give, or consume liquor except in a private dwelling house".

In 1916 and 1917 all but one of the provinces went dry. Quebec, which marches to a different drum in these matters, held out until 1919 and then proscribed the sale of liquor, but not wine or beer.

The Women's Christian Temperance Union of Ontario, the vanguard of the movement, had triumphed but political realities began to nibble away at their victory. Pressure from the strong grape growers' lobby caused the Conservative government to exempt native wines from the provisions of the act. Section 44 stated that wines made from Ontario-grown grapes could be produced by manufacturers who held permits from the Board of Licence Commissioners. This political sleight of hand was to elicit a raised eyebrow—if somewhat belated—from the editorial page of the *Toronto Telegram* (April 21, 1921): "There may be political reasons for protecting wine and banning beer. But there is no moral or social reason. There is no inherent vice in barley which does not also lodge in grapes."

When the Ontario Temperance Act became law there were ten operating wineries in the province. While they were able to vinify wine legally during Prohibition the government saw to it that consumers had a difficult time getting hold of it. Each winery was allowed one store outlet and that on its premises. Customers could only buy a five-gallon quantity or its equivalent in bottles—two cases. An extraordinary piece of double-think by a government dedicated to the proposition that the people must be denied alcoholic beverages!

Another bizarre anomaly of Prohibition in Canada was that while it might have been illegal to sell liquor, it was not against the law to manufacture it. Alcohol was readily available for "Sacramental, industrial, artistic, mechanical, scientific, and medicinal purposes." And it was the medical profession which was to become the barman of the nation. A doctor could prescribe alcohol to a patient if he felt that patient might benefit from such "medicine". Peter Newman writes of those days in *The Bronfman Dynasty*: "As well as selling straight liquor through the drug stores to patients with doctors sympathetic enough to prescribe it, the booze was sold to processors who concocted a variety of mixtures for the drug store trade, including a Dandy Bracer—Liver and Kidney Cure, which when analysed, was found to contain a mixture of sugar, molasses, bluestone and 36% pure alcohol—plus a spit of tobacco juice."

Stephen Leacock summed up the social situation with the observation that "to get a drink during Prohibition it is necessary to go to the drug store . . . and lean up against the counter making a gurgling sigh like apoplexy. One often sees there apoplexy cases lined up four deep."

Nevertheless, during the eleven years of Prohibition in Ontario the only alcoholic beverage that could be sold legally was wine. The natural effect was to spark off a mad scramble by European immigrants who had some brush with winemaking in the old country to get in on the act. And even those native-born Ontarians who could not tell wine from vinegar jumped on the bandwagon. Wineries were started up in basements, at the back of grocery stores, in garages—and one even in the converted pig shed of a Beamsville farm.

The Board of Liquor Commissioners handed out permits with heady abandon to placate the vociferous grape growers' lobby. Between 1917 and October 31, 1927, no fewer than 57 licences for new wineries were issued, in addition to the ten that were already established.

The three major centres for these wineries were the Niagara Peninsula—at the source of the grapes; Toronto—as the largest urban population; and Windsor—to take advantage of the great thirst across the Detroit River. But distance from the vineyards was of little consequence to those early wine-producers. There were two successful wineries in the lakehead cities of Fort William and Port Arthur (Twin City Wine Company and Fort William Wine Co.), one at Kitchener (in the basement of Fred J. Kampmann's house), one at Belleville (John Tantardini who started in Guelph, eventually selling out to the Belleville Wine Company in 1926) and yet another in Sudbury (the Sudbury Wine Company). There were even two Toronto rabbis who made kosher wines: Rabbi M.H. Levy of Bathurst Street was granted a licence in 1921. His company was purchased in 1925 by Canada Wine Products Ltd., which in turn was swallowed by Jordan in 1938. The other was Rabbi Jacob Gordon, who manufactured Passover wine in the cellar of his home at 116 Beverley Street. In 1928 the rabbi's winery licence was purchased by the Oporto Wine Company on Danforth Avenue, which sold medicated wine. After a series of takeovers the rabbinical company—originally called the Concord Wine Co. Ltd. in 1923—ended up as part of Chateau-Gai in 1978.

Only those companies that made a drinkable product survived this extraordinary era—companies like Brights who introduced the first bottling

The antique handblown bottle (left) dates back to the days of the Pelee Island Winery, one of the first wineries in Ontario. The small bottle of "tonic" (right), dating from 1925, was available only through drugstores with a doctor's prescription. Courtesy: London Winery Ltd.

line in Canada, Jordan Wines (a company formed to take over Canadian Grape Products Ltd. in 1926), the London Winery (which purchased a three-year-old licence from Giovanni Paproni in 1925) and the Turner Wine Company. This last enterprise dated back to 1885 when it was founded by a Brantford grocer—no doubt in competition with the enterprising Major J.S. Hamilton. They distributed a product known as "Turner's Tonic Bitters" which was heavy on alcohol and quinine.

As far as most winemakers were concerned there were no quality controls, no government interference and in many cases, little of the basic knowledge of the craft. American equipment and cooperage, hastily bought by the newly-formed companies, was calibrated in US gallons as opposed to Imperial measurements; but this meant nothing to some unscrupulous manufacturers who were simply out to line their pockets at the expense of the public thirst. They squeezed their grapes—literally—till the pips squeaked and with added water they were getting as much as 600 gallons of wine from every ton of grapes. (Today the negotiated limit is 258 gallons per ton.) Sugar was poured into the vats by the sackful during fermentation to bring up the alcohol level. If the colour wasn't quite right after so much dilution there was always coal tar or vegetable dyes like cochineal to deepen it. Blocks of sulphur were pitched into the vats to kill bacteria and one enterprising vintner even used aspirins to control his fermentation.

For all those who made wretched wine under licence there were countless others who did so without the bureaucratic blessing of a permissive government. Unlike moonshine whisky, homemade wine was legal and the hobbyist who had a few hundred gallons of wine could always plead that he had made it for the home consumption of his entire family rather than for selling through the back door. Few such cases ever came to court and the government took a lenient view of new immigrants who wished to make their own wine when the LCBO was created in 1927. All they would require was a home winemaking licence and they could produce up to 100 gallons for their own use. (Today no such permit is required).

In spite of the abysmal quality of most wines available during the eleven-year hiatus, the mere fact of Prohibition had focussed the attentions of Canadians on their domestic wine industry. And Prohibition more than anything else turned Canadians into a nation of wine-drinkers. During 1920-21 Canada consumed 221,985 gallons of domestic wine. A decade later the figure was 2,208,807 gallons—for Ontario alone! And 80% of it was a red port-style wine of maximum alcoholic strength made from the Concord grape.

After eleven years of social dislocation Canada passed through the wilderness of Prohibition. Even those who were loudest in its support saw that Prohibition had failed. Sanity finally prevailed. It was seen by most conservative politicians as a victory for "British values" over "all the evils . . . wished on Canada by agitators who took their ideals not from the motherland but from that hot-bed of political experiment, the American Middle West."

If the politicians could not stop the fermented juice of the forbidden fruit from finding its way down the throats of the people at least they could regulate its use.

Eventually, province after province would adopt a form of government control over the sale and distribution of alcohol—a system which involved a state monopoly, based on the Scandinavian model, and more importantly, control over the quality of the product. The new system meant that each province would decide, individually, which wines of the world they would make available to their consumers and how much they would tax them for that privilege.

With the advent of government liquor stores, consumers now had a focus for their complaints if the wines they purchased were substandard—and they had a lot to complain about. During Prohibition the mere idea of beating the regulations in acquiring wine made the drinker overlook its dubious quality; but now it was legal and the government was held responsible for every bottle that tasted of vinegar, was black with sediment or contained such foreign bodies as spiders and flies. Some bottles never reached the consumer as they exploded on the liquor store shelves owing to a secondary fermentation—much to the consternation of the employees who felt as if they were living in a minefield. And the bottles themselves could be any shape. A.N. Knowles, Vice President of London Winery, recalls seeing the same label of his father's company on three or four different types of bottle. "Winery employees used to visit the junk yards," he said, "buy up boxes of old bottles, wash them out and fill them with wine. Bottles were hard to get in those days."

In Ontario, the government acted after 1928 by bringing in a rudimentary quality control for the products it accepted for sale from the wineries. The new Liquor Control Board under Sir Henry Drayton, a former federal minister of finance, administered the new regulations which set a maximum of 250 gallons per ton of grapes, limiting the amount of water that could be added to the wine. The new restrictions stressed cleanliness of operations above all and fixed the permissable level of volatile acid at 4%, which was still enough to make a wine taste of vinegar. (Even this generous limit was beyond the capabilities of most basement vintners.) But the bureaucrats had to move cautiously since the Depression was looming and the vocal farmers' lobby was concerned about the dropping price of grapes. King Concord had fallen as low as $12 a ton.

In an effort to improve the quality of winemaking, the Board's chief analyst, Bert Bonham, suggested that the Provincial Department of Health set up a winemaking school at the laborator in the east block of Queen's Park. When the more marginal companies found their products were being refused for listing at the liquor stores their winemakers flocked to attend. Many were new immigrants whose command of English was limited and decided that winemaking in the new world was not for them. The courses lasted for two years but they had the desired effect. The bathtub school of winemaking as a commercial proposition quietly died.

Encouraged by the government, viable companies like Brights and Jordan began buying up the licences of these precarious operations lock, stock and barrel at prices as low as $5,000 to $10,000. Over the years Brights acquired 13 such licences, not for the wine which was generally sent to the distillers, nor for the equipment, but for the privilege of owning another retail store. The wineries still had their own single outlet and the government now allowed them to locate these stores away from the facility in the cities of their choice. By this expedient the government eventually reduced the number of Ontario wineries from 51 to eight.

The next problem was to rationalize the sale of tonic wines and patent medicines which were readily available over grocery store counters. As we have seen, doubtful products such as Dandy Bracer, (Liver & Kidney Cure) were extraordinarily high in alcohol and of questionable therapeutic value. The Liquor Control Board came up with an elegant solution. The sale of medicated wines could continue but the makers had to blend in a "certain additive". If the tonic in question were taken without reference to the stated dosage the additive induced vomiting in the would-be patient. Needless to say such nostrums quickly disappeared from the shelves for all time.

But the well-intentioned government did not address the fundamental question of what Ontarians were drinking. Wines made from the Catawba and Concord grapes were selling for 30 cents a bottle. They were sweet and highly alcoholic—twice the strength of European table wines. (In 1932 the government established a 20% limit.) In an effort to help the wine industry and the growers, the Ontario government removed the 50 cent a gallon tax on wines in January 1929 to enable the Liquor Board to sell Ontario products at such a low price. These beverages were known as "Block-and-Tackle" wines—you drank a bottle, walked a block and you could tackle anybody!

Further representations from the grape growers and the wine lobby convinced the Department of National Revenue to allow the fortification of domestic wines. By adding pure grape spirit the producers could now manufacture fortified wines. The new legislation was a godsend for the industry which could now use wine that was badly oxidized. Before, they would have to pour it into the sewer. Now they could distill it for grape alcohol.

The Ontario grape growers, too, were happy because they could sell more grapes and doubly so when in 1931 the government banned the importation of grapes from outside the province. The Liquor Board also insisted that the wineries pay a minimum of $40 a ton for those they bought.

Concerned about the rocketing sales of these new fortified wines—42% of all wines sold in 1933—the government appointed a Wine Standards Committee in an attempt to wean Canadians from such heady products towards lighter wines to be drunk with meals. In its report the Committee suggested that it was the industry's responsibility to supply the marketplace with a range of "good quality light wines". It stated that "The distribution of pamphlets fully describing the merits and low alcoholic content of table wines will unquestionably materially assist in promoting the sale of same."

But the Canadian public was not yet ready for wines of 9 to 12% alcohol; their palates had become accustomed to fortified products which were closer to whisky than wine in their alcoholic strength. It would take another 25 years before the industry would suddenly be caught offguard by the demand for the style of wines consumed by the Europeans. In the meantime, port and sherry would be the mainstays of the Canadian industry, especially during the Depression when disenchantment and despair found solace in cheap alcohol.

The brand leaders at this time were Brights' Catawba sherry, (affectionately known as "Brights' Disease") and Jordan's Bran-Vin.

Without the ability to advertise or promote their products—a legacy of the Prohibition mentality—the Wine Standards Committee loftily reported that "many people in this province associate drinking of any kind of alcoholic beverage with fostering drunkenness"—the wineries struggled through the 1930s to keep their industry alive. No new winery licences were to be granted in Ontario to allow those currently operating to stay afloat.

But in those dismal years between the two world wars a dedicated group of individualists laboured in their respective vineyards to produce wines of quality and if this goal proved to be beyond the capabilities of the native grapes such men were determined to find varieties that could do so.

In the early thirties, Harry Hatch, the new owner of Brights, brought a young French chemist and winemaker, from Montreal to his Niagara Falls winery. A French aristocrat by birth, Viscomte Adhemar de Chaunac de Lanzac was working at Brights' Quebec plant in Lachine at the time. Nurtured on the wines of his native land, he had little time for the company's ports and sherries and set about to make experimental batches of dry table wines from Catawba and Delaware grapes he found in Brights' Concord vineyards. Harry Hatch was so impressed by the results that he gave de Chaunac his head to experiment further, setting aside funds for his winemaker to buy vines from New York State to be planted in the company's experimental plot. In 1937 de Chaunac went to France to find out more about the hybrids the French were experimenting with.

At the same time the Horticultural Research Institute at Vineland was conducting similar experiments to provide the wineries with hardy varieties to resist winterkill. Patiently, the scientists at Vineland had been crossing vines to produce the magic grape free of labrusca flavour. William Rannie writes in *The Wines of Ontario* that the Institute planted and evaluated 57,000 seedlings between 1913 and 1928 and retained only six as "promising for table grapes and five for wine making!"

World War II interrupted this quiet revolution, the fruits of which would eventually change the nation's wine-drinking habits.

Cut off from Europe during the war, the wineries retrenched. All experimentation ceased; it was enough to keep the companies going until the servicemen returned home. As members of a nonessential industry wine-makers found themselves short of bottles and were forced to recycle those they could find.

During the war wineries were rationed by the government as to how much wine they could sell; the figure varied between 75% and 80% of their production in the base year of 1939. Wine drinkers used to line up for three hours outside the liquor stores until they opened at 10 a.m.

The Canadian wine industry marked time and waited for the peace which would signal its renaissance.

four

Post WW II

*"Canadians returned from the Second World War and from
travel abroad with a taste for table wine, and the
postwar flood of immigration has brought millions of people
from the wine countries of Europe, starting a swing
to mealtime wines."*

(Leon Adams, The Wines of America)

When the war was over, Adhemar de Chaunac of Brights was determined to upgrade the quality of the company's table wines. In 1946 he visited France again and ordered 40 European vine varieties—hybrids and such noble viniferas as Pinot Chardonnay (the grape of white burgundy) and Pinot noir (red burgundy). The vines were planted in the spring of that year, some on their own roots, others grafted onto a European rootstock known as Couderc 3309.

Ten varieties, including the two vinifera, adapted reasonably well to their new surroundings. In 1952, Harry Hatch, the owner of Brights, ordered 600 acres of Concord and Niagara vines torn out between the lake and the escarpment to make way for the new varieties. Among them was a hybrid called Seibel 9549 which would be rechristened De Chaunac in 1972 as an accolade to the Frenchman for his contribution to the Canadian wine industry.

De Chaunac also selected a list of varieties for the Horticultural Research Institute at Vineland after discussion with J.R. Van Haarlem who was in charge of grape development at the time. These vines were planted in the spring of 1947. HRIO's initial experiments suggested that a hybrid called

Chelois would be the grape of the future. It took ten years before they found that Chelois was susceptible to a disease called "dead arm".

Other commercial concerns were also experimenting. Parkdale Winery, based in Toronto, brought in vines from Hungary in 1947. Although they proved to be a "dead loss" they did have some success with Gamay Beaujolais on their test farm and with Johannisberg Riesling and a muscat-flavoured Couderc, which de Chaunac had brought in as well. (A young nurseryman in Niagara-on-the-Lake, Donald Ziraldo, would eventually propogate these vines from cuttings, and in 1971 would sell them to other wineries.)

Of all the hybrids planted at Vineland, it was the Seibel 9549 which would prove to be the leading commercial variety for red wines in Ontario, or as we know it today, the De Chaunac.

If Brights thought back in the 1950s that their Pinot Noir vines would give them a wine to rival the best of Burgundy—as Justin de Courtenay had dreamed about—they were disappointed. The vines produced a mere ton per acre, well below commercial viability; in fact, a "nuisance volume". Subsequent attempts to grow Pinot Noir on a large scale by the companies and estate wineries of Ontario have failed. Crops that have been harvested by those who took the gamble are used for blending, particularly in the better sparkling wines. There is hope, however, that the Pinot Noir will flourish in the warmer microclimates of southwest Ontario, so perhaps de Courtenay's dream may one day be realized. (Paul Bosc at Chateau des Charmes has made a valiant stab with his 1982 Pinot Noir.)

But the initial step to plant better grapes had been taken and Brights' Director of Viticultural Research, George Hostetter, can justifiably claim that their 1946 experiment predated the introduction of the finest French grapes to the Eastern United States by that outspoken champion of vinifera, Dr. Constantin Frank.

In 1955 Brights produced the first 100% Canadian Pinot Chardonnay from the vines de Chaunac brought back from France. And now every Canadian winery worth its salt has a Chardonnay among its premium varietal wines.

De Chaunac also brought to Canada 88 vines of a red hybrid called Maréchal Foch, (a cross between Pinot Noir and Gamay). Nine years later, having propogated them and allowed them to reach maturity, Brights put on the market a wine called Canadian Burgundy in 1958, much to the disgust of the French who were unhappy that their finest wines should be impugned with such an adjective (even though the grape's taste characteristics are similar to the lesser wines of the Côte d'Or).

Brights shared their research willingly with the rest of the industry and when de Chaunac retired in 1961 the wineries were nudging their growers to replant their vineyards with the more acceptable hybrid varieties like Seibel, Foch and Verdelet and, where possible, viniferas. They were now in a position to produce the style of products the Wine Standards Committee had called for back in 1933. Only this time, it was the consumers' voice they heard demanding drier wines which resembled those of France and Germany—if

Pressing grapes with the old
hydraulic presses was a time-
consuming business because
of the manual labour involved.
The process today (right) is
fast and efficient.

Courtesy: *London Winery
          Ltd. (l.)
          Jordan & Ste-
          Michelle Cellars
          Ltd. (r.)*

not in complexity and finesse, at least in alcoholic strength and without the
overriding "foxy" labrusca taste. But old Mr. Fox would be a long time a-
dying and a new craze would give him a breath of life again.

Social behaviour is governed by the law of the pendulum and wine
drinking like everything else has its cycles, its fads and its fashions. In the
affluent sixties young people became a formidable force in the marketplace
and the wine companies began to take notice of this new section of society. In
the late sixties, at the request of a Detroit tavern owner a German winemaker
in Michigan created a blended sparkling wine named "Cold Duck" which
immediately took off.* Everybody started making Cold Ducks—a 12%

*There is a European tradition, convivial though unsanitary, which calls for the
guests to pour their glasses into a common bowl at the end of the party. The mixture
of wines of whatever hue are then sampled. This is called in German *das caulde
Ende*—"the cold end". The German word *Ente* meaning duck, very similar in sound,
is a pun which gave the winemaker his name.

alcohol, sparkling wine made from labrusca grapes with sugar and water added.

In 1952 when Brights purchased the Fred Marsh Wine Company one of the products Marsh was working on was a 7% sparkling wine. De Chaunac overcame the problems of instability and developed Brights Winette which was originally sold in a 13 oz. pop bottle. Since it was a sparkling product the champagne tax of $2.50 per gallon was applied. M.F. Jones of Brights argued successfully with the LCBO to lower the tax and the mark-up because of the product's low alcohol level. The tax per gallon was fixed at 25 cents.

The 7% wine was an inspiration: not only did it score Brownie points with those pressure groups who wanted to see less alcohol consumed but it saved the company vatfuls of money. The labrusca grapes which were—and still are—used are the cheapest on the market. The crush is stretched with water and the excise tax is half that of table wines.

For several years Brights had the market to themselves with Winette and Du Barry Sparkling Vin Rosé.

But out in BC, Andrew Peller at Andres was looking for a new product line and, realizing that there were high profits to be made from this style of product, he and his company took the plunge.

Andres created a range of Chanté wines (as in *enchanté*) and one of these evolved as the "wine" that would create a revolution in Canadian taste— Baby Duck. At its peak, two years after its 1971 launch, one out of every 24 bottles of wine sold in Canada was Andres' Baby Duck.[*] The rest of the trade—and by now it was corporate business run by marketing men and Harvard-trained MBAs—scrambled to make a light, sparkling wine. A whole menagerie of pop wines descended on the liquor board shelves as a consequence; their names suggested Noah's ark rather than a wine shop: Little White Duck, Luv-a-Duck, Fuddle Duck, Baby Bear, Baby Deer, Pink Flamingo, Gimli Goose, and Pussycat, were just some of them.

The generation of postwar Canadians may have turned their backs on the whisky-substitutes of the Depression era but there were few Canadian wines of sufficient quality to fill the gap between the ports and sherries and the Ducks. The provincial liquor boards, seeing there were hefty profits to be made by catering to the growing demand for wine, began to increase their imports of European products until in 1975, 3,315 imports were listed across

---

[*]As Winston Collins wrote of the Baby Duck phenomenon: "Most Canadians grow up on soft drinks, and prefer to consume their alcoholic beverages flavoured, sweetened, carbonated, chilled, and diluted—rum and Coke, rye and ginger. Baby Duck was an easy transition from soft drinks to not-too-hard alcohol for the baby-boom generation, young people who may have been attracted to wine but were put off by its "come-alive-for-a-dollar-five" image, or else intimidated by the overly sophisticated aura of something with an unpronounceable foreign name." (*Saturday Night*, June 1982)

the country as opposed to 1,875 domestic products. This posed a new problem for the indigenous wineries that had to contend with a public who knew what it didn't want from Canadian wineries and went elsewhere for what it thought it ought to be drinking—the wines of France, Italy and Germany.

Alarmed by the influx of inexpensive wines from overseas, the grape growers and the wineries appealed to the Ontario government.

In 1976 Queen's Park instituted the Ontario Wine Industry Assistance Programme. The LCBO sent around a memo to all its stores saying "Delist imported wines that are not meeting their sales quotas and thereby make room for Ontario wines ... Urge store managers and wine consultants to mention Ontario wines ... Store managers will rearrange present shelf-facings and thereby make room for additional brands of Ontario wines ...". The government also initiated a program for the growers to help them change over from labrusca to the more desirable hybrids and viniferas so that the wineries could produce European-style wines. The program provided interest-free loans for five years.

The "Big Four" wineries of Ontario—Andres, Brights, Chateau-Gai and Jordan—in searching for ways to sell more of their products began to build bottling plants and blending facilities in non-grape growing provinces. The

In the 1950's, when labour was cheaper, very little machinery was used in the bottling plants.
Courtesy: London Winery Ltd.

initial capital outlay would soon be ameliorated by a grateful province which would now list *all* that company's products in its stores. Their investment was welcomed because the new facilities provided jobs locally. And the companies gained the added benefit of being able to manufacture wines without the regulations that restricted them in Ontario and, to a lesser extent, in BC.

The mid-1970s were a watershed for the Canadian wine industry. The large companies were desperately searching for a table wine which would appeal to the nation's palate to compete with such imported blends as Black Tower, Blue Nun, Colli Albani and Donini.

Indications from south of the border suggested that Americans were drinking white wine instead of red and the same thing would happen here. The sherry and port market virtually collapsed. Diet- and health-conscious Canadians switched their allegiance from red to white and there were hardly enough quality white hybrid grapes in the ground to satisfy the demand.

The Baby Duck drinkers had graduated to Mateus Rosé and the blended wines of Europe. Imports enjoyed a cachet on the strength of their label alone, irrespective of the quality of what was in the bottle.

In 1976 Calona wines in British Columbia entered the field with a wine to compete with the top-selling Black Tower called Schloss Laderheim. It looked suspiciously like a Rhine Riesling in its brown bottle and German gothic script. In 1978 Chateau-Gai launched Alpenweiss in Ontario—the first of that company's wines to contain California grapes blended with the locally grown Seyval. The success of these two wines sent the other companies off in the direction of brand names and labels which were unashamedly European in appearance and style. The age of the packaged wine had arrived. The way the bottle looked was as important as what was in it.

The "Big Four", with their modern plants strung out across the country, not only had to contend with burgeoning imports but also with the arrival of a new source of competition—the boutique wineries. The last licence issued by the Ontario government was in 1930, but the young nurseryman, Donald Ziraldo, so impressed Major-General George Kitching, Chairman of the Liquor Board of Ontario, with his concept of a cottage winery that he and his winemaker Karl Kaiser were given the green light to produce 10,000 gallons of wine from the 1974 vintage. Inniskillin Wines was born that year.

A few months earlier, a Hungarian winemaker named Karl Podamer had been granted a licence to create the Podamer Champagne Company at Clinton, Ontario. These two small wineries were the first since the bad old days of Prohibition and paved the way for other such adventuresome entrepreneurs as Alan Eastman at Charal, Paul Bosc at Chateau des Charmes, Joe Pohorly at Newark (subsequently renamed Hillebrand Estates Winery), and Enzo DeLuca and his winemaker Carlo Negri at Colio Wines in Harrow.

In British Columbia the first estate winery, Claremont, was opened in 1979. This opened the doors for Uniacke Cellars, Sumac Ridge, and Gray

Monk. And in 1980 the tiny Grand Pré Winery began fermenting grapes grown on its own property near Wolfville in Nova Scotia.

These cottage enterprises were dedicated to producing labour-intensive wines of quality from vinifera and hybrid grapes and would nudge the big wineries in both grape-growing provinces to follow their lead. (But it must not be forgotten that it was the research and development done by companies like Brights that provided these new wineries with a source of grapes.) The public, in the belief that small is better, snapped up the wines of Inniskillin and Chateau des Charmes and overenthusiastic nationalists held blind tastings against European products to prove that Canadian wines could hold their own in the international marketplace.

The noted British wine writer, Hugh Johnson, author of *The World Atlas of Wine*, was moved to concede that "even the Canadian Province of Ontario has recently produced some creditable table wines, particularly from the vinifera hybrid vine Maréchal Foch". The wine in question was Inniskillin's 1974 vintage. To show just how good this particular wine has become, Inniskillin sold 650 cases of their 1980 Maréchal Foch to France. Inniskillin has also sold its wines to Germany where Brights has enjoyed a continuing market for its President Canadian Champagne, Baco Noir and Pinot Chardonnay.

While the Canadian wine industry is garnering praise from beyond our borders in international competitions, it still has to convince its own constituents that it has come of age. Wineries both big and small are making wines from domestically grown grapes like Seyval Blanc, Maréchal Foch, Baco Noir and Vidal which have a distinctively Canadian flavour and should be judged for what they are, not against European varieties. The industry can pump millions of dollars into the production and promotion of light wines like Capistro, Club Spritz and Toscano Bianco Light, but ultimately it will be judged on the taste of its table wines.

The "Block-and-Tackle" wines are behind us now. Growers in Ontario and British Columbia are conscientiously upgrading the quality of their grapes, planting more vinifera and hybrids in scientifically selected soils and employing better viticultural practices. The industry is embarking on the most exciting phase of its history. Now it is up to the consumer to forget, or at least forgive, the past. With judicious selection through the dozens of domestic labels available on liquor board shelves from St. John's to Vancouver, the Canadian wine lover can now find products in the range of everyday table wines as palatable as anywhere else in the world.

It must not be forgotten that the Canadian wine industry—in terms of the production of table wines—really only began after World War II. It took the French and the Germans 2,000 years of trial and error to achieve their Lafites and Bernkasteler Doktors. With modern technology and European know-how the Californians, blessed with a better climate than Niagara or the Okanagan Valley, took 200 years to produce their excellent Cabernets and

Chardonnays. Today, the Canadian wine industry is where California was in the late 1960s. We have nowhere to go but up. And as long as it remembers it is a *wine* industry and not a commodities market where the bottom line is all that counts, it can win the respect and admiration of wine lovers across Canada.

five

Ontario

*"Ontario wine means (i) wine produced from grapes,
cherries, apples or other fruit grown in Ontario or
the concentrated juice thereof, and includes Ontario wine
to which has been added herbs, water, honey, sugar or the
distillate of Ontario wine or cereal grains grown in
Ontario, or (ii) wine produced by the alcoholic
fermentation of Ontario honey with or without the
addition of carmel, natural botanical flavours or the
distillate of Ontario honey."*

(Liquor Licence Act, Revised Statutes of Ontario, 1980.)

The Ontario government's idea of wine is rather like the horse designed by a committee which ends up looking like a camel. Wine is nothing more or less than a natural fermentation of fresh grape juice. Begrudgingly, I would add concentrates or frozen juice. This catch-all concept of what wine is in Canada's largest grape-growing province (the annual yield varies from 60,000 to 80,000 tons depending on the vintage) serves no other purpose than to make life easier for civil servants. The Liquor Licence Act makes no mention of secondary fermentation which suggests that Podamer's "champagnes", for example, are not wines. Until we have an appellation system similar to other wine-growing countries a vintage-dated Chardonnay grown in Niagara will be treated in the same manner as Baby Duck, mead, apple wine or vermouth.

The notion as to what constitutes an Ontario wine is further refined in the Wine Content Act of 1972 which has been amended several times over the years as a result of negotiations between the Ontario Wine Council and the Grape Growers' Marketing Board. Following a disastrous harvest in 1972 the Grape Growers agreed to allow 18,000 tons of grapes as concentrate to be imported into the province by the wineries to make up for 80% of the estimated shortfall. (During Prohibition vast quantities of Californian grapes used to be shipped into Ontario but the federal government put an end to the practice in 1931.) With the sudden boom in wine sales in 1975 the wineries again found themselves short of the raw material and the Wine Content Act was amended the next year to permit "the introduction of grapes grown outside Ontario and imported wine manufactured in Ontario without reducing the use of Ontario grapes in the content". A figure of 15% was set which meant that wineries could buy 15% of its total tonnage from California or wherever. But they could only use up to 30% of these imported grapes or finished wines in one blend. At the same time, however, the amount of wine made from a ton of grapes was fixed at 225 gallons either by amelioration or blending.

The reason the large wineries wanted to import grapes was to improve the taste profile of their wines—a laudable sentiment but one which the grape growers saw as threatening their livelihood.

No other wine-producing country in the world would countenance the figure of 225 gallons of wine per ton of grapes. Varietal wines usually run around 160 gallons per ton. But in February 1982, thanks to pressure from the commercial wineries, that amount was increased to 250 gallons and later in

Picking grapes by hand is still practiced today (left), but only at the request of the winery. About 90% of the grapes are now harvested by a machine picker.

Courtesy: London & Ste-Michelle Cellars Ltd. (l.)
London Winery Ltd. (r.)

the year to 258 where it stands today. A winemaker can only get that quantity by adding water during the crush. Known in the trade as "stretch" or, more euphemistically, "amelioration", some water may be necessary to soften the high acidity of Ontario grapes but ultimately the quality suffers. The basic constituent of the 7% pop wines comes from a tap. Commercial wineries do not generally ameliorate their varietal wines (those made from a single grape type and bearing that name on the label).

Happily, the practice is not widely employed by the cottage industry where winemakers can produce small batches of varietal and blended wines and court the consumer's favour by a quality comparison with imported wines. The large concerns have to answer to shareholders and accountants more interested in volume sales than the plaudits of critics. But even the "Big Four" realise that they have to keep a toe in the water against the time when the public palate begins to demand wines of superior quality.

The Liquor Control Board of Ontario

The day-to-day regulation of the industry has been in the hands of the Liquor Control Board of Ontario since its foundation in 1927. At that time the Board had 80 stores, since its mandate was to distribute and sell liquor throughout the province. Today it has 597. If any winery, domestic or foreign, wants to sell its products through the LCBO (and this is the only game in town), samples must first be submitted for tasting and quality control. The Board has one of the most sophisticated oenological laboratories in the world and subjects all products to rigorous analysis once they have passed the first hurdle of taste-testing by the Wine Standards Committee at the Horticultural Research Institute in Vineland.

Once approved, the Board will put the wine on its shelves if over 200 cases are produced. Less than this amount must be sold either through the two Rare Wine Stores in the province (in Toronto and in Ottawa)—if accepted—or through their own retail outlets. Between 200 and 1,500 cases will be made available to the All-Brand stores (8 in the province in areas of high-volume business) and over that amount can receive listings in any LCBO store that requests them. In addition there are two airport duty-free stores controlled by LCBO regulations.

Under the Liquor Control Act of 1975, the LCBO was incorporated as a Crown Corporation. Its monopoly on the sale and distribution of beverage alcohol also included the obligation to recommend policies "in line with changing social and economic conditions; *and to raise revenue for general government purposes*" (my italics). In the year 1981-82 the LCBO provided the government with $613.5 million from the sale of alcoholic beverages— almost 25% of all revenue resulted from domestic and imported wines. (The Liquor Licencing Board provided a further $85 million.)

The price we pay for wine wherever we live in Canada is determined by provincial governments who set the mark-up and taxes. Apart from generating revenue these mark-ups can also be manipulated to cushion the local industry against "foreign" competition. Wines made in Ontario conforming to the Wine Content Act currently carry a 45% mark-up. Those entering the province from other parts of Canada (i.e., British Columbia and Quebec) are marked up at 85% with a 25-cent per 750 ml bottle handling charge. At present, imports from the United States and Europe bear a punitive 110% mark-up but this may change.

As William Rannie has written in *The Wines of Ontario*, "the influence of the LCBO upon the industry has been all important, first in imposing standards and "cleaning up" the mess caused by unregulated licencing during the period of the Ontario Temperance Act, later in using its powers to assure fair treatment of wine growers during Depression years, and more recently in easing its import policy to give Ontario wineries a better competitive position in fighting for sales of domestic wines." But its emphasis has always been on *control* not only of the industry but of the consumer as well. Shades of Prohibition mentality linger still. As late as 1961, Allan Grossman, who was then the Commissioner of the LCBO, wrote in the Board's annual report: "We take the view that our citizens desire, subject to reasonable controls, to be able to purchase alcoholic beverages in convenient and pleasant surroundings without feeling that they are committing any wrongdoing." Pleasure and guilt are closely allied in the minds of government functionaries.

The government's hunger for tax revenue forever runs up against its pious attitude toward what it perceives to be the public good. On the one hand the treasury rakes in millions of dollars from a provincial monopoly of alcohol sales which provide 3% of the annual budget; on the other it pretends it is not in the "booze business" at all by instructing the wineries what they can and cannot do in promoting their products.

This squeamishness was unwittingly expressed in Grossman's 1961 annual report: "It should be emphasized that the increase in the number of (Liquor Board) stores ... in no way indicates an attempt on the Board's part to promote the increased sale of liquor. The Board's policy has been and remains aimed at controlling the orderly sale of alcoholic beverages." That year the sale of Canadian wines alone rose 8.6%

The LCBO stores themselves used to be as inviting as a railway lost property office. Before 1960 no bottles were displayed and customers had to fill out a form and hand it to a clerk. The bottle was shown briefly to the buyer to ensure it was what he had ordered and then slipped into a brown paper bag. And in many cases this was the last time the label saw the light of day.

A limited number of Ontario wines were eventually put up behind glass in selected stores, a revolutionary marketing concept which drew this laconic statement from Commissioner Grossman in the 1962-63 annual report: "In addition to the usefulness of such displays, they have added to the general improved appearance of store interiors." The following year imported wines were included. And in 1968 the first self-service stores were introduced into the province.°

Responding to the consumer demand for a wider choice of quality wines—and prompted by the success of a private wine club called The Opimian Society which imported interesting wines for its members—the Board opened the first Rare Wine Store in Market Street in Toronto. The well-appointed underground cellar offered 236 listings of imported wines and spirits.

If the Board did little to promote the Canadian wine industry at its major point of sale, the executives further hamstrung the wineries by its Draconian directives on how they could advertise their products. In 1971, the Chief Commissioner, General George Kitching, sent around a code of ethics which operated "on a brand performance basis rather than an increase in the use of alcohol."

The regulations governing where and how Ontario wineries can advertise their products were revised in October 1980 but the spirit of the Women's Christian Temperance Union still informs each reluctant concession to the twentieth century. All advertisements, print or broadcast, must be approved by the Liquor Licencing Board. "In print media brand reference will be limited to an illustration and use of the brand slogan, not to exceed 25% of the total space of the advertisement . . . In broadcast media, brand reference is limited to an illustration, brand copy and jingle, not to exceed 25% of the length of the commercial". Within the limits of "good taste and propriety" advertisers cannot compare their products with those of their competitors'; no well-known personality can endorse wines on television (as Orson Welles did in the United States for Paul Masson wines), and "actors and musicians employed in the production of advertising shall not imply that their talent or ability is dependent on the use of the company's product". Nor, heaven forbid, should they "imply directly or indirectly, that social acceptance, personal success, business or athletic achievement may be acquired or result from the use of the product being advertised".

The companies are not allowed to give the price of their product nor tell an audience where it can be purchased and never, never must anyone be seen actually consuming the product in a TV commercial. If a visitor from another planet were to tune in to a Maria Christina or a Capistro commercial he might think that wine is something Canadians use to wash out glasses. (In Saskatchewan, New Brunswick and Prince Edward Island, our mythical little green man would not get the chance because none of these provinces allow such TV commercials, nor radio and magazine ads.) Every province has its own caveats against certain kinds of public advertising of wine, beer

---

°In March 1982 LCBO general listings showed 517 Ontario products, 27 from other provinces, and 672 imports.

PRESENTING GRANDE CUVÉE.

GRANDE CUVÉE
DRY WHITE WINE/VIN BLANC SEC

A FINE CANADIAN WINE IN THE FRENCH TRADITION
FROM STE-MICHELLE.

Also available in Jordan & Ste-Michelle wine stores

and spirits. For instance, Newfoundland is alone in permitting billboards and posters, and Quebec is unique in allowing point of sale advertising in its stores. Recently, BC has relaxed its regulations to permit brand advertising on anything from business cards to T-shirts, promotional gimmicks still frowned upon in Ontario.

Not only does the Ontario government regulate the size of ads and their frequency ("only one advertisement per company shall appear in any issue of a daily newspaper") but they also tell us that "no more than four advertisements for beverage alcohol products will be permitted in any subway station. In addition, only two such advertisements shall face any subway platform"!

Small wonder Ontario's wineries have trouble getting the message across that their products have improve 400% over the "Block-and-Tackle" wines most Canadians remember.

ONTARIO WINERIES

ANDRES WINES, Winona, Ontario

The company that brought you Baby Duck—that uniquely Canadian beverage—is now the largest vintner in Canada with plants in six provinces. But Andres is something of a latecomer to the Ontario winemaking scene. The other commercial wineries can trace their lineage back at least sixty years; Andres arrived in Ontario in 1970—after establishing itself for ten years in BC—when it bought the Beau Chatel Winery, formerly known as Welland Wines and, before that, Subosits Wines.

The Beau Chatel winery was first offered for sale to the Ontario Grape Growers' Marketing Board at a time when "Concord was coming out of our ears," confesses former chairman, Keith Wiley. The grape growers did not want to get into the winemaking business and the facility was eventually bought by Andrew Peller. That purchase "was a godsend to the Ontario grape industry," says Wiley. "Until Andres hit the market our wines were dead."

When Victor Subosit acquired the original licence in 1930, the future president of Andres Wines, Andrew Peller, had not yet become a Canadian citizen. Peller sailed to Canada from his native Hungary in 1927; he opened a grocery store in Toronto and subsequently moved to Chicago to learn the brewer's trade, after working as a maintenance man at Cosgrave's Brewery. In the 1940s and 50s Andrew Peller set up a variety of businesses, including the Peller Ice Company and the Peller Brewery in Hamilton.

After ten years in the business, Peller sold his company and for two years flirted with journalism as the owner of the *Hamilton Daily News*. In 1959 he bought Skyway Motors but that enterprise did not last long either. Casting around for a new idea, Peller hit upon the wine trade—at the suggestion of his son, Joe. In the light of his brewing history the Liquor Board of Ontario was not too receptive to his overtures for a licence; so Andrew Peller turned his attentions to British Columbia.

In 1960, after much lobbying, he was granted a licence and a year later began operations in a small plant at Port Moody. With a supreme lack of imagination and comprehension of the wine market, Peller's directors wanted to call the company "The Vancouver Winery" or "The British Columbia Winery". Andrew Peller had other ideas: "I proposed that we call the winery 'Andres'. This was my baptismal name and sounded French. French wines sold. Andres would be top of the list in the liquor stores because everything was listed alphabetically." An image of "Andre, the little old winemaker," was created by a commercial artist (a plump-cheeked smiling face with a cartoon Frenchman's moustache) and the stylized letter "A"—the company's logo—was conceived by Peller himself: the three-barred cross on top of the letter "A" is an Egyptian fertility charm worn by women hoping to become pregnant.

The success story of Baby Duck, the product that made Andres the most profitable wine company in Canada, is told elsewhere in this book. Suffice it to say here that since 1973, the year the engaging little yellow duckling took flight, it has commanded centre stage on the Canadian wine scene and sent competing companies scrambling to develop a taste-alike product. Over the past decade, the duckling on the label has begun to look more mature and elegant as befits an aging bird whose appeal is on the decline but who can still pull in a healthy profit for Andres, particularly in Quebec and the Maritimes.

In 1982 Andres brought out a white version of Baby Duck, after much internal agonising, in order to compete with the growing sales of Jordan's Spumante Bambino, a wine which sold largely because of the slapstick antics of an athletic blonde and a lugubrious pianist in the TV commercial.

For many years Andres has put all its eggs in the Baby Duck nest, but now that sales of the 7% "fun" wine have peaked in most provinces, the company is beginning to concentrate on table wines and on diversifying its product base. Even though it is trying to distance itself from the Baby Duck-Quack Pack image, it still stresses the importance of sparkling wines by listing them first in all its company brochures and literature.

Under its chief executive officer, Andrew's son Joe, who gave up medicine to take over the running of the company in 1965, Andres has moved aggressively forward, opening up facilities to enable it to get maximum liquor board listings in six provinces. In 1975 the company introduced the bag-in-box (4 litre) concept into Canada with its Cellar Cask wines. These now sell over 400,000 gallons annually.

Hochtaler, the company's answer to Schloss LaderHeim, was vinified in BC first (like most of Andres' products), and the blend was changed to accommodate Ontario's 30% imported wine regulation. As a result of this ruling, Ontarians cannot get the full range of Andres' premium Richelieu wines made from California grapes in BC. But the Auberge screw-top litre bottles, both red and white, are among the best inexpensive table wines made in the province.

In an effort to move the enormous quantity of red grapes available from the 1981 harvest, Andres winemaker, Barry Poag, created a white wine from the ubiquitous De Chaunac grape. The grapes were picked young before they had developed a deep skin colour and only the free run juice was used.

As the consumer palate shows signs of drying out the company has the Domaine D'Or red and white blend which are well made and attractively priced French-style products. And following the spurious trend to light wines—a market largely created by the wineries rather than the demands of the market place—Andres has introduced a light "champagne" and a white at 9% called Franciscan Light (the Germans have been doing this for centuries!).

But perhaps the most innovative and controversial of Andres' corporate decisions has been to vinify wine in California under its own label and to acquire two Toronto agencies which import Italian and French wines respectively.

Originally called Andres California Cellars, a company oenologist, David Hojnoski, made six wines from Californian grapes at the Souverain winery in Sonoma. The wines, four whites and two reds, were vinified to Canadian tastes and sold as Californian products at the same mark-up as other American imports. But the public could not understand why an Ontario winery should be in the business of selling Californian wine. The Andres label on the product suggested that the wines were made in Ontario, so the company decided to change the name of this range to Jalger (an acronym of Joe, Andres, Lena—Andrew's wife—and Gretchen—Joe's sister. The "er" comes from the Peller name).

This venture into the importation business upset other winery executives, all the more when Andres announced in 1982 that it had acquired control of two small import agencies, Superior Wines, founded by George Piscitelli three years earlier to import Italian wines, and Watleys Ltd., an established Toronto company run like a traditional English wine merchant's by John Watley. This agency imports a range of European wines and spirits.

With these two importers under the Andres umbrella, the Peller family had done in a small way what the Seagram empire had achieved on a large scale with Paul Masson and the Barton & Guestier labels—instant diversification with a ready-made wine list. Not only does Andres make its own wines but it is looking to the future when European imports will gain an even larger share of the market than they already command (53%).

Andres did not seriously enter the table wine market until the late 1970s. The company needed to generate a reputation beyond its sparkling wine image and the Andres California Cellars label was to be that entrée into the market. Unfortunately it backfired as consumers were unsure what the bottles contained. Certainly, the acquisition of the wine-importing agencies has made life more difficult for other Ontario wineries who see Andres in the role of gamekeeper-turned-poacher. As one rival executive put it: "We, as an industry, have been making representations to Queen's Park about the dumping of Italian wine in our market and Joe Peller goes out and gets into the game himself as a big player. He's harmed our credibility as an industry." But the Peller family has always howed their own row. They introduced Baby Duck to the public when the Canadian consumer needed something different from the sweet heavy alcohol dessert wines and the other commercial wineries followed suit. So no doubt we will see other companies eyeing the importers of European wines with a view to marrying into a growth market.

David Ringler, the Director of Marketing for Andres, thinks that his company should be competing in both the domestic and imported sectors of the wine business. "We should be separating ourselves from our Canadian competition as much as we possibly can, even with our Canadian production. We believe we should compete for the import share of the market because it's there." But whatever direction the company takes, according to Ringler, Baby Duck will never disappear from its list.

Andres figures in the March 1982 Annual Report show sales of nearly $47 million and a net earnings of $4.85 million, an increase of 41% over the previous year. From a corporate point of view the company must be doing something right.

Storage capacity: 3,100,000 gallons

BARNES WINES, St. Catharines, Ontario

In 1873, just six years after Confederation, George Barnes created his winery on the banks of the old Welland Canal. It is Canada's oldest continuously run winemaking operation. At first it rejoiced in the name of "The Ontario Grape Growing and Wine Manufacturing Company" and bought in grapes from farmers in the St. Catharines area to augment its own production from 52 acres of vineyards surrounding the property, known as Barnesdale.

The original cut-stone building still stands today and is used as storage for holding tanks; another part of the historical building has become a tasting room, museum and retail store. The outside deck was made from the oak staves of the nineteenth-century vats when the winery changed to stainless steel fermentation. A few of the 5,000 gallon vats dating back to 1875 are still kept for sherry and red wine production.

In the museum you can see a bottle of Barnes' Golden Diana Sherry dated 1887 and a Port "by Appointment to his Excellency the Governor General of Canada" in a screw-top, flask-shaped bottle. Wines such as these were favourites of the Great Lakes ships' captains whose sailing vessels were hauled by mule team through the canal in the latter part of the nineteenth century. The boats would tie up below George Barnes' winery to sample his products and barrels of his wines were rolled down the embankment to be stowed below deck for the captain's table. By 1894 the company had a storage capacity of 250,000 gallons. Today that volume has multiplied five times, although the sprawling complex of buildings belies the size because half of Barnes' cellaring is underground.

Two years after the company changed its unwieldy name to Barnes in 1934, it bought up the licence of the Fort William Wine Company and, in 1939, the Sunnybank Winery in St. Catharines. Barnes itself was bought in 1973 by Reckitt & Coleman (Canada) Ltd. who sold it to a private company called Keewhit in 1981. Keewhit in turn sold 49% of its shares to the large

British distillery, Gilbey's, in 1982. Using Gilbey's 100-strong national sales force across the country, Barnes products have been aggressively marketed and the company is represented in all but one of the provincial liquor boards (British Columbia).

When Reckitt and Coleman acquired the company in 1973 its business was 85% sherries and ports. In the following ten years, Barnes made the shift into table wines which now account for 90% of its list. According to its president, Jeff Ward, "We've had to convince the consumer that the same winery that produced Catawba for 120 years can now put out a Riesling of what we consider to be excellent quality. For that reason we are tending to sell our wines under a brand identification rather than a corporate one." This means that the Barnes name appears in the smallest print on the bottom of the label—a marketing pattern now common to all commercial wineries.

The major line is Heritage Estates—an umbrella brand which includes five blended wines: Chablis, Burgundy, Claret, Rosé, Rhine Wine and four sherries. Apart from the obligatory German-style white, Weinfest, and an excellent sturdy red called Beauvoir, the company also lists four champagnes (made for Barnes by another producer) and the more traditional labrusca-based white wines like Sauternes and Bon Apetit, as well as a sweet Spumante and the ubiquitous Crackling Cold Duck.

Because of the Gilbey connection (part of an English-based conglomerate, IDV, which owns Piat in Burgundy, Chateau Loudenne in Bordeaux and the Stellenboch wineries in South Africa among others), Barnes now has access to the technical services of winemakers around the world in the future development of its viticultural practices. This augurs well for the introduction of flagship products like its 1982 Johannisberg Riesling made from Ontario grapes with sweet reserve added.

In 1976 Barnes introduced the first light table wine on the market at 9% alcohol. Government regulations at the time proscribed the use of Light Wine as its name so the company subsequently called it Bon Apetit. But, following the success of light wines like Chateau-Gai's Capistro and Jordan's Maria Christina Light, Barnes will be taking the plunge into the market with its own, as yet unnamed, light white product soon.

Most of the Barnes' white wines have 30% Californian base wines blended in and the red Beauvoir gets its backbone from Petite Sirah grown in California.

Storage capacity: 1,350,000 gallons

BRIGHTS WINES, Niagara Falls, Ontario

M.F. Jones, who was associated with Brights for 29 years, the last four as company president until 1963, remembers the co-founder, Thomas Bright, as something of a martinet. "He didn't hold with government interference and didn't believe he should be made to keep books. When I joined the winery a year after he sold out in 1934, there were no accounts. The old boy kept them all in a small book which he carried around with him." At that point in its history Brights was the largest winery in private hands in the world, with a storage capacity of 4 million gallons.

Brights was founded in 1874 in Toronto, a year after George Barnes opened his winery at St. Catharines. The young Thomas G. Bright, a wealthy lumberman, started the business with his partner F.A. Shirriff. They called it the Niagara Falls Wine Company and sixteen years later they moved to the outskirts of that town to be near their grape supply. Their original capacity of 50,000 gallons was housed in a two-storey building of 10,000 square feet which is still part of today's gigantic plant.

In 1911, the company changed its name to T.G. Bright when the founder bought out his partner. By then the winery had grown to 300,000 gallons. In 1933 Harry Hatch, who controlled the Hiram Walker distillery and owned Jordan Wines, bought the company from the Bright family and immediately undertook a massive reorganisation which would eventually make Brights Canada's leading winery. He hired a Virginian-born microbiologist from California, Dr. John Eoff, who in turn brought in a young French chemist named Adhemar de Chaunac. The two men virtually single-handedly were to turn the Canadian wine trade around and create the basis of the industry we know today.

When de Chaunac joined Brights, the company, like its rivals, was producing sweet ports and sherries from five or six varieties of labrusca grapes. De Chaunac's low opinion of these products was expressed in his customary colourful language; and he began to look at the possibility of making *dry* table wines from Ontario-grown grapes for the first time since the nineteenth century. He pressed two experimental batches from Catawba and Delaware grapes which so impressed his employers that he was given the green light to make commercial quantities of these wines.

The Second World War interrupted de Chaunac's intention to bring French vinifera and hybrids to Niagara and it wasn't until 1946 that he was able to plant Riesling, Pinot Noir and Chardonnay in Canadian soil. Perhaps his single most important contribution was the cultivation of the grape that now bears his name—the grape that has become the backbone of Ontario red wine production.

Since those early pioneering efforts, Brights has an impressive list of "firsts" in the development of the Canadian wine industry: the first non-labrusca red table wine, Manor St. Davids Claret (based on the Chelois grape, one of the hybrids de Chaunac imported); the first Canadian vinifera

*The main entrance of Brights Wines Limited in Niagara Falls, Ontario. This
distinctive entrance is often used as a symbol for the winery.*
Courtesy: Brights Wines Ltd.

varietal, a Chardonnay produced in 1956; the first 7% sparkling wine, Dubarry
Rosé and Winette (in 1953, long before Baby Duck uttered its first quack); the
first bottle-fermented sparkling wine, Brights President in 1949, (although the
Jules Robinet winery at Sandwich had made a little sparkling wine during
Prohibition, but legislation proscribed its sale and distribution); the first
champagne from exclusively Chardonnay grapes (in 1955); and the first
Canadian sherry to be made by the Spanish method using flor yeasts and the
solera system.

But the company's greatest contribution has been its development of
grape breeding programs that are still carried out on its experimental acreage
at St. Davids and on a 15-acre plot at Harrow in the Kent-Essex region of
southwest Ontario. The current Director of Research, George Hostetter, is

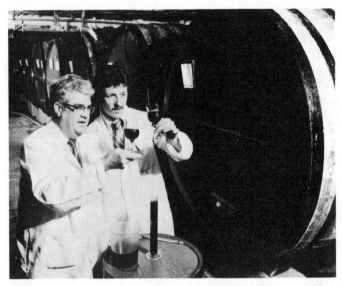

Laboratory supervisors at Brights testing wine for colour. The casks behind them date from 1880, making them the oldest in North America.
Courtesy: Bright Wines Ltd.

justifiably proud of his company's record in improving grape varieties for winemaking. Brights has spent millions of dollars over the years to this end and has generously shared its knowledge with the industry, to the betterment of Ontario and Canadian wines in general. Its research into the production of white wine from red grapes in 1979 is especially impressive. The widely planted De Chaunac has become something of an albatross around the necks of the commercial wineries at a time when the public demands white wines. This blanc de noir juice makes up 30% of Brights Dry Home White.

As the second largest producer in Canada after Andres, Brights has a massive list of 75 different labels vinified at its facilities in Ontario, Quebec and British Columbia; the full gamut of wines from 7% sparklers to table wines, port, sherries, ciders, vermouths, premium vinifera varietals and sacramental wines. One oddity is the 5% alcohol, Club Spritz, a labrusca-based beverage with spring water added. But the company fortunes are founded on its champagnes—two of every three bottles purchased in Canada bear the Brights label—and its national sales of House Red and House White. These blends differ in their taste profile from province to province depending on regulations governing the use of Californian wines and also on the sophistication of provincial palates. Ontario's version is a shade drier than that sold in BC.

While products such as Entre-Lac White and Entre-Lac Red suggest French-style wines, the company offers three German imitations—Liebes-

Heim, WarnerHof, and Baron Ludwig (the undiluted Club Spritz blend at 9% alcohol).

One of Brights' best wines is the varietal Baco Noir. The grapes are left on the vine as late as possible for maximum sugar. In good years (like 1978, 1979 and 1982) it is labelled as a 'Late Harvest'. Other red varietals are Seibel and Maréchal Foch. The company also produces three well-made vintage-dated viniferas: Riesling, Pinot Chardonnay and Gewurztraminer; and a Seyval Blanc, L'Entre-Côte White.

In 1980 Brights brought out an Ontario-grown Gamay Beaujolais Nouveau (released in early November) along with Chateau des Charmes—the only two Ontario wineries currently indulging in this annual craze. This wine tends to vary according to the vagaries of the Niagara climate.

Storage capacity: 6,500,000 gallons (wooden cooperage)
2,500,000 gallons (stainless steel)

CHARAL WINERY & VINEYARDS,
Blenheim, Ontario

Allan Eastman is the third generation of his family to farm in Kent county. This area used to be a thriving winemaking region before Prohibition but grapes gave way to more profitable crops in the 1920s and the Niagara Peninsula became the grape-growing centre of Ontario. Now the wine-makers are turning their attentions once more to southwest Ontario where Eastman has pioneered some excellent vineyards, in a very favourable microclimate.

The winery complex at Porky's Corner on Highway 3 between Bleinheim and Cedar Springs, produced its first 1,000 gallons of wine in 1975, a varietal Dutchess and Pinot Chardonnay (which won the 1977 gold medal at the Wines Unlimited Competition in Lancaster, Pennsylvania beating out 200 entries of North Eastern American Chardonnays). The grapes were grown on the Eastman fruit farm—three acres of Concord and Niagara and one with thirty different varieties of hybrids and viniferas. Following the success of those first bottlings, the winery received its licence in 1977 and began to expand the vineyards.

Today Charal has one-third of the 300-acre farm under vines and produces some fourteen labels. (Charal, incidentally, is the composite name of Charlotte and Allan Eastman.) In 1982 the winery produced 50,000 gallons from 15 grape varieties.

Although Eastman does have some Riesling, Gewurztraminer and Char-donnay in his vineyards, the bulk is French hybrids. Following the market dictates, in 1982 he produced 85% white wines, some of it from red grapes. To ensure the freshness of his juice, he purchased a destemmer machine which is linked to a mechanical harvester. This allows him to crush the grapes in the field and transport them within an hour to the presses or fermenting tanks. Charal is the first Ontario winery to employ this system, one that is extensively used in California.

Apart from the varietal whites like Seyval Blanc, Dutchess and Vidal, the winery puts out a useful blend called Cuvée Blanc which is based on a German hybrid, and a Chandelle Blanc made from Aurore grapes with 30% Californian French Colombard added. Eastman admits that he is still looking for a style for his white wines although they are all clean and well made. "As far as the reds are concerned," he says, "we started off with fruity wines and now we're giving them a little wood by barrel aging in American oak and adding some back to the tanks."

Charal offers a varietal Baco Noir and Maréchal Foch as well as two red blends—Premiere Rouge (De Chaunac and some Baco Noir) and Chandelle Rouge (De Chaunac and Villard Noir).

The rest of the list is made up with a light white Spumante (made for the company by Brights) and two fruit wines based on apples, strawberries and pears—called Vinacopia, red and white.

Some products, like Pinot Chardonnay and Riesling, are only available through Charal's retail outlets. One is at the winery and is a mini farmer's market in itself, selling a variety of fresh fruit and vegetables, as well as cheeses, jams, pickles, baked goods and cider (8,000 gallons a year are fermented at the winery.) The other retail store is located in London, Ontario.

Storage capacity: 60,000 gallons.

CHATEAU DES CHARMES,
Niagara-on-the-Lake, Ontario

"When my family and I lived on the Algerian coast," Paul Bosc has written, "we owned a small villa. In traditional style each one was named. Our home was called Charmes." And when he started his own small winery in 1978 Bosc recalled that era in the name of his company. He emigrated to Canada from his native Algeria in 1963, having studied oenology at the University of Dijon in Burgundy and having grown grapes in North Africa. This training was to colour his approach to winemaking because, today, Chateau des Charmes comes closest to the French style, particularly in its Chardonnay and Aligoté (the only one of its kind available in Ontario). And nothing could be more

Burgundian than the use of carbonic masceration as a winemaking technique for some of his reds. After his arrival in Canada, Bosc worked for the Liquor Board and then joined Chateau-Gai as a winemaker, a position he held for fifteen years, presiding over the creation of Alpenweiss before he left to start up his own operation.

From the wines he had made experimentally at Chateau-Gai, he was convinced that the best European grapes could be grown successfully in Ontario and superior table wines made from them. He also owned a small farm in Upper New York State where he grew a variety of vines including such difficult grapes as Cabernet Sauvignon, Cabernet Franc and Merlot. In 1979 he made a very respectable Medoc-style wine from equal parts of all three grapes.

The winery at Chateau des Charmes is an unprepossessing cement block house, standing in fifty acres of vinifera vines planted in 1978. While Paul Bosc had visions of creating a list of wines vinified from only the top European varieties like Chardonnay, Riesling, Aligoté, Auxerrois, Gamay Beaujolais and Pinot Noir, the dictates of the marketplace have forced him to pay attention to more bread-and-butter products such as blends based on that most Ontarian grape, the white Seyval, and reds from Maréchal Foch, Chelois, Villard Noir and Chancellor.

Charmes bought in 18,000 gallons of Seyval in 1982 to improve its white blend Sentinel Blanc (with Vidal and Californian Chenin Blanc). Further down the scale is La Cour Blanc, based on the Alpenweiss "recipe" in which the homely Elvira predominates over some decolourised reds and the mandatory Californian base white.

The red version of the Sentinel and La Cour blends have 25% Petite Sirah from California mixed with four Ontario grapes—Maréchal Foch, Chancellor, Chelois and Villard Noir.

Primeur Rouge, the company's best blended red is part Gamay, part Villard Noir (both vinified by carbonic masceration) with 10% Pinot Noir.

Paul Bosc has perfected his use of carbonic masceration after years of producing Gamay Beaujolais Nouveau. Currently this over-rated wine is made only here and at Brights. Bosc had the audacity to send a few bottles over to Paris out of the 850 cases he made in 1982 for a tasting days before the official release date of November 15th. The wines were tasted in Paris and diplomatic courtesy was observed.

Chateau des Charmes has learned the benefit of publicity from Inniskillin and has pulled off some notable coups of its own. In 1980, Bosc's Riesling 1979 was judged the best Canadian wine by *Today Magazine*. (There was no explanation as to how this decision was reached, but immediately everyone wanted to get hold of that particular wine.) Even better, to my mind, are the two 1980 Chardonnays—Nokara Estate (grown by a neighbouring farmer) and Estate (Bosc's own grapes) which provided wines of great character and good fruit quality. The first was vinified in stainless steel and the second had

Oenologist Paul Bosc of Chateau des Charmes in Niagara-on-the-Lake, Ontario. His training in France is reflected in the wines, which come closest to the French style. Courtesy: Chateau des Charmes Wines Ltd.

three months in oak. The 1982 Estate Chardonnay I tasted from the barrel will be first-rate, probably the finest white wine yet made in Canada. This particular vintage also produced Aligoté and Auxerrois. The winery is moving more and more into individual bottling of its better vineyards, fermenting some in tanks, some in wood and aging in both stainless steel and French oak.

Paul Bosc treats his grapes and his wines like a first-time father and his pricing policy, as a result, can be somewhat eccentric. If he is happy with the wine he charges accordingly as though it were a work of art (which it is). And if anyone is capable of growing a serious Chardonnay in Canada that can stand next to Meursault and Corton-Charlemagne without blushing, it will be Paul Bosc at Chateau des Charmes. While his heart seems to be in his white wines, Bosc has produced in 1982 a Pinot Noir and a Cabernet Franc which, though light in style, are encouraging portents for the future if the vines survive.

Storage capacity: 135,000 gallons (including 6,000 gallons in French oak).

CHATEAU-GAI WINES, Niagara Falls, Ontario

The early years of Ontario wineries are one long history of small fish being swallowed by bigger fish who are in turn swallowed by even bigger ones. Such is the story of Chateau-Gai, which can date its ancestral beginnings back to 1857 when a certain Achilles Rougemous opened a winery in Cooksville where Johann Schiller and Justin de Courtenay had been before him. The Rougemous winery was taken over by the Canadian Vine Growers' Association in 1926, which itself had been acquired by Canadian Wineries Limited. This latter company brought together five small winery operations including the Stamford Park Wine Company, created in 1890 by the Marsh family in the township of Stamford, Niagara Falls. In 1941 the company changed names from Canadian Wineries to Chateau-Gai, giving prominence to the marketing brand of its Canadian champagne.

In 1973 Chateau-Gai was taken over by John Labatt who brought Chateau Cartier, formerly Parkdale Wines, into the organisation and amalgamated the two wineries under one roof at the Niagara Falls plant. The new owners financed the changeover from port and sherries to table wines in 1978. Eight million dollars were spent to remove the wooden cooperage and replace it with stainless steel jacketed cooling tanks and the latest technology. But some of the ancient wood vats still remain from the Marsh family era of 1898. These are used to age the company's sherries and red wines. The vats survived the inactivity of the Prohibition era by being filled with water to ensure that their staves would not shrink.

But forty-five years before Labatt's took over, the company, under the innovative direction of a former newspaperman, Alec Sampson, was already looking for new technology. In 1928 Canadian Wineries, as it was then, bought from France the patented "Charmat Methode" with its equipment and formula for producing sparkling wines—the first of its kind in Canada.

It was Alec Sampson, with his sense of public relations, who changed the name of the company to Chateau-Gai. As M.F. Jones, the former President of Brights, recalls, "When Alec Sampson took over Canadian Wineries it had no flair whatsoever. He recognised that and hit on the name Chateau-Gai, boosting it wherever he went. He even took his champagne to France and stuck it up in a street in Paris, saying that it was the equal of French champagne." This was too much for the French. In 1964, fifteen champagne houses took Chateau-Gai to court to prevent the company from using the term "champagne" on its labels. As William Rannie wrote in *The Wines of Ontario*, "The claim was based upon a trade agreement of 1933 between Canada and France. Chateau-Gai argued that it had been making authentic champagne under the Charmat process for five years prior to the trade agreement, its labels approved by both federal and provincial governments."

At that time there were seven companies in Canada making champagne; but Chateau-Gai was singled out because of the tub-thumping chauvinism of

Alec Sampson who had the nerve to challenge the French on their own turf. The champagne houses, backed by the French government, had cleverly brought their action in Quebec and it was heard before a judge of French descent who, in 1967, found against Chateau-Gai. The case went to the Supreme Court of Canada on appeal and in 1974 the original verdict in favour of the French champagne makers was upheld.

Why, then, do we still see the term "champagne" on Canadian sparkling wines in every province but Quebec? The answer is that in December 1977, the Canadian government abrogated the 1933 trade agreement which had never been formally ratified by France.

Chateau-Gai also crossed swords with the sherry makers of Spain. In 1968 the company had to change its labels on sherry products shipped to Britain because the winemakers of Jerez, like their French colleagues in Champagne, objected to anyone outside the delimited area using the generic name of their product. So Chateau-Gai sherry was shipped to London as "Ontario Cream Appetizer, Solera Canadian Appetizer and Dry Canadian Appetizer".

In the early 1970s Chateau-Gai made a commitment to produce premium dry red varietal and French hybrid wines. More interesting than the Maréchal Foch, Seibel and Gamay Beaujolais offered to the public were the experimental wines produced by its oenologist Paul Bosc (who now runs Chateau des Charmes). Bosc made limited batches of Pinot Noir, Chardonnay and the first white wine from Gamay Beaujolais grapes; but unfortunately the company did not exploit them commercially. Chateau-Gai did, however, draw up a set of wine standards which it hoped the industry as a whole would adopt. But this encouraging idea was not taken up and the company had to wait until 1979 to see its concept put into practice as the Ontario Wine Industry Standards Act.

For the last five years Chateau-Gai has made a reputation on its white wines, particularly Alpenweiss, Alpenweiss Sparkling and Capistro. But this concentration of whites at the expense of reds is a direct result of catering to market demands. Alpenweiss, for example, was unashamedly modelled on Black Tower and in 1979 it won out over that German EEC blend in a blind tasting organized by the now defunct *Wine Press* magazine—the first Canadian-made white wine to triumph over a European import, however dubious the quality of the competition.

Alpenweiss, made with Ontario-grown Elvira and Ventura grapes, was the first Chateau-Gai product to have Californian wine blended into it—a mix of Thompson Seedless, Chenin Blanc, French Colombard and sweet Muscat. The wines were purchased from another John Labatt holding, Lamont Winery in Di Giorgio, California. In BC the predominant grape is Okanagan Riesling and in Alberta and New Brunswick, the two other provinces where it is made, the product tastes slightly different from either Ontario's or BC's.

Chateau-Gai was the first of the major wineries to follow the Californian lead and introduce a light wine to the Canadian market in October 1981. Capistro, with its 8% alcohol, innocuous flavour and dreamy pastel label, was aimed at diet-conscious women who like a glass of wine with lunch, but one with some residual sweetness. A year later the company brought out a sparkling version of Alpenweiss at the same alcoholic strength of 10.5% but a touch sweeter. The other German-style product on its list is Edelwein, an offspring of Alpenweiss.

The move to whites has meant that the company has neglected its reds. Princiere and various Italian-sounding products like Chianno Rosso (to try to capture some of the Castelli Romani market) make up a rather lacklustre list which now includes a red Alpenweiss. But, following the 1982 vintage, the company will be putting out a varietal Maréchal Foch in its attempts to upgrade its red wine offerings.

While Donald Campbell freely admits the company is in the *vin ordinaire* market, Chateau-Gai has not turned its back entirely on the production of premium vinifera wines. Under the Lincoln County label are three well-made wines—Pinot Chardonnay, Johannisberg Riesling and Gamay Rosé. First produced in 1980, these wines need two or three years of bottle age to show their best. And the company has been flirting with a Merlot which eventually will see the light of day on the Liquor Board shelves.

The labels of the Lincoln County series (featuring Ontario's provincial symbol, the trillium flower) and Capistro's dreamy landscape are the most imaginative of all the commercial wineries' and will no doubt make other companies take a second look at their packaging. After all, there is no reason why a wine label should look and read like an invitation to a mortician's convention.

Chateau-Gai—under the Labatt's holding company, Ridout Wines—owns Casabello in BC and two other facilities: Chateau-Gai Wines (Atlantic), Scoudouc, New Brunswick and Stoneycroft Cellars/Chateau-Gai Wines, Calgary, Alberta.

Storage capacity: 3,500,000 gallons.

COLIO WINES, Harrow, Ontario

In 1977 a group of Italian businessmen living in Windsor visited that city's twin in the Friuli region, Udine, to discuss the possibility of importing wines of the Cantina Il Castello into Canada. As Colio's president, Enzo DeLuca, remembers it, "When I told them the problems, they threw up their hands and said why don't we build a winery instead?" In 1980, even before the company had received its licence they began to build their facility on four acres of ground in the town of Harrow. The total investment for the plant and Italian equipment was $2 million.

This part of Essex County had been a thriving grape-growing area until the Depression when farmers turned to more lucrative cash crops like tobacco. Grape growing began to revive in the early 1970s and the crops were trucked east to the Niagara wineries. Local farmers had a commercial incentive with the creation of the Charal Winery in Blenheim and Colio at Harrow. Now there are 300 acres under vine in the immediate area around Harrow. As the "sun parlour of Canada", the nation's most southerly town, it enjoys a longer growing season than Niagara and its grapes have a higher sugar reading in consequence.

For its first crush, Colio used 60% grapes from Essex County, mainly Seyval Blanc, and leapt boldly into the marketplace with 120,000 gallons of wine under ten different labels.

The company winemaker is Carlo Negri who comes from Trentino in northern Italy where he spent seventeen years learning the art. His style is uncompromisingly Italian and commercial. Everything is fermented and aged in stainless steel—even the reds—so they are fresh, fruity and market-ready. Negri's wines are soft and mellow at one year old; he does not look for great personality and vinifies labrusca grapes expertly to avoid foxiness. A good examples is his Fragolino (100% Concord)—a sweet, fruity dessert wine with a flavour of strawberries.

The main grapes used in various combinations are Seyval Blanc, Aurore and De Chaunac for the whites, and Maréchal Foch and De Chaunac for the reds. Many of the products are too similar in style to warrant so many labels which again are confusing in their similarity. But the basic red and white blends, Colio Rosso Secco and Colio Bianco Secco are well structured and clean. The more expensive "Riserva" label is a misnomer; it does not refer to barrel age, as under Italian wine laws, but to the winemaker's selection. The Riserva Rosso 1981, a blend of Maréchal Foch, Chelois and some Californian Cabernet, is flavourful but not as successful as its white counterpart—the pride of Colio's list.

The winery has planted its own vineyards in the Harrow area which will be available for commercial harvesting in 1985. In 1982 Carlo Negri produced some excellent Johannisberg Riesling Seyval Blanc and Maréchal Foch; the company ultimately plans to import vines from the Alto-Adige region of Italy. The emphasis, says Enzo DeLuca, will be on reds rather than white wines.

Storage capacity: 250,000 gallons.

HILLEBRAND ESTATES WINES,
Niagara-on-the-Lake, Ontario

When engineer and teacher Joe Pohorly created Ontario's eleventh (and smallest) winery in 1979, he called it Newark—the original name of Niagara-on-the-Lake in the late eighteenth century. That same sense of history is enshrined in the colonial style of the two-storey wood building that houses the retail store, laboratory and tasting room and in the names he chose for his first wines: Wellington Rouge, Chevalier Rouge, and Comtesse Blanc. (Newark's Elizabeth Rosé was named for Pohorly's wife, Betty, who acts as company treasurer as well as helping out around the winery with their two teenage daughters.)

Situated smack on Highway 55 just west of Virgil, Newark was ideally placed to catch the flow of tourists to the Shaw Festival. "Without the tourists," he confesses, "we would have gone bankrupt with the high interest rates on bank loans."

Joe Pohorly had farmed the 35 acres of the family property since the early 1960s, tearing out peach trees and strawberry beds to make way for vines in 1967. A self-taught winemaker, he determined to devote himself fulltime to the creation of a cottage winery. "I decided to leave the teaching profession," he says, "because I wasn't challenged. Wine was a part of my life as a hobby. I just decided to develop it into a business." His original vines were mainly French hybrids—Maréchal Foch, De Chaunac, Seyval Blanc, Seyve-Villard, plus some experimental Chardonnay, Gewurztraminer and Aligoté. His intention was to concentrate on white varietals as well as some blended reds.

The whites were vinified in stainless steel and the reds in four wood vats purchased from Barnes when they released some of their wood cooperage in favour of steel fermentors. The first harvest in 1979 yielded 5,500 gallons; in 1980 the figure rose to 13,000 (including some Johannisberg Riesling the winery brought in from a neighbouring farmer). These two vintages were bottled by Inniskillin but by 1982 Newark had its own bottling line to cope with a greatly increased capacity. In that year they made 47,000 gallons of wine.

In the summer of 1982, Joe Pohorly was approached by the German winemakers Scholl & Hillebrand of Rüdesheim in the Rheingau with the object of buying into the Niagara company. The offer was finally accepted and early in 1983 Newark changed its names to Hillebrand Estates—although the Newark logo (which Pohorly himself designed) is still used on most of the products he created.

As Newark, the company aimed at French-style wines, especially the whites as exemplified by the dry, acidic Seyval Blanc, the crisp Chardonnay and Riesling and the Alsatian-type Gewurztraminer 1980.

With the Scholl & Hillebrand investment in the company, Pohorly, who acts as winemaker and president, will have access to German experience and technology. A graduate of the Geisenheim school, Jurgen Helbig, has been hired to assist him in the winemaking. Consequently, the new emphasis will be on Riesling rather than Chardonnay. Already such German grape types as Kerner, Müller-Thurgau and Morio-Muscat have been planted in the company vineyard.

As Joe Pohorly sees it, "Niagara-on-the-Lake will become the Rheingau of Canada". The first fruits of the collaboration has been the introduction of a Rhine-style blended white wine, Schloss Hillebrand, made from decolour-ised De Chaunac, Seyval Blanc with some Dutchess and Morio-Muscat is the most successful attempt to create a German-style wine from Canadian-grown hybrid grapes. A drier style is also planned.

The company also plans to market two house blends, Le Baron Rouge and Blanc. The red will be of Beaujolais character, a mix of Maréchal Foch and Le Commandant and the white a blend of Dutchess, Seyval Blanc and Riesling in a Rhine style.

Pohorly made his first red varietal in 1982—a Baco Noir. The Gewurz-traminer of that vintage had a very pleasing, spicy aroma when I sampled it out of the barrel early in 1983.

At the side of the winery are ten 40-gallon barrels which stand outside in all weathers. These are Pohorly's sherry casks which produce two styles based on the Agawam grape—one medium dry, the other sweet with added caramel. The sherries are "built up" to 18.5% alcohol by adding sugar to the fermentation over a period of time and aging them for three years in the oak casks. These products are available only at the winery store.

Storage capacity: 70,000 gallons (including 10,000 gallons in wood).

INNISKILLIN WINES,
Niagara-on-the-Lake, Ontario

Inniskillin is a film-maker's idea of what a farm winery should look like: a gleaming white plant surrounded by weathered barns and old barrels set in a sea of vines; large enough to look opulent, yet small enough to be run by two partners—one a taciturn Austrian winemaker, the other an extroverted young agronomist with a penchant for white suits, white sports cars and beautiful women. Falconcrest revisited, or Robert Mondavi Canadian-style. But it was not always so. The original winery was an old tin shed on the Ziraldo nurseries two kilometres away from the present site just off the Niagara Parkway. It was once a farm called Inniskillin by an early settler in the Niagara region.

The impact that Inniskillin has had on the Canadian wine industry in its ten years of operation is out of all proportion to its size. Its glamorous image, fostered by the public relations acumen of its founder, Donald Ziraldo, and supported by the quality of Karl Kaiser's wines, has chivvied the major companies into reassessing their own lists and upgrading the quality of their products. Inniskillin proved that there was a market for Ontario-grown hybrid and vinifera wines of a single variety, and equally important, it created a climate of interest and excitement among Ontario's consumers that made it possible for other small wineries to follow in its footsteps. Inniskillin was Ontario's original cottage winery—the first wine licence to be issued in the province since 1929.

The story of how Inniskillin came into existence has taken on the proportions of a legend in the Canadian wine world. As Donald Ziraldo tells it, "One day in 1973 Karl Kaiser came to my nursery to buy grape vines. In

Some vineyards at Inniskillin Wines in Niagara-on-the-Lake, Ontario. In the foreground are vinifera vines bearing Gewurztraminer grapes from Alsace. In the background are hybrid Vidal vines.
Courtesy: Inniskillin Wines Inc.

Austria he used to help his grandfather make wine and despaired of the Canadian products available at the Liquor Board. He came back with a bottle and my initial reaction was 'You made this from those!' The wine was terrific." The two men began to discuss the possibility of creating their own winery and they were joined by a French oenologist, Alain Rigaud, who soon dropped out of the picture. Their idea was to make limited quantities of quality table wines from hybrid and vinifera grapes.

In 1973 Ziraldo approached the head of the Liquor Control Board, General George Kitching, who was suitably impressed by the concept of a cottage winery in the province. The General had a vision of a string of such small operations in southern Ontario and endorsed Inniskillin as a pilot project to this end. He even donated ten Portuguese oak barrels, albeit damaged ones, to age the wines. The issuing of a licence to the new enterprise depended on the first batch of experimental wine which had to be submitted for testing by the LCBO.

The wine they chose to submit to the Board was a varietal De Chaunac rosé and on the strength of that they received a licence in 1974 to produce 10,000 gallons. But their tiny facility with its stainless steel tank, Portuguese barrels and glass demi-johns was only capable of producing half that amount. The first wines to be marketed under the Inniskillin label were 500 bottles of 1974 Maréchal Foch, 500 bottles of De Chaunac and 5,000 bottles of Vin Nouveau (a blend of these two wines with Chelois and Chancellor.) They were all red because the winery could not secure any white grapes.

When General Kitching telephoned Ziraldo to ask what he was going to call his operation, the young owner suggested "Chateau Inniskillin" for its historical value; but, as he confessed, after a moment's reflection, "that sounded too pretentious. So I told the general—who obviously appreciated the military connection—I'd simply call it 'Inniskillin House Wines'." (The 'House' was subsequently dropped.)

Inniskillin's early success must be attributed to one of the greatest public relations coups since Canada sent Yvonne de Carlo to Hollywood.

In February 1976, Toronto wine writer Michael Vaughan took a parcel of Ontario wines to England where they were tasted at Ontario House by such educated palates as Harry Waugh, Michael Broadbent and Hugh Johnson of *Wine Atlas* fame. Three years earlier Johnson had endeared himself to the Canadian wine industry by his pronouncement on Ontario wines: "The foulness of taste is what I remember best—an artificially scented, soapy flavour." Having sampled the selection, Hugh Johnson commented: "My favourite without doubt was the Inniskillin 1974 Maréchal Foch."

With this transatlantic endorsement Inniskillin's wines quickly sold out and it became a mark of social prestige to exhibit the label at smart dinner parties. But this instant cachet did not impress the better Toronto restaurants when Donald Ziraldo tried to convince them to list his wines. "They thought I must be joking," he says "Maitre d's showed me the door in no uncertain terms. But things have changed now."

Inniskillin moved from its Heath Robinson tin shed on the Ziraldo nurseries property in 1978. (A sign over the laboratory door read: "Employees will please wash their feet before returning to work".) By this time Ziraldo had added a rosé to his list as well as estate bottled Chardonnay, Gamay and Riesling from vines planted in 1974 in the company's vineyards (now the Seeger Vineyard). The present site of the winery, on what used to be the Brae Burn farm, boasts 20 acres of vines. Today, Inniskillin has 250 acres to supply its needs, including the Rief, Seeger, Klose, and Montague vineyards which now feature on the labels of vinifera bottlings like Chardonnay, Riesling, Gewurztraminer and Merlot.

This is the direction in which the winery is moving: limited editions of single European grape varieties under vineyard designations. In 1982, for example, Chardonnay from the Seeger and Montague vineyards was fermented in stainless steel and two styles of French oak (Limousin and Nevers), as well as blends of both—enough combinations to produce eight different Chardonnays. The object of the experiment is to find which grapes produce the best wines using different vinification and aging techniques. (Inniskillin purchased 100 of its 225 litre oak barrels from Chateau Margaux in the Médoc as well as 100 new French, Yugoslavian and German casks). While it was the first winery to take advantage of the 1977 Wine Content Act which

Donald Ziraldo and Karl Kaiser of Inniskillin Wines assess the quality of their Leon Millot.

Courtesy: Inniskillin Wines Inc.

permitted Ontario companies to import Californian juice or blending wine up to 15% of the amount of locally grown grapes they crushed, Ziraldo feels very strongly that Canadian products have to be just that. He has phased out the Californian Cabernet and Petite Sirah from his Brae Rouge blend and French Colombard from the Brae Blanc. Gone, too, from the list are the varietal De Chaunac, Villard Noir and Dutchess, but Inniskillin, in its persistent attempts to find the right grapes and the right soil, offers a large range of hybrid and vinifera wines such as Chamburcin, Leon Millot, Millot-Chamburcin, Chelois, Merlot, Maréchal Foch and Gamay Noir in the reds: and in whites, Seyval Blanc, Vidal, Chardonnay, Riesling, Gewurztraminer, and two styles of decolourised Gamay Beaujolais (one dry "French style", the other with sweet reserve in "German style"). The white wines, given Karl Kaiser's Austrian background, tend to be Germanic in style, but the reds are definitely Burgundian.

Ironically, Karl Kaiser made Inniskillin's reputation on its reds and he is currently experimenting to find the right style for his whites. The 1982 vintage has provided him with such high sugar Vidal grapes that he can produce a sweet dessert wine of *Spätlese* quality.

The winery's 1980 Maréchal Foch, which I contend is the best red wine yet made in Canada from domestically grown grapes, was bought by the Burgundy negociants, F. Chauvenet, in Nuits St. Georges in 1982. Six hundred and fifty cases were ordered but they are still waiting to be shipped. French law requires that all wines bear an appellation of origin and as yet the Ontario industry has not instituted the most fundamental regulations governing its products in terms of viticultural areas, grape types and production methods.

In addition to this French sale, Inniskillin wines enjoys a limited export market in Germany, Switzerland, England, Japan and the United States. The company has 4,000 bottles of sparkling wine made from high acid Chardonnay grapes in 1978 resting in its attractive champagne cellar above the wine boutique. Ziraldo plans to celebrate the company's tenth year of operations with this wine in 1984.

Apart from the well-designed wine boutique in the old Brae Burn barn, Inniskillin has a retail outlet at First Canadian Place in Toronto, where many of its limited edition wines not available in LCBO outlets can be purchased. And most recently the company has opened a small outlet in a "wine cellar" below a health food store in St. Catharines.

Storage capacity: 200,000 gallons

JORDAN & STE-MICHELLE CELLARS,
St. Catharines, Ontario

The history of Jordan Wines is a bewildering story of takeovers and mergers which ultimately brought together two large operations in Canada's only grape-growing provinces. The Ontario saga began in 1870 when Clark Snure and his son Eldrige set up an apple-drying business in a fieldstone house at the village of Jordan.

After changing ownership and operations many times, the company was taken over in 1926 by a Scottish distiller named William Cleland who changed the name to the Jordan Wine Company and subsequently purchased the Welch's grape juice plant at St. Catharines. In the same year Fred Torno founded Ontario's fifty-second winery called Danforth Wines in Toronto. Following the death of Cleland, the two companies merged in 1948 when Torno convinced Sam Bronfman's Distillers Corporation to acquire Jordan Wines.

The new company was known as Jordan-Danforth Wines until 1953, the year it bought the assets of the St. Catharines Winery, whose licence dated back to 1922. Danforth finally lost its identity in 1964 when Jordan bought it out. In 1971 Bronfman sold Jordan to Carling O'Keefe and in 1976 Ste-Michelle Cellars in BC was brought under the corporate umbrella.

When Jordan's chief oenologist, Bill Anderson, joined the company in 1950 the leading seller was Branvin, a sweet sherry, which had enjoyed popularity since the 1930s.

Like other commercial wineries up until the 1960s, Jordan produced 90% sherries and ports. These products made from Concord, Niagara, Agawam, Buffalo and Veeport grapes were highly baked and heavy on the alcohol and sugar. One of its early winemakers was Ralph Crowther at Danforth Wines who subsequently left the company in 1951 to work at Ontario's Horticultural Research Institute where he developed a speedy method to produce flor sherry.

Jordan's table wine production in those years was based on the Delaware, Catawba and Buffalo grapes. The winery also produced a "champagne"—a carbonated version of its white Sauterne.

Today the company has placed its confidence in the German school of winemakers, hiring its oenologists from Geisenheim in the Rheingau. This emphasis is reflected in the vinification techniques and style of its whites. Even the Zinfandel made from California grapes in Surrey, BC by Ste-Michelle Cellars resembles a German red in its light fruitiness compared with the more robust versions generally made from this grape.

Much of the technology at Jordan is German and the company has recently acquired a juice concentrator—the first in Canadian winemaking—which, through heat exchange, removes the esters from labrusca grapes responsible for the "foxy" aroma and taste. The Elvira grape, the mainstay of Ontario white wines, is improved immeasurably by this process. Until Jordan has better white hybrids to vinify in sufficient quantity, the winery will rely on such hardware as cold fermentation tanks and advanced filtration techniques for its bread-and-butter products like Toscano, Maria Christina and the new Interlude.

But in the first analysis better wines are made from better grapes and to this end Jordan has set up two experimental vineyards—one 20-acre plot at the St. Catharines winery and another 38-acre plot near Vineland—to propogate suitable winter-hardy varieties for its contracted growers. In addition to the mother block at the St. Catharines nursery, the company also has acreage in the Inkameep Vineyards in B.C.; these three vineyards will ultimately provide stock for superior table wines in the future.

While the company's thrust is currently in light Germanic-style white wines with sweet reserve added, like Falkenberg and Rhine Castle, it also markets varietals such as Pinot Chardonnay, Seyval Blanc, Vidal and an interesting dessert wine called Pinot Muscato.

Mindful of a swing back to the popularity of reds, the winery has removed

Reisling vines planted at Jordan & Ste-Michelle Cellars' 30-acre experimental vineyard, "Glen Elgin," located in Vineland, Ontario.
Courtesy: Jordan & Ste-Michelle Cellars Ltd.

its entire wood cooperage from the old plant at Jordan Station and, after refurbishing and cleaning, has reassembled it in a vast oak cellar (the largest in Canada) with a capacity of 1.3 million litres.

In future all the reds, as head winemaker Josef Zimmerman says, will be "kissed with oak". The company produces a Maréchal Foch and two blends called Jordan Valley Burgundy and Claret as well as red versions of Maria Christina and Toscano.

Jordan offers two sweet rosés, three champagnes under the Gold Seal label, a variety of 7% sparkling wines, crackling wines, vermouths, ciders and from its large stocks, two ports and six sherries. The Branvin label is still represented in these last two categories, but the best of the sherries are the vintage dated De Chaunac's (1966 and 1969) which were released to celebrate the company's 60th anniversary and Christmas 1982 respectively.

Apart from the Ste-Michelle operation in BC, Jordan also has a facility in Calgary, Alberta which is used as a blending plant for bulk wines from California and Ontario.

Storage capacity: 5,000,000 gallons

LONDON WINERY, London, Ontario

In the company's museum is a cutting from the London Free Press, dated September 2, 1925. The headline reads: "New Winery to Open Plant in Few Weeks. Will Utilise 55 Tons of Grapes to Manufacture Wine this Year." Those first wines included Vinroi Blanc, a patent medicine with grape alcohol added, which was sold in 6 ounce bottles on presentation of a doctor's prescription at the local drug store. Vinroi Blanc is still on the London Wine list but without the added grape brandy. Today it's a blend of three North American varieties—Delaware, Elvira and Niagara.

The winery was founded by two brothers, A.N. Knowles and J.C. Knowles, originally from Nassau in the Bahamas. They bought the licence and assets of Giovanni Paproni of Welland. A.N. Knowles was an electrical engineer who set up a successful contracting business while acting as president of the new winery. His brother ran the plant since he had experience of winemaking, acquired from his father-in-law who had worked in a winery in Ohio and later owned one in Oakville, Ontario.

A. Neville Knowles, named after his father, is the Executive Vice-President of London Wines today, with forty years of service to the company behind him. "When my father and my uncle started the winery in 1925," he recalls, "there were no liquor stores. It was the final years of Prohibition, but they must have known it was going to end and liquor stores would open or

Wineries used to use wooden cooperage for storing all their wines, but now it is used mainly for storing red wines.
Courtesy: London Winery Ltd.

they'd never have gone into business. When Prohibition was repealed in 1927 they had a good supply of mature wine ready for the new Liquor Board stores." At the time he joined the business during the Second World War, its big volume brands were Westminster Sherry and Westminster Port. The sherry still exists but the drop in demand for port has decimated the list. In the late 1950s the company introduced its first table wines (two whites: Windsor Castle and Green Gables, both made from Niagara grapes). At 13% alcohol they were stable products but, according to Knowles, did not sell well.

As an efficient going concern in the 1930s London Wines was encouraged by the Board to buy up the licences of less reputable companies; over the years the Knowles Brothers bought eight companies including the assets of J.S. Hamilton and Company in 1945. This winery at Brantford could date its continuous operations back to 1871 when it was founded on Pelee Island by Thaddeus Smith and later controlled by Major J.S. Hamilton. This acquisition made London technically the oldest wine company in Canada.

This notion has somehow worked its way into the corporate psyche because London Wines is one of the most traditional in its thinking. The company fortunes are still founded on its sherry production which accounts for almost 60% of sales. A wine that stretches back to the days of Major Hamilton over 100 years ago is still on the list: St. Augustine Communion Wine, a product which the energetic major exported to Britain, the West Indies and the United States. London has cornered the market on mead (having purchased the licence of Strawa Honey Wines in 1965) and has more fancy bottles than you can shake a stick at. (Its Dinner Wine, for instance, comes in a glass container which looks like a bottle resting in a cradle. The

Temperature-controlled stainless steel tanks are replacing wooden tanks to meet the increasing demand for table wine in Canada.
Courtesy: Brights House of Wine

table wines look like chianti bottles in glass.) The reason for this exotic collection is to attract the American market. This sounds suspiciously like a beads-and-mirrors approach to marketing, but London has found that the only way to penetrate the US market (which makes up 10% of their sales) is to package their sherries and meads so that they stand out of the crowd.

For all its atmosphere of history, London does have some impressive achievements in furthering the technology of the Canadian wine industry. The company was the first to introduce the process for making flor sherry (invented by Ralph Crowther at Vineland's Horticultural Research Institute), the first to put on the market sherry in a decanter with a glass stopper (London Cream Sherry), and the first to bring in the "millipore filter".

In order to extend its range, London is developing premium table wines, particularly reds. In 1981, the company's Scottish winemaker, Jim Patience, made 500 cases of Maréchal Foch and 1,000 cases of Baco Noir, both light and fruity in style. Its best white is London Chablis which won a gold medal at the International Wine & Spirits Competition in England in 1980.

The company, apart from sherries, ports, table wines and meads, makes a range of sparkling wines, vermouths, a still cider and a juniper-flavoured cocktail called Riki.

Storage capacity: 2,500,000 gallons

MONTRAVIN CELLARS and PODAMER
CHAMPAGNE COMPANY, Beamsville, Ontario

In September 1973 the LCBO granted Karl Podamer a manufacturer's licence "to produce authentic French-style champagne in Canada". In his fiftieth year, Podamer had four decades of experience with sparkling wines behind him. His father, Ferenc Podamer, owned a successful champagne house in Hungary where he worked from the age of nine. The original plant was bombed during the Second World War and then taken over by the Communist government when it was subsequently rebuilt. Karl Podamer had studied the art of champagne-making in France and applied the time-honoured method of secondary fermentation in bottle to his Hungarian products.

When he emigrated to Canada as a refugee he worked as a butcher but longed to get back to his trade as a champagne master. With the help of a consortium of Niagara businessmen and an investment of $930,000, Podamer set up his sparkling wine operation at Beamsville. In its first year of operations the company produced 120,000 bottles under three labels—Rouge, Extra Dry and Brut from Delaware, Dutchess and Seibel hybrids. The wines were fermented in large Austrian white oak casks which had been sent over from that country as bundles of staves and reassembled in the plant by Austrian coopers. The winery was granted its formal licence in 1975, twenty-four days after Donald Ziraldo and Karl Kaiser at Inniskillin received theirs.

Today Podamer uses steel temperature-controlled tanks for first fermentation and produces his sparkling wines by hand following the same traditional process of vinification, bottling, handling and storage used in the Champagne region, even down to employing the Epernay yeast cultures to create the secondary fermentation in the bottle. The riddling process is all done by hand, as is the disgorging process. In virtually all champagne houses this is done by freezing the neck of the bottle so that the undesirable matter is shot out as a plug of ice, but Karl Podamer prefers to use the ancient room-temperature method. His style is rigorously French and traditional. The bottles are then topped up with a dose of brandy and sugar and selected wines before corking and wiring.

As champagne master, Podamer now devotes himself exclusively to the production of the company's sparkling wines, leaving the business and operational concerns to the president, Sam Fuda, and the chief oenologist, Ernst Fischer. Fischer himself has a long history with sparkling wines. He was formerly the head winemaker at Chateau-Gai and spent several years as a champagne master in Germany and at the Gold Seal Vineyards in Hammondsport, New York.

Only Ontario grapes are used in Podamer's five sparkling wines and the best of them, the Blanc de Blancs Brut, is made from a single grape

Karl Podamer, the champagne master at the Montravin Cellars and Podamer Champagne Company in Beamsville, Ontario. Podamer champagnes are made strictly according to the traditional French methode champenoise.
Courtesy: Montravin Cellars and Podamer Champagne Co.

(Chardonnay), the variety used in France for this style of champagne. The company's best-selling brand is the Cuvée Speciale, a blend of Seyval and Dutchess. As in the case with French champagnes, these wines are a blend of two or three different years, but Podamer is moving toward single vintage wines in good harvests. Unlike still table wines which need high sugar grapes to produce the requisite alcohol, champagnes rely more on acidity; the fermentation process adds one degree of alcohol or more to the finished product.

Although its current list is all made by the Méthode Champenoise, the company plans to put out an inexpensive sparkler using the Charmat process (where the secondary fermentation occurs in a sealed steel tank).

Sam Fuda says that all their champagnes use only free-run juice; the juice from the grapes when they are pressed is directed to still white wine production under the Montravin label. (The quality of the wines suffers as a result.) The company currently markets three varietals, Maréchal Foch, De

Chaunac and Seyval Blanc and two house blends called Concerto (red and white). In future Montravin will offer a semi-sweet white and a rosé from hybrid grapes, as well as a vintage Chardonnay and Riesling from grapes grown in the Grimsby area.

The company changed its name early in 1983 to Montravin Cellars when it expanded its still wine production. The champagnes will still be marketed under the Podamer label, but the new Charmat process sparkler soon to be on the market will bear the Montravin label.

Storage capacity: 350,000 gallons

RIEDER DISTILLERY, Grimsby, Ontario

Ontario has several cottage wineries but only one cottage distillery. The company is run by a genial Swiss, named Otto E. Rieder, who is perhaps the best friend the fruit and grape growers of the Niagara Peninsula have. Rieder's distillery buys red and black cherries to make kirsch, Bartlett pears for Poire William, apples to make vodka and grapes to produce three qualities of brandy.

Rieder, a former mechanical engineer, came to Canada in 1953. He grew up on a farm near Basel where his father distilled eaux-de-vie from the fruit grown in the family orchards. The Rieder name itself goes back over a thousand years. In Switzerland there is a town called Ried and a nearby mountain, Rieder Alp. The crest which graces many of the distillery's products was the family coat-of-arms, except that a large gold R has replaced an heraldic gryphon breathing fire—hardly the image a brandy-maker would like to project.

The company was formed in 1970 but did not begin to distill in its premises beside the Queen Elizabeth Highway at Grimsby until two years later. By the terms of his licence (and in order to call his grape products Canadian Brandy) Rieder had to use exclusively Ontario-grown grapes, a proscription that would ensure growers in the Peninsula a market for low sugar berries rejected by the wineries. Government regulations demanded that no sugar or alcohol could be added to the brandy to increase the yield.

Rieder brandies, like the eaux-de-vie, are double distilled by a continuous process (unlike cognac, which uses the traditional copper pot still). The three labels in order of quality are Trillium, Bordulac and Ontario Small Cask. The latter is the second largest seller in Ontario after the South African Paarl Brandy.

If Rieder takes up the slack in times of grape surplus, the distillery suffers when there is a short-fall in the crop. In 1982, the company could only buy 800 tons of grapes for processing (Foch, De Chaunac and Le Commandant) when it wanted 2,500 tons. The large wineries can pay higher prices for grapes and have first call on the growers' harvest. It takes one ton of grapes to make 240 bottles of brandy on average, but if the grapes have a low sugar content, more are required to bring up the alcohol level to the statutory 40% level.

Unlike the wineries, Otto Rieder prefers the cheaper labrusca grapes over hybrids. "They make a lovely fruity brandy," he says. "In the distilling process we take out all the taste components which would be offensive to wine drinkers." The spirits are aged in either American white oak, Limousin oak or old sherry casks, depending on the flavour requirements. Small Cask spends a minimum of two years in wood before bottling; Bordulac from three to four and Trillium at least six years. This particular brandy is aged in Limousin oak as used in Cognac "to impart an oily, soapy flavour."

"Canada," states Rieder, "is the only country in the world where brandy is less expensive than whisky. But the raw materials for making it are more expensive."

The company has recently purchased a traditional copper pot still from the Black Forest region of Germany to make limited quantities of framboise and a superior version of the kirsch and Poire William it already markets in the distinctive square-shouldered bottles. These eaux-de-vie are extremely well made and deserve a wider appreciation. "The problem is," according to Otto Rieder, "people take our clear white products home and when they find they're completely dry we get phone calls saying 'How dare you put something like this on the market!' They're expecting a sweet liqueur. What we're giving them is the sublimated perfume of the fruit."

NEW ONTARIO WINERIES

In this imperfect world of ours there are always people—thank heaven—who are willing to make wine, in spite of the vicissitudes of weather, the economy and consumer indifference. Four provisional winemaking licences were granted in 1982. If samples submitted to the Horticultural Research Institute of Ontario and LCBO for taste-testing are up to snuff then we will have more new wineries in the province.

One licence has already been granted to a grape grower (Ewald Rief, who has supplied Inniskillin with vinifera grapes). Rief's tiny winery will be the fourth in Niagara-on-the-Lake. Two substantial importers of Californian grapes, Darrigo Brothers (owners of Les Vignobles du Québec winery at Hemmingford), who have subsequently dropped the idea, and Pietro

Culatto, are also in the running. The fourth contender is Pelee Island Vineyards. One hundred acres of vinifera vines, including Johannisberg Riesling, Chardonnay, Gewurztraminer and Pinot Noir planted in 1980 by Austrian winemaker Walter Strehn will provide the basis for the new operation on the site where the Canadian industry virtually began. Wines from other grapes grown on Pelee Island have been vinifed at the company's winery just east of Kingsville. But it is Strehn's intention to build a facility on the island itself once the operating licence is secured.

The future for quality Ontario wines is rosy indeed.

six

British Columbia

*"Let every person plant one vine at least next their door,
and let them remember as they press the earth around its
roots and give it a final touch that they have not only
provided a lasting pleasure for their own household, but
they are handing down a source of health and happiness to
the inmates of their home for generations to come."*

(G.W. Henry, a leading BC botanist, 1899.)

More wine is consumed in British Columbia than in any other
province. According to the Canadian Wine Institute's annual
statistical report of 1982, BC drank 13.5 litres per head as opposed
to 9.5 in Quebec and 8.5 in Ontario, and they have maintained this number
one spot on the wine consumption league since the 1960s. What's more, they
consistently favour their own domestically produced wines two to one over
imports.

In general terms, BC differs from Ontario in climate, soil and grape
varieties. Ontario's industry is much older than that of BC and is based on
North American varieties. The BC industry having been developed com-
paratively recently, established itself on French hybrids. Not only are the
grape varieties of the two provinces different, but the flavours of the same
varieties vary dramatically because of the vast differences in growing
conditions. Ontario never experiences the intense heat, low humidity and
cool nights of the desert summer and the Okanagan, situated as it is on a
latitude roughly equivalent to Timmins, enjoys significantly more hours of
sunshine during summer days. While Ontario is moving slowly to vinifera
vines, the BC industry started with vinifera and is now expanding with the
next generation of new hybrids. BC wines, as a result, tend to be highly

flavoured, fruity, and full-bodied with good acidity, especially the whites which resemble those of the Rhine rather than the softer Californian style.

The wine industry in BC did not really start until the 1930s. While the combined insanity of Prohibition and the Depression almost destroyed the Ontario wineries, ironically it provided the impetus for the birth of BC commercial winemaking in the Okanagan and Similkameen River valleys.

The story goes back to the 1860s when the Oblate Fathers built a mission seven miles south of Kelowna and Father Charles Pardosy planted a few vines at the mission. But the farmers who followed were more interested in fruit crops like apples, peaches and apricots than in grapes. The first commercial vineyard in the province was planted by W.J. Wilcox some 90 kilometres north of Kelowna, at Salmon Arm. This three-quarter acre plot yielded such Ontario varieties as Concord, Niagara, Delaware and Agawam for the table trade. Six years later Jim Creighton planted a small vineyard in Penticton, an area which would ultimately prove to be one of the best sites for grape growing along the shores of Okanagan.

The narrow, serpentine lake, carved out by prehistoric glaciers, stretches north for over 100 kilometres and the land rises steeply from the water on either side. Technically the area is a desert since there is little rainfall (the southern end of the lake around Oliver gets no more than six inches of precipitation a year). In terms of latitude the Okanagan Valley is in the same belt as the Champagne region of France and the Rheingau of Germany—a fact which seduced many pioneers into believing that they could produce wines to rival the great Reislings and sparkling Chardonnays—but the climate is very different from Europe. During summer days the Okanagan vines experience tremendous heat and at night the temperature drops dramatically. Intense sunlight builds up the grape sugars and the freezing nights do not allow the acids to metabolise so the berries have very high acid readings. Because of the lack of rainfall the vineyards have to be irrigated during the growing season.

The Okanagan experiences long, mild autumns, as does northern Germany, but by mid-October, the temperature has fallen to a point where the grapes will no longer mature and they have to be harvested. On the plus side, British Columbian summers, like those in California, are consistent and predictable which ensures an even quality of grape from year to year. In spite of fluctuating temperatures, there are pockets along the valley's southern slopes which protect the vines from the killing frost that rolls down the lake from October on, and the body of water ameliorates the air temperature on the coldest of nights. Many of these microclimates have yet to be identified by infrared aerial photography, a program currently being conducted by the Summerland Research Station in conjunction with the provincial government.

Without the advantage of such technology the early grape growers could only plant their vines, sit back and pray.

The first wines in British Columbia were not made from grapes at all, but from loganberries which flourished in southern Victoria Island on the Saanich Peninsula. They rejoiced in such names as Slinger's Logan and Logana. But in 1926 a farmer by the name of Jesse Willard Hughes, encouraged by the Hungarian oenologist Dr. Eugene Rittich, bought a 45-acre vineyard in Kelowna near the Oblate Fathers' mission and planted vines which had been locally propogated. He also purchased a 20-acre site on Black Mountain. The larger vineyard near Kelowna prospered to such an extent that four years later wines made from these grapes were vinified at the Growers' Wine Company in Victoria. Encouraged by his success, Hughes was to expand his vineyard to 300 acres. But the experiment at Black Mountain proved a disaster since the vines were wiped out by winter kill.

Rittich, however, was convinced that grapes could be grown on Black Mountain. It was just a question of finding the right variety and employing the correct viticultural practices to prevent winter kill. As the first champion of vinifera grapes in the province, he experimented with forty-four varieties on this site and one in the barren Oliver region. In 1930 he imported from Hungary a winter-hardy vine which would revolutionize the BC wine industry and provide the basis for its future development—a grape that has come to be known as the Okanagan Riesling.

In the same year Rittich was hired as the winemaker for the Growers' Wine Company, which had previously specialised in loganberry wine. And a freak of nature was to give the fledgling industry the boost it needed. Successive abundant harvests of apples caused a glut on the market and many farmers were forced to tear up their orchards and plant grapes instead. Growers' Wine Company was paying $100 a ton for grapes (compared to $65 a ton in Ontario) while apples were left rotting under the trees. "A cent a pound or on the ground" was the farmers' anguished cry. "A dollar a box or on the rocks."

At the height of the Depression in 1932, an immigrant Italian winemaker named Guiseppe Ghezzi came to Kelowna with the idea of creating a winery to use the worthless apple crop. The idea had also occurred to a local hardware store owner, William Andrew Cecil Bennett who had discussed just such a possibility with his neighbour on Kelowna's main street, an Italian grocer, Pasquale "Cap" Capozzi. Both men were teetotalers but they joined with Ghezzi to form a company called Domestic Wines and By-Products. The company would manufacture not only wines but a whole gamut of products including "apple cider . . . brandy, alcohol, spirits of all kinds, fruit juices, soft drinks, fruit concentrates, jelly, jams, pickles, vinegar, tomato paste, tomato catsup, tomato juice and by products of every kind." The debonair Guiseppe Ghezzi stayed long enough to set up the winery before emigrating to California where he established a champagne plant.

Bennett and Capozzi set about raising money to finance their new operation. At a time when soup kitchens meant more to the public than wineries, they began selling $1 shares in the company; they raised $4,500 and although they were undercapitalised, they bought fermenting tanks and other equipment to begin this multifaceted business. In September 1932 they took up residence in an old rented building on Kelowna's Smith Avenue. The following year they hired Guiseppe Ghezzi's son Carlo as winemaker to complete their staff of eight employees. Their initial production included four apple-based wines—Okay Red, Okay Clear, Okay Port and Okay Champagne. But the products were far from "okay". Even the company's official history records that the wines "were a bitter disappointment. Many bottles refermented on liquor store shelves and had to be thrown out. Liquor stores were reluctant to stock the ill-famed *Domestic* wines and people were reluctant to buy them." Sales in the company's first full year of operation were a disaster, amounting to a mere few thousand dollars.

After three years of ineffectual competition against the genuine wines of the Growers' Company, Bennett and Capozzi realised that BC consumers just did not want apple wines. They switched to grapes which they bought in California and soon Growers' and the Victoria Wineries on Vancouver Island did likewise, perpetuating the fiction of making domestic wines by using what local grapes as were available.

With the change of style the former apple winery needed a change of name and in 1936 the directors chose a phonetic spelling of the Indian place name where the company was born: Calona Wines Limited. Okay Clear apple wine became Calona Clear grape "wine"—a white semi-sweet product whose label read ominously, "When Fully Mature: About 28% Proof Spirit."

In 1940 W.A.C. Bennett left Calona to pursue a career in politics. One year later he was elected to the BC parliament and he sold his shares to Capozzi; and when he became premier of the province in 1952 he took a serious look at the wine industry he had helped to create. If the wineries were to sell their products through the government-controlled liquor stores then they should do their part in promoting the grape-growing sector, he argued. In 1960 the BC government passed a law stating that wines vinified in the province had to contain a minimum percentage of locally grown grapes. Since there were only 585 acres under vines in the Okanagan Valley that figure was set at 25%. To encourage the planting of new vineyards, the Liquor Board stated that the quota would rise to 50% in 1962 and 65% by 1965. (Currently the figure is 80%).

Farmers in the Okanagan began planting vines with a vengeance and within four years the total acreage had risen by 400%.

In 1961 Andrew Peller built himself Andres' spanking new winery at Port Moody; six years later a company called Southern Okanagan Wines of Penticton opened for business, but soon changed its name to Casabello. At the same time the beautifully situated Mission Hill Winery was built on a ridge overlooking the Okanagan Lake at Westbank. This facility was acquired in 1969 by the ebullient construction king and brewer, Ben Ginter, who promptly renamed it with characteristic flamboyance (if little understanding of consumer sophistication) Uncle Ben's Gourmet Winery. He also put a portrait of himself on his labels. Among the products Ginter was to market were such crass items as Fuddle Duck and Hot Goose.

In 1973, the Growers' Wines Cooperative, which had merged with

Victoria Wineries, and changed its name to Castle Wines, was acquired from Imperial Tobacco by Carling O'Keefe. Another corporate name change was in store. Castle Wines became Ste-Michelle Wines—a subsidiary of Jordan and Ste-Michelle Cellars Ltd.—in 1974. The company had long outgrown its facility in Victoria and looked to the mainland to build a modern winery to service the growing demand in the province for table wines. Four years later they began building at Surrey just south of Vancouver, and opened operations in April 1978.

In March 1977, the BC Ministry of Consumer and Corporate Affairs, responding to a strong lobby from the wineries and grape growers, announced a new liquor policy "to recognize the health and social costs caused by the abuse of alcohol on the one hand and consumer demand for better products, better prices and better premises in which to have a drink, on the other." The thrust of the new legislation was to encourage the consumption of wine, both imported and domestic, at the expense of hard liquor and beer.

To help the provincially-based wineries compete with low-cost imports, the government lowered the mark-up on table wines from 66% to 46% (at the same time reducing imports from 117% to 100% mark-up).* To give their products a sales boost, BC wineries were allowed to open a retail store on their premises and under the aegis of the federal and provincial Ministries of Agriculture a five-year grape-growing program was introduced at a cost of $133,000 to upgrade the quality of the grapes they had to use. The program was directed by the world-famous viticulturalist, Dr. Helmut Becker, head of the Research Institute of Grape Breeding and Grape Propogation at Geisenheim in West Germany. Dr. Becker selected twenty-seven European varieties for testing in the Okanagan, including Riesling, Gewurztraminer, Pinot Noir, Pinot Gris, St. Laurent and Limberger.

Two three-acre plots were chosen for the experiment—a southern site on light, sandy soil near Oliver, and a northern site in the heavier soil at Okanagan Mission. The first wines made from these grapes were vinified by the Summerland Research Station in 1980, but it will take some years before consumers will be able to buy the products of the new stock as the most promising vines are not yet available to the industry.

Looking south to the Napa and Sonoma Valleys of California, the BC government realised that there was great tourist potential for a thriving wine industry in the beautiful Okanagan Valley setting.

After years of bureaucratic foot-shuffling they finally agreed to the creation of cottage or estate wineries; the first in the field was Claremont. In 1979 Bob Claremont and his wife, Lee, took over a facility built by Marion John who had planted vineyards on a steep slope just north of Peachland

---

*As a further incentive to the wineries the government relented over its ban on TV advertising and on October 1, 1982 the companies were allowed to promote their products on the air.

nineteen years earlier. John's first wines were made and bottled at Mission Hill Winery, but Claremont, who had worked as a winemaker at Calona as well as at Jordan's Ontario plant, set up a crusher, fermentation tanks and a bottling line, and began to vinify BC's first estate bottled wines in 1979.

The BC Liquor Control and Licencing Branch, not knowing how to deal with the novel enterprise, hastily introduced regulations which both encouraged and inhibited the new winery. To be an estate winery, the company could only make a maximum of 30,000 gallons. All the grapes used in the wine had to be grown in the province and 50% of these had to come from Claremont's own vineyards. The winery was allowed to open a retail store on its premises and could sell directly to licencees without having to pay the government mark-up of 46%. Claremont could sell two products through the specialty liquor stores only, but these would only carry a mark-up of 15%. These regulations are still in force for all estate wineries. However, the two listings can now be carried in all 210 liquor store outlets depending on shelf space and demand.

Within the next three years Bob Claremont was joined by four other small producers in the Okanagan—Sumac Ridge, Vinitera (which subsequently

A map of the Okanagan Valley wineries in British Columbia. After the Niagara Peninsula area of Ontario, the Okanagan is the major grape-growing region in Canada.

went into receivership in 1982), Uniacke Cellars, Gray Monk, and in the spring of 1983, Divino Wines in Oliver. There is a feeling of cameraderie among the operators of these small wineries and they help one another out when they can by sharing facilities and equipment, such as hand-labelling machines, or storing one another's wines. They are the pioneers of a new phase of BC's growing wine industry.

Meanwhile, Uncle Ben's Gourmet Wines, suffering the consequences of marketing dubious wines, fell foul of the banks and re-emerged briefly under the name of Golden Valley Wines. But its reincarnation did not help its balance sheet; thanks to union animosity following troubles at Ginter's Red Deer Brewery, Ginter was forced to sell and the company was bought in 1981 by Anthony Von Mandl's Mark Anthony group, a successful Vancouver-based firm of wine importers, who immediately gave it back its original name of Mission Hill and began a massive reorganisation.

The newest commercial winery to open in BC belongs to Brights. On land leased from the Osoyoos Indians south of Oliver near the American border, the company built a spectacular modern winery in 1981 to ferment grapes grown by Indian growers on the Inkameep vineyards. The building alone cost $2 million funded by development money from the provincial and federal governments. Brights has invested $3.5 million in equipment for the new facility.

In total there are now eleven wineries (large and small) operating in British Columbia. While the estate wineries have to use locally grown grapes, the large commercial concerns can get the raw material where they please. Technically, they are obligated to use 80% of BC-grown grapes and under an agreement with the province's Grape Marketing Board the entire commercial production is contracted to the wineries. They must buy them in the corresponding percentage to their market share whether they need them or not. However, the grape crop in BC represents a mere 65% of the total grapes used for wine in the province. The balance comes from California, Washington or Oregon, giving BC wines a taste profile very different from Ontario-made products, particularly when the wine can contain 100% Californian grapes and still have a BC label.

The reason is that BC's 3,300 acres of vines in the Okanagan and Similkameen areas are just not large enough to supply the wineries with the grapes they need, particularly white wine grapes. Like Ontario, the industry was caught with too many red grapes in the ground when consumers switched their preference to white wines.

Sixty percent of the vines are red grapes (mostly De Chaunac and Maréchal Foch); 25% are white hybrids, with Okanagan Riesling by far the largest tonnage; and the remaining 15% is divided between the noble European varieties (mostly on estate winery properties) and labrusca, such as Bath and Concord.

In 1982 BC's commercial wineries had a five-year supply of red wine in their cellars, close to seven million gallons. This sort of sorry situation can occur in any of the wine-growing countries of the world. The domestic wine lobbies in both the grape-growing provinces of Ontario and BC have called on their respective governments to help them out of their financial bind. They have demanded price increases on highly competitive European imports, particularly from Italy, to make Canadian-grown reds more attractive to the consumer. But protectionism is not the answer. The industry must produce the wines the public wants and this means a concerted effort by the growers and the wineries to ensure that the preferred grapes are planted. The problem is one of time. It takes at least four to five years before a newly planted vine can produce a commercial crop of sufficient quality to make a drinkable table wine, and the growers would not tolerate any loss of income while they waited for new vines to mature.

For all of this, the growth of the estate wineries in the Okanagan and the efforts of the Summerland Research Station to find the best clones for planting in the region, have had a marked effect on the quality of wines available to BC consumers. So far the commercial wineries have been careful not to be seen as the elephant ready to step on the mouse: they have assiduously avoided making the costlier vinifera wines from grapes imported from the United States to compete with the estate wineries' home-grown viniferas. Most of the BC vinifera vines are controlled by the cottage industry but, if they felt so inclined, the commercial wineries could easily bring in Chenin Blanc, Riesling and Gewurztraminer from California and Washington. According to Calona's oenologist, Elias Phiniotis, the reason they don't— at least for their own provincial market—is that "it would be wrong to market them. We don't want to put out a wine grown from grapes below the border when we've got Gray Monk, Sumac Ridge and Claremont up the road, all working their hearts out to make a go of it, bottling estate-grown varietals and viniferas in this province, in this valley. You could see the consumer backlash it would cause."

The BC wine industry, in spite of its glut of red wine, is so confident about its future that in 1982 it held its first BC wine festival competition at Penticton, called Septober Wine Festival, at which an international panel of five judges tasted 47 locally made wines. Their recommendations were sampled blind by the winemakers themselves who awarded medals in eight categories. The medals were divided almost equally between the commercial and estate wineries.

BRITISH COLUMBIA WINERIES

ANDRES WINES, Port Moody, BC

Andrew Peller wanted to start his winery in Ontario in the early 1950s but it took him nearly 20 years before he realized that dream. Rebuffed by the LCBO each time he applied for a licence, Peller turned his attention to British Columbia. In 1958 he bought a 40-acre farm at Cawston, on the banks of the Similkameen River, between Oliver and Keremeos. Here he intended to plant Ontario grapes to impress the provincial bureaucrats of his good faith when he applied for a winery licence. Efforts to purchase an already existing winery had failed (including overtures to Pasquale Capozzi at Calona), but eventually the tireless Peller was granted his licence and Andres—Peller's baptismal name—was born. In 15 years it would become Canada's largest and financially most successful winery with facilities in six provinces.

The first winemaker was Wallace Pohl of Lodi, California, who set up the cellars with equipment and wooden vats purchased from a winery in Madera. In 1961, Andres Wines opened its plant off the Barnet Highway on the shores of Burrard Inlet at Port Moody; appropriately enough, the address is 2120 Vintner Street. With no locally grown labrusca grapes available to the new enterprise (they were all contracted to Growers', West Coast Wine and Calona) Peller brought in Californian. In April 1962 the first Andres wines were presented to the BC Liquor Control Board. Among them were such bogus names imported from the Niagara Peninsula as Claret and Rhine. All six were listed but because they were not made from Okanagan grapes the Board raised the price fifteen cents a bottle above the retail cost of other locally made wines. (This was a foretaste of protectionism that was to come in both BC and Ontario against each other's wines as well as European imports).

But that was not the company's only headache: in January 1963 it suffered the ignominy of having its wines explode all over the LCB warehouse. The cellar master had neglected to add stabilizer to the wine before it was bottled to stop refermentation. The entire consignment had to be shipped back to the winery. But in spite of that early mishap, Andres struggled to hold its own against competition from the established BC wineries. The company decided to find a better way: they expanded into other provinces on the assumption that if they invested in facilities a grateful provincial government would list all their wines. In 1964 Andrew Peller opened up in Calgary, Alberta (originally called the Anjo Winery after Andrew and his son, Joe), and Truro, Nova Scotia (Abbey Wines) in specially constructed premises which resembled the original Port Moody facility. A year later Peller enticed Joe, who was then Chief of Medicine at the Hamilton Civic Hospital and also on the Board of all three wineries, to become the growing company's president and chief executive officer.

Joe Peller and his father understood that in order to establish Andres as a major Canadian winery, the company needed a base in Ontario so that they could compete successfully in that large market. All attempts to get the products on the LCBO shelves from the West had failed and the Pellers had to secure themselves some real estate in the province to get listings there (real estate with a winery licence to go along with it). Eventually, they managed to buy the Beau Chatel winery at Winona, from the Imperial Tobacco Company. This company had been in operation since 1930, originally as the Subosits Winery and subsequently the Welland Winery. At one point Welland had produced what it called a Grande Estate Canadian Champagne (Extra Dry). At the time of the takeover, Beau Chatel marketed a sparkling cider called "Light and Easy" which joined Andres list and is still sold in Ontario.

In 1970 Andres moved its headquarters from Port Moody to Winona. But the boldest innovation made by the company—and one that would catapult it into the No. 1 position and have enormous repercussions on the Canadian wine trade as a whole—was the invention of Baby Duck. Winston Collins in his well-documented article on Baby Duck in *Saturday Night Magazine* (June 1982) wrote:

> ". . . At the time of the company's move its share of the market was less than one per cent. Today, with . . . a market share of 10% it is Canada's largest and most profitable producer. Although Andres turns out more than 70 different wines,

A view of the Andres Wine plant in Port Moody, BC. With facilities in six provinces, Andres is Canada's largest and financially most successful winery.
Courtesy: Andres Wines Ltd.

from Richelieu Champagne to Similkameen Red, it owes its standing largely to a single product . . . Baby Duck (which) accounts for about a fifth of total sales which in 1981 exceeded $42,000,000."

Since it made its reputation on light sparkling wines, Andres' BC facility puts great emphasis on this sector of the trade. Baby Duck, the Chanté wines, Moody Blue and Perle ("Light and delicious with the sparkle of a sunny Okanagan day" reads the label) are still big sellers in the province, although the company has been putting more effort into developing table wines to meet the consumer demand, especially for whites. In 1980, alarmed that they had nothing in their armoury to compete with Calona's Schloss Laderheim, the marketing people put their heads together to come up with a German-style white wine. Dave Ringler was marketing manager in BC at the time and his thinking behind the creation of the new product reflects the industry's approach to satisfying the public taste. "We had identified the need for a German-style table wine. Schloss Laderheim was selling as if there was no tomorrow and we didn't have anything to compete with it. We went to our winemaker and said we're going to use Blue Nun as our model (the top-selling Liebfraumilch). But we couldn't make it as expensively as Blue Nun because we couldn't afford to sell it at the price it would cost us to make. I worked very closely with the advertising agency to come up with a name and the label and we advertised it very heavily." The result was Hochtaler, a blend of three Californian grapes—French Colombard, Chenin Blanc and Semillion. The label (like Schloss Laderheim's) could easily be mistaken for a Rhine table wine.

Hochtaler, a well-made product, carved a healthy niche in the white wine market, second only to the ubiquitous Schloss Laderheim, and the company soon brought out a sweeter version using the Okanagan Riesling called Wintergarten.

Domaine D'Or was Andres' answer to the need for a French-style white, an all-Californian product based on French Colombard and Chenin Blanc grapes. (These wines have a different taste profile in Ontario where the company must use 70% of grapes grown in the province.)

In the early 1970s Andres developed 300 acres of French hybrid and vinifera vines on Indian land near Oliver, called Inkameep Vineyards. The red and white wines vinified from these grapes appear under the Inkameep label. Perhaps the best known Andres wines in Ontario are the Similkameen red and white, named after the river on whose banks the grapes are grown. When the red wine was first introduced in 1968 it was called Canadian Beaujolais, (to the fury of the French who saw to it that the name was changed).

The company's best wines are marketed under the Richelieu label. A limited number of these varietals were introduced to Ontario in 1980, made from locally grown grapes, such as Johannisberg Riesling and Chardonnay. In BC, they have been marketing this prestigious line since the late 1960s, bottling 100% Californian wines such as Cabernet Sauvignon, Zinfandel, Petite Sirah, Gamay Beaujolais and Chenin Blanc, as well as BC-grown products such as Johannisberg Riesling, Gewurztraminer and an interesting German grape called Ehrenfelser (two versions in 1980, one a late harvest at 7.5% alcohol.)

Following the hefty 1982 harvest, Andres, like all the commercial wineries in Canada, had an ever-increasing lake of red wine on its hands. In an effort to move stocks, the company lowered prices in BC and started on November 3, what *The Province* newspaper called "a price war" among the wineries. The company also put out a utility label simply called Red Wine—an insipid product to match its no-name brand packaging (extolling it on the brown paper label as "a quality red wine made from French hybrid grapes grown in the Okanagan Valley") in a desperate attempt to deplete its store of De Chaunac and Maréchal Foch.

The company also markets four sherries and a Lambrusco-type, sweet, low-alcohol red called Botticelli, reminiscent of the top-selling wine in the United States, Reunité. House wines are marketed under the Eagle Ridge and Pacific Coast Cellars in 1.5 litre bottles and 4-litre bag-in-box for BC and Alberta.

Encouraged by the "Becker Experiment" with German varieties in the Okanagan, Andres is currently undertaking an experimental grafting program at Mission to improve the winter hardiness and disease resistance of white grape vines. The company hopes to enhance the complexity and flavour of the finished wines with the sturdier root stock.

Storage Capacity: 3,000,000 gallons.

BRIGHTS HOUSE OF WINE, Oliver, BC

Brights' contemporary-rustic 45,000 square-foot building stands in splendid solitude in a wilderness of pine-clad granite mountains and arid plains in southern British Columbia. On the wall by the entrance hangs a framed photograph showing the Chief of the Osoyoos Indian Band, Sam Baptiste, shaking hands with the Managing Director of Brights, Ed Arnold. It is dated May 14, 1982, the official opening date of the winery although its 1981 wines were already on the market.

That handshake symbolizes the cooperation which made the facility possible, because the winery stands on 17 acres of Indian reserve land and it was the Osoyoos Indians who built it at a cost of $2 million to the federal and provincial governments. The building has been leased to the company for five years.

The whole enterprise is a joint venture between Brights and the Osoyoos company, Inkameep Vineyards Ltd. The Indians will plant and harvest the grapes and Brights will buy them and produce the wines.

For its part, Brights had to invest $3.5 million in equipping the new winery but the investment no doubt appealed to the company accountants who could see profits down the road from the expanding wine sales in the province.

The Osoyoos Band owns 6,000 acres of land between Oliver and Osoyoos which is suitable for the planting of vines. If this happened, the grape tonnage of the Okanagan Valley would virtually double. Currently 250 acres of this property are under vines but these are contracted to Andres and Ste-Michelle. Brights has committed itself to buy the crop from the next 200 acres planted, but so far funds have only been forthcoming for 20 acres of Baco Noir.

According to the General Manager of the plant, Rob Domville, (formerly with Calona Wines): "Somehow we managed to crush in our first year. There was only half a building over our heads and literally the tanks were being installed as the grapes were coming through the door." Brights had a problem securing those initial 400 tons of locally-grown grapes. Some were borrowed for a year from other wineries, and in order to get immediately into the BC market, the company was forced to buy finished wine from its competitors as well as trucking in great quantities from its Ontario base.

While Brights produces several of its national brands like House Wine and LiebesHeim here for BC consumers, the wines have a taste profile all their own. Two products unique to the province are labelled Entre Montagnes red

Edward Arnold, President of Brights House of Wine, and Sam Baptiste, Chief of the Osoyoos Indian Band, agreeing on the final details of the leasing agreement which permits Brights' BC facility to be located on the Inkameep Reserve.

Lynn Stark, winemaker for Brights in Oliver and the first female winemaker in BC, in the laboratory testing wine.

Courtesy: Brights House of Wine

An aerial view of the 250-acre Inkameep Vineyards, which, in a joint venture with Brights, produces the grapes for the company's BC winemaking operation.
Courtesy: Brights House of Wine

and white. The label features a stylized drawing of the winery in its rugged setting. The white is a blend of Chenin Blanc (from California), Verdelet and "three other components". The red is 100% BC grown Maréchal Foch and De Chaunac, which is not necessarily anything to boast about.

Brights is concentrating on planting premium white hybrids like Vidal and Seyval which have proved successful in Ontario and the company has high hopes for a clone of Baco Noir which was isolated on its 60-acre experimental farm in Niagara. The grapes from this particular vine were shown to have a lower acidity than others of the same variety.

The winemaker at the Oliver plant is one of the few women in the industry—Lyn Stark—who spent several years with Andres at Port Moody before joining Brights.

Storage capacity: 800,000 gallons (all stainless steel).

CALONA WINES LTD., Kelowna, BC

When Guiseppe Ghezzi, Pasquale Capozzi and W.A.C. Bennett started their winery in 1932 the most sophisticated piece of equipment they had was a hand-operated grape crusher. Originally it was created as Domestic Wines and By-Products Ltd. to take advantage of the surplus apple crop and produce a variety of apple wines, but the directors soon realized that it could not compete with the burgeoning Growers' Wine Company and switched to grapes they brought in from California.

In 1936 the company changed its name to Calona Wines and from its humble beginnings has become the largest winery in British Columbia, with an enormous modern plant covering 140,000 square feet. It now commands nearly 40% of the provincial market in domestic wines.

After its shaky start in the Depression, Calona survived the 1930s thanks to its sale of sacramental wine (St. John) to the Catholic Church. In 1935 a Kelowna priest, Father W.B. MacKenzie, suggested to Archbishop W.M. Duke that instead of importing Canada's communion wine from Spain, the Church could buy it cheaper and more easily from Calona. After rigorous canonical tests by a chemist at the Université de Montréal, His Excellency W.M. Duke received a badly translated report that Calona wine could be used "with at least as much safety (not to say more in my experience of Mass Wine trade) as any imported sweet wine from Spain, and with as much safety as your Excellency can humanly expect, unless She makes the wine Herself or under Her direct supervision"!

Up until the end of the 1950s Calona relied on winemaking techniques usually associated with cottage wineries. Bottles were washed by hand, individually filled and labelled one at a time. With the sudden consumer boom in table wines, the company bought automated equipment from a bankrupt BC brewery and directed its energies to satisfying the public's taste for a lighter, drier style than the 28% proof alcohol products it had marketed up until then. "Cap" Capozzi secured a majority interest in Calona at this time and took over the management himself after initial thoughts of selling the entire operation. Two of his sons, Tom and Joe, joined him in running the family business.

Marketing wines through McGuinness Distillers, Calona expanded its market into the Prairie provinces, the Northwest Territories and Ontario, and established its own distillery to make brandy for fortified wines. In 1971, Pasquale Capozzi, who had arrived penniless in Canada from the Italian village of Santo Stephano del Sole in 1906, retired as a multimillionaire from the company he had built: the family sold its shares to Standard Brands of Montreal.

In the early 1970s the successful mass market house wines Sommet Rouge and Sommet Blanc appeared on the market and even an abortive incursion into the Quebec market (its screw-cap wines fermented on the shelves and the company sold its facility to Andres in 1974) did not check its growth. As more Canadians jumped on the grape bandwagon, the company devised a product which would be a stepping stone for those who wanted to convert from beer and spirits to wine—an easy drinking white with a touch of sweetness, called Schloss Laderheim. Its label, sporting an heraldic shield and gothic print, could easily be mistaken for a German product, especially since it also contained the words, Weisslact Riesling. The wine does contain Johannisberg Riesling grapes grown in California as well as some Okanagan Riesling, Aurore and Delaware. Schloss Laderheim overtook Baby Duck in 1981 to become Canada's largest selling wine. That year it sold some 5.5 million bottles without listings in the Maritime provinces.

Most of the whites produced at Calona have more than a touch of residual sugar. Festspiel, for example, was introduced as a younger sister of Schloss Laderheim, a touch drier with one degree less alcohol. A notable exception from the house style of fruity German imitations is Haut Villages White, which is to Burgundy what Schloss Laderheim is to the Rhine. Based on Californian Chenin Blanc grapes with added Aurore, Haut Villages is well-made dry wine with a floral, grassy nose and a faintly perfumed taste. It, too, has some residual sugar but much less than Calona's other products. (There is also a red Haut Villages.)

The red brand-named blends are Italianate or Bordeaux in style, light and fruity, vinified for immediate consumption.,

Calona is the only BC company with any penetration whatsoever in the Ontario market, in spite of the present mark-up of 85% on these wines compared with 45% for locally made Ontario products. BC wines also carry a handling charge of 25 cents per 750 ml. bottle which makes them less attractive in competition with the indigenous wines of the province. This tariff imposed against BC wines in 1975 was a direct result of Calona's aggressive marketing policy in Ontario. The sales of its wines—especially Schloss Laderheim—were perceived as a threat to the local industry and the Ontario government acted accordingly. As a result, Calona's sales in the province plunged by 50%.

The company lists eleven labels in Ontario, including Schloss Laderheim, the Sommet twins, and Haut Villages White and Red, as well as two ferociously sweet 7% sparklers and the well-made, dry Cuvée Blanc. The strategy, according to marketing director, Bruce Walker (formerly with Andres in Winona, Ontario), is to produce "a broad range of wines which will be acceptable alternatives to low priced imports"—nothing fancy, very much geared to the market place. Calona does, however, give a passing thought to premium wines and spasmodically puts out some varietal products under its Winemaster's Selection label which benefit from additional bottle age. The company began with De Chaunac in 1977 and Maréchal Foch 1978. In 1982 winemaker Elias Phiniotis bottled Rougeon, Chancellor, Maréchal Foch and Johannisberg Riesling—all from BC-grown grapes.

For the company's fiftieth anniversary in 1982 it brought in grapes from the Yakima Valley, Washington, to produce five prestige varietal whites: Chardonnay, Gewurztraminer, Fumé Blanc, Chenin Blanc and Johannisberg Riesling.

The company also produces a range of sherries of varying sweetness, and three fruit wines: Berry Jack (blueberries and blackberries), Black Jack (blackberries) and—in memory of its early days—Double Jack, made from apples. A dessert Muscatel, a port and four sweet sparkling wines (the best is Cuvée Blanc made from Riesling and Muscat by the Charmat method) make up the list.

Storage capacity: 4,500,000 gallons.

CASABELLO WINES, Penticton, BC

In 1966 a new company called Southern Okanagan Wines Ltd. crushed their first grapes and produced 60,000 gallons of wine. They called themselves "a small premium winery" dedicated to producing wines "equal to European wine standards". One year later, around the time of their second crush, Evans Lougheed, the founder of the company changed the name to one with more flair: Casabello. Today they are one of the giants of the BC wine industry with sales approaching one million gallons, half of which is bag-in-box, inexpensive blends.

The winery is located on Penticton's Main Street, formerly set in seven acres of experimental vineyards. The company acquired a further five acres for future expansion. In 1977 they built a new bottling plant. Today only one acre of vineyard remains. And this is only a token gesture to appease the tourists who don't feel they are visiting a winery unless they see vines and piles of oak barrels in the cellars.

Casabello now gets its grapes from eighteen contracted growers in the Summerland area and around Oliver to the south.

Casabello is owned by John Labatt Ltd. through a holding company called Ridout Wines which also controls Chateau-Gai's operations. This means that Chateau-Gai's national brands such as Alpenweiss, Edelwein and Capistro carry the Casabello name in British Columbia.

Along with these top-selling lines, Casabello lists over thirty products, all of which are basically vinified from the same five grape types. The way these grapes are pressed, fermented and aged gives the company winemaker, Roberta Jordan, some flexibility in the blending permutations to prevent all their wines from tasting the same. This same game is practiced by all the large commercial wineries and is certainly not unique to Casabello.

For its premium line—the red and white Estate Selection (similar to Chateau-Gai's Lincoln County series in Ontario, with the same style of labels featuring the dogwood flower of BC rather than the trillium)—Casabello uses first run juice from Californian and BC grapes. The middle range Casabello wines have some first run juice from locally grown grapes blended with Californian wines for the whites. The third line is the inexpensive Gala wines which are made from second-pressings (after the free-run juice is taken off, the skins are washed with a sugar and water solution and then pressed). The water "ameliorates" the acidity; it also allows the winemaker to get the last cent's worth out of his grapes.

Casabello is one of the largest bag-in-box producers in Canada, if not North America. In 1982, the company sold 600,000 gallons in the four-litre size alone. The drier Gala whites are an equal blend of Okanagan Riesling and California base white, and the medium sweet varieties are fermented dry with some cane sugar added later.

Most of the reds, such as Osoyoos Select or Burgonay, have Maréchal Foch and De Chaunac as their major constitutents, with a little Chancellor or Rougeon in the blend. And the Estate Selection Canadian Burgundy has a healthy backbone of Carignan grapes from Washington State mixed into the basic Foch, De Chaunac and Chancellor blend. The company also markets a sweet pink Chablis and a Sangria.

Storage capacity: 2,800,000 gallons

CLAREMONT WINES, Peachland, BC

In 1977 and 1978 wines were made from the vineyards Marion John had planted twenty years ago on land cleared of pine trees on the Trepanier Bench at Peachland. But at the time there was no facility to vinify them on the property. The grapes were crushed and fermented at nearby Mission Hill. In 1979 John built the present ranch-style home and the concrete block winery on the 34-acre site, but, being unfamiliar with the technology, he approached Bob Claremont and asked him if he would be interested in buying the business. Claremont had recently left Calona Wines to start his own winery. After graduating as an oenologist from Guelph University in Ontario, he went to work for Jordan and then moved west to join Mission Hill. With some 15 years of commercial winemaking under his belt, he felt he and his wife Lee were ready for the challenge. "We're old veterans by Canadian standards," says Bob. "I haven't ever done anything else but make wines."

Claremont has eighteen acres currently under vine in rocky, sandy soil, facing south, surrounded by pine trees. Apart from Okanagan Riesling and Rougeon, which make the company's bread-and-butter wines, there is also Maréchal Foch, Verdelet, Pinot Blanc, Sauvignon Blanc, Gewurztraminer and Merlot, as well as Johannisberg Riesling and Muscat. Claremont's wine production will eventually be equal parts hybrids and viniferas.

The style of the whites is big and intense, very close to the Californian taste. Apart from the Muscat Riesling blend, the range is very dry and assertive, particularly the Vin Blanc (a mix of Vedelet, Chenin Blanc and Semillion) which is one of the driest BC wines on the market. The reds are robust, full-bodied and deep in colour from fermentation on the skins and a minimum of two years in small French oak casks.

In 1983 Claremont plans to release its first Merlot, a blend of two vintages (1981 and 1982), Pinot Noir and Johannisberg Riesling.

Every Mother's Day weekend the winery holds an arts and crafts show, a predilection of Lee Claremont. It was she who chose the art work for the winery's Maréchal Foch, Gewurztraminer, Sauvignon Blanc and Pinot Blanc labels (paintings by the New Denver, BC artist, Les Weisbrich).

Bob Claremont is extremely pleased with the quality of his 1982 grapes and the wine he is proudest of is his 1980 Gewurztraminer. Only 126 cases were made, and these quickly sold out.

Storage capacity: 60,000 gallons.

GRAY MONK CELLARS, Okanagan Centre, BC

George and Trudy Heiss own one of the most beautifully situated wineries in Canada; the facility, set in 24 acres of vines, sloping down to the lake, looks out onto the water and the mountains behind. George, who was born and raised in Vienna, started building the classically simple farmhouse-style winery in January 1982, ten years after he had torn out acre upon acre of aged orchard and planted his first European vines.

The name he chose for the winery is the English translation of what the Austrians call the Pinot Gris grape—Gray Monk. "Heiss Wines doesn't sound like anything," he confesses, although Jo Heitz in the Napa Valley did rather well with *his* name!

The Pinot Gris was one of the first varieties he put in the ground, along with Auxerrois and two varieties rare to North America, Kerner and Bacchus, which suggests that George's heart is in white wines. In 1980 his first year of operation (aided by Brights' BC winemaker, Lyn Stark) he produced wines of excellent quality, and the following year his Pinot Auxerrois 1981 and Gewurztraminer 1981 won four medals at BC's Septober Wine Festival after nine months in bottle.

In 1982 the winery offered five whites (Pinot Auxerrois, Kerner, Pinot Gris, Johannisberg Riesling, Bacchus and Gewurztraminer) and one varietal rosé, the little-known Rotberger. Half of the 10,000 gallon production was made from grapes grown on the property; the rest were purchased from other family members in the neighbourhood.

George Heiss wants to concentrate on white wines made from vinifera grapes and the red Seibel hybrids and Maréchal Foch which were already on the property are slowly being torn out to make way for the better varieties at the rate of 2 to 3 acres a year. These grapes are currently sold to commercial wineries although George is experimenting with a tank of Foch.

In contrast to its burly owner, the style of Gray Monk wines is one of almost porcelain delicacy; their colour is virtually water-white and their flavour edges towards Spätlese and Auslese sweetness, although light in alcohol.

Trudy drives a tractor in the fields while George takes care of the cellars. The Heiss' middle son is at present studying winemaking in Weinsberg, Germany, which will ensure family continuity of the style of these excellent wines in the future.

Storage capacity: 42,000 gallons.

JORDAN & STE-MICHELLE CELLARS,
Surrey, BC

Carved on the head of a great oval vat in the company's showcase maturation cellar are the letters 'SL' which stand for Slinger's Logan. The vat dates from the 1920s and it embodies the story of the winery itself. In 1923 Steve Slinger of Chemaius moved to Victoria to pursue his hobby of fermenting wine from loganberries on a commercial basis in Victoria. He called his company Victoria Wineries and began marketing Slinger's Logan. The former jockey and entrepreneur began fermenting wine from grapes ten years later and put out two labels—Slinger's Grape and Slinger's Port. In 1936, on the strength of his winemaking expertise, the irrepressible businessman was brought into the Growers' Company which would continue to market the Slinger products under the Victoria Wineries label, and even added a new one to the list— Slinger's Gin Cocktail: a blend of gin, rum and grape wine.

Steve Slinger joined the company after Dr. Eugene Rittich had established its pre-eminence in the grape-wine field with such Okanagan-grown products as Bon Red and Bon White two years earlier. As these highly alcoholic sweet wines gained more acceptance Growers' put out a prestigious line in 1940—Regal Port, Regal Muscatel, Regal Sherry and Empire Vermouth. Because of wartime restrictions the company had to cut its production and in 1941 it allowed the storage area of its Vancouver plant to be used for the training of the Pacific Coast Militia Reserves.

In 1955 Growers' (which included the Richmond Winery in Vancouver, Slinger's old Victoria Wineries and the largest loganberry farm in the British Empire at Saanich) was taken over by a Vancouver syndicate headed by a retired banker, Francis Lumb, sportsman Coley Hall and investment dealer and racehorse owner, Don Lauder. Five years later the company purchased a small winery at Langley, BC, specifically to produce two sparkling wines—Muscada and Donetelli.

In 1965 the company was to be bought by Imperial Tobacco who saw in its proliferation of products a sound business base. In that year alone Growers' brought out fourteen new products on the basis of its market research, including such questionnable labels as Beau Sejour Canadian Chianti, Beaujolais and Chablis. And for the first time it introduced the Ste-Michelle line of wines.

As grape wines grew in popularity the company had to ensure a reliable supply of the raw material so it bought the 130 acres of the picturesque Schmidt vineyard (Beau Sejour) in the Okanagan-Mission area. The winery had been buying these grapes for thirty years and had conducted the company's viticultural research here. With control of the vineyard the research program was greatly expanded.

In 1973 Growers' Wine Company and its subsidiaries were acquired from Imperial Tobacco by Carling O'Keefe and finally it was to lose the name it had used for over 50 years. The next year Growers' became Ste-Michelle Wines, part of the Jordan & Ste-Michelle Cellars in Ontario.

The company had outgrown its facilities at the Quadra Street Winery in Victoria and in 1977 they began to build a new winery 12 miles north of the American border at Surrey.

Today Ste-Michelle Wines, like all the large wineries, has divested itself of its vineyards and prefers to buy the grapes it needs rather than grow the crop themselves. But the Beau Sejour name is kept alive on the labels of four wines (two reds and two whites).

The company is very proud of its oak maturation cellar, one of the largest in Canada, where Maréchal Foch wines age in 1,200- to 1,800-gallon vats alongside sherry casks set up in a solera system.

The winemakers of Ste-Michelle have all come from the Jordan operation at St. Catharines in Ontario and virtually all of them have been trained in Germany—a fact reflected in the style of their white wines particularly. Following the dictum that most people prefer dry white wine as long as it's a little bit sweet, the company markets a number of screw-top whites with residual sugar using Chenin Blanc, French Colombard and Thompson Seedless grapes from California to augment the Okanagan Riesling and other hybrids, such as Verdelet.

The Ste-Michelle Zinfandel and Chenin Blanc are made from 100% Californian grapes, as are the Ruby Cabernet and Cabernet Sauvignon. The premium wines vinified exclusively from Okanagan grapes bear the Maîtres Vignerons neck label. The best is the Johannisberg Riesling, which has good fruit character but tends to be over-sweet. This same characteristic works well for the 1981 Special Reserve single vineyard bottling because of its better acid balance.

Harking back to the old days, the company still sells two berry wines (Villa Berry Cup and Vin Supreme) as well as a dry and medium cider marketed sentimentally under the Growers' label.

Storage capacity: 4,000,000 gallons.

MISSION HILL VINEYARDS, Westbank, BC

The California-style winery built in 1966 by orchardist R.P. (Tiny) Walrod commands one of the finest views in the Okanagan. From its position high above the town of Westbank, it overlooks a patchwork of orchards and vineyards with a spectacular view of the lake and surrounding mountains.

Following the death of Walrod, the company experienced financial troubles and was sold to Ben Ginter in 1969. Ginter had made his fortune in the construction business and was responsible for building roads into the northern interior. After an ill-fated foray into the brewing business where he fell foul of the beerocrasy, Ginter turned his attentions to the wine industry at the time of the Baby Duck boom. Not known for his humility, Ginter changed the name of Mission Hill to Uncle Ben's Gourmet Wines and proceeded to produce such abominations as Fuddle Duck (to compete with Andres' Baby Duck), Hot Goose, Queenie, Yellow Bird and an acceptable sparkling Foch. Self-portraits of the owner appeared on the labels of his products and hung in the offices around the winery. But the public was not interested in Uncle Ben's menagerie and soon the company was in financial trouble again. Brights considered purchasing the winery in 1979 for $750,000, but a fresh injection of capital by the irrepressible Ginter breathed new life into the business. Uncle Ben's became Golden Valley Wines, but after it limped along for another two years he was forced to sell.

The purchaser was an aggressive young entrepreneur, himself a controversial figure in the BC wine trade, named Anthony Von Mandl, whose Vancouver-based company imported German, French, Italian and Californian wines. The reputed price paid for the winery was $4 million and the two businessmen settled the final figure by flipping a quarter, best of five, at $25,000 a throw.

Immediately Von Mandl changed the name back to Mission Hill Vineyards and set about establishing the concern as a quality winery. At midnight on June 1, 1981, the day the deal was signed, Von Mandl and Nick Clark (who

A stylized view of Mission Hill Vineyards located above Westbank, BC. This
California-style winery, built in 1966, commands one of the finest views of the
Okanagan Valley.
Courtesy: Mission Hill Vineyards, Inc.

now runs the winery) were hosing the fruit flies off the fermentation tanks
and cleaning up years of neglect.

They began to phase out the Golden Valley wines and introduce a number
of subsidiary labels not associated with the Mission Hill Vineyards' name to
generate cash flow. After eighteen months, the addition of three Eureopean
winemakers and a major investment in new equipment, the first Mission Hill
wines were released. According to Von Mandl, "we have entirely patterned
the winery on Robert Mondavi's operation in the Napa Valley. That's exactly
what we want to be."

The style of the winery with its eighteenth-century antiques, tiled floors,
and whitewashed walls is reminiscent of the Mondavi model, as is the
owner's penchant for associating his enterprise with cultural events such as
support for the Vancouver Symphony Orchestra. And more importantly, the
Mondavi method governs the range and presentation of the company's
wines: the current Klosterburg and Chauvignon labels (for the burgundy-
style wines) will go in favour of a three-tiered system based on the Mission
Hill name. The blended table wines, red and white, will appear under the title
Mission Ridge; the varietals are under the Mission Hill Vineyards label
(including a Chenin Blanc and a Johannisberg Riesling as well as a generic red
and white); and the top of the line will be Mission Hill Private Reserve,
featuring five vinifera varietals—Gewurztraminer, Johannisberg Riesling,
Chenin Blanc, Pinot Noir and Cabernet Sauvignon.

Currently the two reds (the most expensive of Canadian wines) are made
from grapes grown in Washington, but the company has contracted growers
in the Osoyoos region to plant Pinot and Cabernet vines in soil and climatic

conditions very similar to those in the Yakima Valley, 200 miles south in Washington State.

The white grapes for Mission Hill's Gewurztraminer and Johannisberg Riesling are brought in from Dave Mitchell's vineyards at Uniacke. A second label, Pandosy Cellars (named after Father Charles Pandosy, an early settler in the valley at Okanagan Mission during the mid-1800s) has been released for the wines made from hybrid grapes.

Mission Hill has a sense of style: from its beautifully designed corporate symbol (a mission cross of vine leaves with grape clusters) to its tasteful decor and imaginative labels, it reflects a desire to produce wines of quality. A large commercial operation, it thinks in the same terms as an estate winery, babying its wines along and looking to the future when the Okanagan will become the Napa Valley of the North. Its quest for new products has led to a Maréchal Foch Nouveau in 1982 and a Pineau des Charentes-style aperitif made from free-run labrusca juice with grape alcohol added. The company has recently acquired a copper pot still for the distillation of eaux-de-vie and brandies.

Storage capacity: 575,000 gallons.

SUMAC RIDGE ESTATE WINERY,
Summerland, BC

In 1979 Harry McWatters and Lloyd Schmidt—who had over forty years' experience in the BC wine industry between them—bought a nine-hole golf course off Highway 97 at Summerland and turned it into a winery. By shaving the fairways of the par three course and shortening it from 2,500 to 1,600 yards, they were able to plant ten of the 38.5 acres with Johannisberg Riesling, Gewurztraminer and Chardonnay vines. The first wines produced by Sumac Ridge in 1980 came from grapes grown across the lake on their Naramata vineyard and a small amount brought in from other local growers. That year the fledgling company put out two whites (Vedelet and Okanagan Riesling) and a red (Chancellor).

These debut wines were crushed and vinified at Casabello where McWatters and Schmidt had worked before leaving to create their own estate winery.

Schmidt's father used to own the 130-acre Beau Sejour Vineyard in Kelowna which supplied Growers' Wine Company (subsequently Ste–Michelle). He sold it to the company in 1965. Lloyd Schmidt stayed on to manage the vineyards until 1971, then worked for the Department of

Agriculture for a couple of years before joining Casabello. Here he met Harry McWatters who had been hired as the company's first salesman in 1966.

The golf course and its restaurant—which must be unique in the world of wines—gave the company cash flow at the beginning and enabled the partners to finance the purchase of equipment and, in 1981, the building of the fermentation cellar. The two families run the golf course, the restaurant and the winery between them.

In the second year of bottling Sumac Ridge added a Gewurztraminer, a Chenin Blanc and a Summerland Rosé (a light, sweetish blend of Okanagan Riesling and Chancellor) to its list and in 1983 a Chardonnay and a Johannisberg Riesling.

The modern cellar is a very compact operation capable of being run by one person. The stainless steel tanks have been augmented with 25 oak barrels (58-gallon capacity) purchased from the Heitz Winery in Napa Valley where Lloyd Schmidt's son worked. The oak cooperage is used to give barrel age to the vinifera whites.

The Sumac Ridge style is for dry white wines, apart from the Okanagan Riesling which has some residual sugar as does the Verdelet—to offset its high acidity. The year 1982 provided the company with some botrytised Chenin Blanc grapes which they hope to vinify in *Auslese* style and market in half bottles. And taking advantage of the consumer craze for Beaujolais Nouveau they released a Chancellor Nouveau in 1982.

Lloyd Schmidt says the list will eventually split fifty-fifty between viniferas and hybrids, although his ultimate dream is to make an oak-fermented and aged Cabernet Sauvignon from the one acre of newly planted vines. (His target date for this is 1990.)

The Club House restaurant, which stands over the aging cellar, the bottling room and the quality control laboratory, features on its wine list other estate and commercial winery products "as long as they contain 100% BC grapes." And any player who gets a hole-in-one receives a congratulatory bottle of Sumac Ridge wine.

Storage capacity: 38,600 gallons.

UNIACKE ESTATE WINES, Kelowna, B.C.

The winery is owned by a fruit farmer, David Mitchell, and his wife, Susan; a builder, David Newman-Bennett; and a photographer in Calgary, Al Savage. Mitchell's grandmother was a Uniacke, a name dating back to fourteenth-century Ireland when a member of the Fitzgerald clan was recognized for service to his king as being "without peer", or "unique". Fitzgerald took the compliment to heart and used it as his family name and it passed to Nova Scotia in 1775 with settlers from County Cork. In memory of that ancient compliment the family crest on the company labels bears the motto "Unicus Est".

Originally trained as a geologist, Dave Mitchell started growing grapes around Kelowna in 1974 and made a little wine on the side, importing vinifera grape vines from Germany and Washington State.

David Newman-Bennett, who acts as cellar master, designed and constructed the bijou winery, in contemporary Mediterranean style above the existing tiny cellar. Thirty acres of grapes and twenty acres of apples rise on a steep gradient from the lakeshore road on both sides of the white-painted winery office. The vines vary in age from 4 to 20 years old. In 1980 Uniacke made its first crush from Okanagan Riesling, Johannisberg Riesling and Chelois grapes. Since then they have expanded their varietals to include Chasselas, Gewurztraminer, Pinot Noir, Merlot and a little Chardonnay. The Pinot and Merlot spend one year in small oak casks. In 1983 the company bottled a Merlot-Pinot Noir blend.

The Okanagan Riesling, which won the gold medal at the 1982 September Wine Festival, had sweet reserve and a little Gewurztraminer blended in, which suggest the Germanic approach of the house style. In fact, the company hired Tilman Hainle, a young German-trained winemaker, for the 1982 crush, so no doubt sweet reserve will be the order of the day since 85% of Uniacke's production is white wine.

Hainle has a small barrel of 1982 Johannisberg Riesling Late Harvest in the cellar so we may see some quality dessert wines from Uniacke in future.

In 1982 Uniacke made 12,000 gallons of wine.

Storage capacity: 17,000 gallons.

seven

Quebec

*"To illustrate the new identity of the Quebec Liquor
Corporation, a basic consumer symbol was needed. We
chose the wine glass. Besides expressing the concept
we had in mind, the wine glass reflects elegance, refinement
and good dining . . . Not to exclude other spirits
we have designed the glass so as to suggest the general
idea of . . . a drink."*

*(From the 1973 Annual Report of the Quebec Liquor
Corporation.)*

Quebeckers have for centuries marched to a different drum and in matters of the grape they will not be swayed by trends outside the province. While they continued to drink two glasses of red wine for every one of white—and the vast majority of this was imported from Europe—the rest of Canada and, indeed, the wine-drinking world in general, had switched their allegiance to white with a vengeance. And while the SAQ sold a meagre 1.58 percent of wines made elsewhere in Canada for the year 1981-82 the rest of the country's winedrinkers shared their favours almost equally between domestic and imported products.

The reason that Quebec—a non grape-growing province—consumes little Ontario and no BC wine is that it has a valuable if somewhat bizarre wine industry of its own.

La Société des Alcools du Québec

The history of wine in *la belle province* is virtually the story of the Quebec Liquor Commission itself. In 1921, following Prohibition, La Commission des Liqueurs de Québec was established as the sole authority to sell alcohol in the province. Up to this time tonic wines were readily available through drug stores and shops; these were products fulsomely advertised as offering all the benefits of a panacea that medical science had not yet succeeded in discovering.

The Commission put a stop to the tonic wine traffic and, with admirable foresight, immediately opened an office in Paris so that it could control the purchase of French wines at the source, in order to procure "the best wines at the best prices", without the intervention of a middle man. Today the SAQ is the largest bulk buyer of wines in the world and has a capacity of 2,600,000 gallons at its Montreal bottling plant.

In 1960 the Commission changed its name to La Régie des Alcools du Québec, dividing itself into two bodies: one to issue liquor licences, the other to regulate the sale of wines and spirits. The two functions were separated bureaucratically between Quebec City and Montreal. But lack of planning and budgetary projection caused such confusion that most of the products sold by the Régie cost more in Quebec than they did in Ontario.

In 1968 a worried provincial government set up a board of enquiry whose findings were published three years later as the Thinel Report. Acting on its recommendations the government introduced several far-reaching reforms.

Under the new title of La Societé des Alcools du Québec, it would now be responsible only for the sale and distribution of wines and spirits. Quebec cider (which had been fermented and sold "under the blanket" for generations) was legalized and by 1972 there were eleven cideries in the province busily fermenting and selling a variety of apple ciders in grocery stores. Their sales immediately skyrocketed.

And most significantly, the government, acting on the advice of the Thinel Commission, decided to create a Quebec wine industry. The SAQ, in its previous existence as La Régie, had been buying wines in Europe and bottling them under its own label for years; now they would have competition from private enterprise.

The symbol of La Societé des Alcools du Québec (the province's liquor board, known as the SAQ) is a glass set in a square suggesting the letter "Q". The purple colour of the square is highly significant. According to the SAQ's annual report of 1973, "It had to be warm, suggestive and refined at the same time. Burgundy, naturally, was our choice."

As a corporate symbol it speaks volumes about Quebec's predilection for wines. Over the past six years there has been a dramatic growth in the consumption of wine throughout the province, thanks to its ready accessibility through some 10,000 grocery store outlets. In the year 1977-78 (before the government allowed wine to be sold in _magasins d'alimentations et dépanneurs_) the sales of spirits amounted to $337,200,000 as opposed to $164,700,000 for wine. In 1982 the figure was $402,100,000 for spirits against $320,500,000: a steep rise in wine consumption at the expense of hard liquor.

There is an old joke in wine circles about the dying vigneron who calls his son to his bedside to deliver his last words. The boy bends down over the old man. "Son," he says, gasping for breath, "I have something very important to tell you . . . It can also be made from grapes."

The problem was that Quebec does not grow grapes. In spite of efforts by such pioneers as Justin de Courtenay and Mr. Menzies of Beaconsfield in the last century, the province has had no success to speak of in the cultivation of wine grapes on a commercial scale. So Quebec wines had to be made from grape juice or concentrates imported from Europe, California and South America. Or, for those who were more adventurous, from fresh grapes shipped across the water in refrigerated containers.

In 1971 the SAQ not only sold wines imported from Europe but also the wines it had bought in bulk and bottled itself in Montreal. They were not going to give up the monopoly they had on the inexpensive house wine market that easily. Those companies that were issued licences to make "Quebec wine" had to ferment at least 70 percent of the products in the province.

As every home winemaker knows, fresh grapes make the best wine and they must be crushed as soon as possible—within hours of leaving the vine—for the best results. Grapes which have been refrigerated lose some of their flavour aromatics over the period of time that it takes to transport them to Canada under ideal conditions, let alone the exigencies of dock handling at either end where they could be left standing outdoors in all weathers.

Juice concentrated by rapid evaporation and reduced to 40% of its volume can make adequate homemade wine when reconstituted and fermented, but it does not bear comparison with the humblest winery product in terms of bouquet alone. And juice which has been treated with sulphur dioxide gas to stop it from fermenting during transportation loses volatile esters when heated to remove the gas. (These esters carry the perfume of the wine.) Often the wines still taste of residual sulfur.

To make such products acceptable, the government of Quebec allowed its commercial wineries to add up to 20 percent of finished wine from Europe or 30 percent from California. This would give them certain characteristics which could not have been developed during fermentation; that is, the proper balance of acids, tannins and sugars as well as the requisite depth of colour to suit the style of the wine.

But in the first analysis it is the quality of the grapes that counts and it all boils down to the silk purse-sow's ear syndrome: when a Quebec business-man approaches a European or Californian broker to purchase juice or con-centrate, he knows in his heart of hearts that he will not be offered the top grade since the best grapes will obviously go to the wineries of that particular country. The Quebec buyers will be getting what is left unless they make special arrangements with local growers themselves.

Quebec labels do not tell you the contents of the wine (where the grapes come from and the origin of the finished wine added after fermentation to bring the product up to snuff). The amazing thing is that the Quebec wineries could produce drinkable products under these Draconian regulations. But the major problem facing the smaller wineries is consistency from year to year since they cannot afford to hold large stocks for blending to produce a product that will have the same taste profile with each vintage.

Undeterred by such inhibiting factors, several Quebec companies took the plunge and by 1974, five manufacturers of Quebec wines formed a pressure group called La Societé de Promotion de L'Industrie Vinicole du Québec, or SOPROVIN for short. The first permit had been granted to Vin Geloso Inc. whose owner, Vincent Geloso, had been importing grapes from Italy for Montreal's Italian community since 1965. Today there are eleven companies around the province making a full range of red, white, rosé, sparkling and aperitif wines as well as ciders.

Among this number are two of the big four—Andres and Brights. Brights was the first Canadian winery to establish itself in Quebec in 1933. The company had a production plant at Lachine where Adhemar de Chaunac worked as an oenologist, making sherries like Vin St. Georges from Ontario grapes which were bottled by the Quebec Liquor Board. In 1972 they were the second company to receive a licence to produce Quebec wines under the name of Les Vins LaSalle at St..Hyacinthe. In December 1978 they bought the ailing cider cooperative called La Cidrerie Deux Montagnes at St. Joseph du Lac. They needed the extra capacity to take advantage of a dramatic new development: the Quebec government had decided to allow Quebec wineries to sell their products through corner grocery stores and Brights had no bottling line in their St. Hyacinthe plant.

But even with this radical departure, the SAQ was to keep its competitive edge because the companies were allowed only a maximum of three products for sale in grocery stores as opposed to 15 bottlings by the SAQ.

This revolution in wine sales came about because of pressure from the grocery store owners themselves, who had been feeling the financial pinch from the large supermarket chains in the 1970s, and from the growing plight of the cider manufacturers. In 1921 the government had overlooked cider as an alcoholic beverage when it passed laws governing the sale of beer, wine and spirits. Until 1971 cider was illegal in the province, even though most of the apple growers made and sold it. A typical example is the case of Fernand Dufour, a chemist at St-Antoine-Abbé, who fermented apples from his farm orchard. His neighbour, Claude Lussier, who managed his own apple orchard under the company name of Lubec, assisted Dufour by buying up his surplus crop. Lussier went further and actually purchased the cider-making facility from his neighbour in 1966. For the next four years he began selling the "forbidden fruit" on a commercial scale until the police finally put a stop to his illicit enterprise by padlocking the cidery.

Lussier complained that cider was legal in every other country in the world and began to lobby the government for a change in the law. He argued that it would merely formalize already existing practices in the province and legitimise a local industry. The government acquiesced and even allowed the product to be sold through grocery stores. Immediately the shelves were full of cider in various forms—sparkling, semi-sparkling, still, sweet, semi-sweet and dry with an alcoholic content of some 10 or 11 percent. There were over 100 brands on the market and no quality control. Through a process of natural selection, the fly-by-night operations began to fold. One by one they went bankrupt or were taken over by more viable concerns. By the mid-1970s only two companies remained. Lubec and Cidrobec in Rougemont. Quebeckers wanted wine rather than cider and both concerns saw the writing on the cellar wall.

In 1976 a wine company called Les Vignobles Chantecler at St-Augustin near Quebec City bought Cidrobec and transferred its manufacturing operation to Rougemont. The transition from the production of cider to wine involved little capital investment since the same vats can be used for the fermentation of both apple or grape juice, as well as the same bottling line. However, Lubec did have an initial setback in the grocery stores since the company marketed their wines under St-Antoine-Abbé, the same brand name as its ciders. This confused consumers into thinking it was apple wine. The company corrected this marketing mistake by withdrawing these labels from the grocery sector.

The new wineries may have been off and running but they were shackled by further regulations on what they could name their products. Mindful of the 1974 Supreme Court decision upholding a judgment against the use of the term "champagne" for sparkling wines made in Canada, the Quebec government declared that any title which suggested the wines of France could not be used. Terms like Chateau, Domaine, Côte or Clos were not to be used by Quebec wineries. But the mind of man is ingenious and resourceful; the label writers came up with any number of French terms which suggested the forbidden words (Manoir, Castel and Cuvée made admirable alternatives).

In a province where most villages were named after saints one would have thought that such a designation would have worked well on a wine label. But not so. After their initial disaster with St-Antoine-Abbé wines, Lubec hired a psycho-sociologist to find out what went wrong. Apart from the confusion with cider in the public mind, they were told that the name of a hallowed saint on a label had little appeal to wine drinkers since "saints don't have much fun".

As Jean Legault, sales manager of Lebuc, explained, "We are not selling wine, we're selling the mood." And this sentiment is reflected in the brand names that grace so many Quebec wines today—La Nuit D'Amour, Plaisir D'Amour, La Nuit Volage' ("Flighty Night"), and Réve d'Été (featuring Edouard Manet's nude picnic scene on the label), Plaisir Divin, Du Barry Rosé d'Amour.

Lubec even has a series of saucy maxims on its neck labels. ("Wine is familiar with every virtue. But it ignores them all because it knows that at the bottom of a glass love sings more strongly." *Maximes Libertines VI*). And Les Entreprises Verdi features a series of nine drinking songs on the back labels of its Cuvée des Moines de l'abbaye wines. The front labels depict a bibulous monk with a red nose, obviously worse for spending more time in the cellar than the crypt.

For all their gimmicks the Quebec wineries had to contend with the monolothic SAQ which not only regulated their activities but competed with them for sales in grocery stores and its own liquor stores.

SOPROVIN has long challenged the inequities of the system and as of January 1983, the eleven-member wineries have scored a victory of sorts. They can now be represented by up to five labels in the lucrative grocery store market (some 10,000 outlets provincially) as opposed to the 15 allowed the SAQ. And what is more important, they will no longer have to import grape juice and concentrates; from the 1983 vintage they will now be able to bring in finished wines and bottle them themselves—subject to the proposed legislation now passing through the Quebec legislature. These new regulations would undoubtedly improve the quality of the wines at the cheaper end of the scale and give a boost to the flagging financial fortunes of seven of the eleven Quebec wine manufacturers. But, at a stroke, it would effectively kill the fiction that there is an indigenous wine industry in the province of Quebec and would make the less viable of the small enterprises easy prey for the large distillers who might sense a handsome profit under the new legislation. Existing winery licenses now have an asking price of 1.5 million as a result.

There is, however, one visionary Frenchman (from Montpellier) who believes that Quebec can make wines from locally grown grapes. Christian Barthomeuf owns a small fruit farm in Dunham, south east of Montreal near the American border, where he has planted some ten acres of Seyval Blanc, Maréchal Foch, Gamay, Chardonnay and Pinot Noir vines. He calls his winery Domaine des Côtes d'Ardoises. *Ardoise* means slate and the microclimate he enjoys is similar to that Beaujolais and Alsace. His growing season, apparently, is as long as Vineland's in Ontario—with 200 more heat units per year. Christian Barthomeuf has already produced an experimental Seyval Blanc which augurs well for the possibility of some authentic québécois wines by 1987.

QUEBEC WINERIES

LES ENTREPRISES VERDI,
Saint-Leonard, Quebec.

Verdi offers thirteen wines and has the distinction of making them entirely from fresh grapes shipped in from California, Chile, Mexico and Argentina. The company was established in 1967 as an importer of grapes by its president, Vincent Cacciatore, but did not receive its winemaking licence until 1979. The oenologist is Laurent Vivès, a Frenchman who worked many years in the south of France as the director of a large wine-producing cooperative.

The company's five white wines are made from the Ugni Blanc grape and the reds from several varieties such as Carignan, Cabernet Sauvignon, Alicante, Grenache, Ruby Cabernet and Ruby Red. The wines are vinified in stainless steel and have no wood aging. Verdi boasts the most modern bottling line in North America, with a capacity of 6,000 bottles an hour.

The winery also produces four kosher wines (two reds and two whites) under the Kineret label. This range came about when Cacciatore choked over the sweet kosher wine he was served at the home of his son's godfather, Montreal lawyer, Rubin Strauber. He was convinced his company could vinify a much more palatable product. Challenged by Strauber to do so— and with the blessing of the Montreal Jewish community council—he went ahead. The Kineret range was ready for Passover 1980.

Apart from the kosher wines, Verdi porduces a full-bodied Rhône-style red called Le Vieux Manoir and a good blanc de blancs called Tourbillon d'automne, which is one of their grocery store listings. Another is Portneuf, a red wine which suffered oxidation problems and had to be withdrawn by the SAQ. That fault has subsequently been rectified. The base for all the wines is the same combination of grapes, blended in different proportions.

Storage capacity: 600,000 gallons

JULAC INC., Dolbeau, Quebec.

This company could justifiably claim to be the most québécois of all, were it not for the fact that its principal product is not made from grapes at all, but from blueberries picked in the Lac St-Jean area. It manufactures a popular aperitif called Dubleuet. Recently the company has begun to vinify grape juice. It markets a well-made white called Cuvée Val-Jalbert.

Storage capacity: 325,000 gallons

LUBEC INC., St-Antoine-Abbé, Quebec

Claude Lussier turned his cider business into a winery in 1978, but he did not foresake the apples which grow so well in this corner of Quebec in the county of Huntingdon.

Just over half the production of Lubec is based on the fermented juice of apples—25 percent cider, mainly under the St-Antoine-Abbé label (a dry sparkler is available in Ontario) and 30 percent apple-based aperitif vermouths. One version, called Mundial, is flavoured with blackcurrant juice and called a vermouth cassis.

The winery is part of an old farm with outbuildings acting as fermenting rooms and storage space. The original cellar in front of the apple orchard is a cement block basement, half underground, where the cider was fermented illicitly in barrels before the practice was legalized in 1971.

Lubec's French oenologist, from the University of Bordeaux, makes his white wines of Greek grape juice from the island of Crete and has lately switched from California to Argentina as a cheaper source of Cabernet Sauvignon, as well as buying concentrates from the Rioja in Spain.

The best wines are La Nuit Volage, a cold-fermented wine, well balanced and clean, and the red Le Cellier des Châtelains.

The company has a penchant for using reproductions of old masters on their labels (Antoine Watteau on La Nuit Volage and Auguste Renoir on Tourne Joie and Tourne Fête). They also make a rosé called Le Fou du Roi.

Storage and fermenting capacity: 750,000 gallons.

LA MAISON SECRESTAT LTEE,
Dorval, Quebec.

Bordering the Trans-Canada Highway on the outskirts of Montreal, Secrestat is housed in an ultra-modern plant owned by the Bronfman empire.

The company's eleven products (a carbonated sparkling wine called Glockenspiel is soon to be added to the repertoire to make a round dozen) run the gamut from red, white and rosé to sherry, vermouth and Sangria. They are all made from grape concentrates from two California companies, one controlled by Seagrams and the other by Labatts, and a small amount from Valencia in Spain, Argentina and Chile.

The finished wines for blending, after the fermentation of the juice, are purchased through the Californian giant, Paul Masson whose vineyard the late Sam Bronfman acquired in the early forties. The concentrates come in at "base 10" or "base 15"; that is, 10 or 15 percent of the original volume. Montreal tap water is added once the chlorine is filtered out and the fermentation lasts from 10 days to two-and-a-half weeks, depending on the style of wine. Sugar is introduced during the fermentation to bring up the alcoholic strength.

For the white wines a blend of Muscat-Riesling and French Colombard is added up to 30 percent by volume. For red wines, it is Cabernet Sauvignon and Ruby Cabernet.

The company's medium sweet Granada Sherry is produced by adding sugar syrup to a white wine base until the alcohol level is raised to 16 percent. The wine is baked for four weeks and then added to a white wine blend in a proportion of 35 to 40 percent.

Their San Mareno vermouth (red and white) is a masceration of the sherry with certain herbs or "botanicals"—a tank process which takes about one month. The wine is filtered and left for six months in barrels with sugar to adjust the alcohol. The alcoholic strength of the white San Mareno is to be vinified up to 18 or 19 percent from its current 16.5 percent to be in line with its competition.

The company has an annual sales volume of $5 million and operates a store on the premises run by an SAQ employee. Secrestat's grocery store listings are Chambord (red) in a carafon and Pica Rosé.

Storage capacity: 600,000 gallons.

LES VIGNOBLES CHANTECLER,
Rougemont, Quebec.

Chantecler is really three companies—a cidery (Cidrobec), a distillery (Dumont Ltée) and a winery. The original company, called Les Vins Chantecler, was founded in 1971 at St-Augustin near Quebec City when the province legalized cider. The distillery operation started three years later. In 1976 Cidrobec acquired Chantecler and transferred its equipment to Rougemont to begin its winemaking operation. Jean-Denis Coté bought the company and changed its name to Les Vignobles Chantecler in 1977 on the strength of a three-acre experimental vineyard planted on the slope of the Rougemont mountain. The company speaks optimistically of producing a truly québécois wine from Aurore and Maréchal Foch grapes grown there, perhaps in 1984. They also have vinifera vines selected from such cold weather regions as the Jura in western France, not far from the Swiss border.

Chantecler produces eight reds and five whites and a white sparkling wine. They buy grape juice from Spain, France, Italy, California, Greece, Argentina and Chile and make all their products—whether wines, ciders or spirits—in stainless steel tanks.

They have the dubious distinction of being the first winery in North America to use the traditional straw-covered chianti flask for their popular Rossini, a blend of Ruby Cabernet, Italian Merlot and filler from Argentina— a fact which has not pleased the Italian government. A white version will soon be introduced. Rossini, along with Rêve d'Été (a 9% light white wine) and Cuvée Table Ronde (a semi-sweet white available in Ontario) are sold in grocery stores, as are three apple-based vermouths under the name of Bellini.

Cidrobec has been exporting its cider products to Japan since 1973 and more recently opened up the American market with a light product called Apple Amber (5% alcohol). They also produce Grand Sec d'Orléans cider and the lighter Double Six for the home market.

Les Distilleries Dumont made its first product in 1974—an eau-de-vie from cider called Calvabec, trading on the generic name of the more famous apple brandy from Normandy. They now produce a range of spirits and liqueurs, including gin, vodka, rum, Amaretto, Creme de Menthe, a Triple Orange cognac and a Prunelle de Bourgogne. These distilled products are manufactured by the continuous still method.

Storage capacity: 1,500,000 gallons

LES VIGNOBLES DU QUEBEC,
Hemmingford, Quebec.

Vignobles means vineyards, but this is something of a misnomer since the company's three wines (two red and one white) are made exclusively from fresh grape juice and sulphited juice shipped in from California. The original concern was founded in 1974 by a French *vigneron* named Michel Croix who was convinced that vinifera grapes could grow in St-Bernard-de-Lacolle when he discovered some old gnarled vine-plants there in the early 1970s. (Grapes had been grown at Lacolle in the eighteenth century.) Croix planted Pinot Chardonnay, Gamay, Cabernet and some De Chaunac on a three-acre site, and actually produced some wine in 1978 from two metric tons of grapes capable of making 1,660 litres. The following year a Vintage Festival was held at the winery but the vineyards were wiped out after two successive cold winters. The enterprise had been taken over in 1977 by John Darrigo, owner of the Toronto-based grocery chain as well as a grape-importing business. In 1978 Michel Croix left the company following a disagreement over the winemaking. Les Vignobles du Quebec has its own juice processing plant near Fresno in California.

The winery is currently housed in an old cidery which used to be known as Cellier St. Bernard, leased from Lubec Inc.

The wines, Petit Prince (red and white) and Seigneur de Beaujeu, are sold in the grocery stores as well as the SAQ which bottles the products for the company. The Italian winemaker, Claudio Bartolozzi intends to produce varietal wines from Californian juice in future.

Les Vignobles du Quebec has six employees and will soon be moving to new premises.

Storage capacity: 400,000 gallons.

VIN GELOSO INC. Laval, Quebec.

Vincent Geloso, the founder of his family company, has the honour of holding permit 001, the first winemaking licence issued by the Quebec government. He emigrated to Quebec from Caserta province in Italy in 1957 and eight years later founded the wine company, although at that time it merely imported grapes and juice. In his lavish brochure the ebullient Italian winemaker writes: "When we settled in Quebec, we brought with us the age-old traditions and knowledge of winemaking of generations of Italian vintners. The Canadian climate is, alas!, unclement to the vine, so we decided to bring in from our homeland the marvellous Italian grapes, bursting with sunshine, with which we make truly Italian wines here in Quebec. We call them "Quebetalian" wines." The name should not be held against the company however, since all the juice comes from the Veneto, Lazio and Pulia regions of Italy and Vinent Geloso himself selects them each harvest time on a trip back home. He ships into Quebec both juice and finished wine from such grape varieties as Cabernet, Merlot, Sangiovese, Verduzzo, Malvasia, Rabaso, Trebbiano and Negramaro.

When they began producing wine in 1971 they delivered 150 cases to the then La Régie des Alcools, packed by hand by the entire family. Today they have an annual sales of some $10 million. Their modern plant at St. Vincent de Paul in Laval covers an area of 75,000 square feet as a result of a $2 million expansion in 1979, and includes tanks for the production of a sparkling wine called Brutus, made by the Charmat method.

Geloso produces eleven red wines, eight whites, a rosé, three sparkling wines and two vermouths. La Romaine, Cuvée Rouge and Cuvée Blanc are sold in grocery stores.

All the wines are Italinate in style, the reds are big and tannic, the whites generally dry and crisp. Their best red is named after the founder, La Réserve à Vincent, which is kept in wood for three to five years and comes in numbered bottles. The best white is Orfée Blanc, which features three nymphs on the label. They also offer a light white with the engaging name of Entre deux Poissons. Their Cuvée Blanc and Cuvée Rouge are available in Ontario.

In addition to the Italian grape juice he ships in, Vincent Geloso also imports Californian grapes for Montreal's home winemakers through a company called Ruviano.

Storage capacity: 2,000,000 gallons.

LES VINS ANDRES DU QUEBEC LTEE,
St. Hyacinthe, Quebec.

Set in the flat corn-land forty kilometres east of Montreal, Andres' Quebec plant was bought lock, stock, barrel and grape crusher from Calona Wines in 1974. The BC-based company had made an abortive attempt to crack the lucrative francophone market in 1971 with screwcap wines, but they ran into problems with bottles exploding after secondary fermentation.

Outside the modern white facility just off the main highway is a cruciform sign with the name 'Andres' printed in large letters across the arm. Below it is the Baby Duck emblem, the symbol of the company's successful penetration of the Quebec market: Baby Duck is the largest selling wine in the province after the SAQ's own bottling, Cuvée des Patriotes—thanks to its presence on grocery store shelves. Andres virtually dominates the sparkling wine segment of the Quebec market with Baby Duck and the Chanté wines.

Unhampered here by the need to use Ontario grapes, Andres imports juice and grapes from California rather than finished wines since the government levies a 20 percent per gallon duty on imported bulk wines for blending. (The juice for Baby Duck and the white and rosé Chanté wines comes almost exclusively from Ontario labrusca grapes, however, and two of the company's lesser reds—Moulin Rouge and Cuvée Vieux Marché do use De Chaunac grapes from Niagara in their basic California blend.)

They bring in sulphited Riesling for their carbonated sparkling wine, Richelieu Brut, and French Colombard and Chenin Blanc for their whites. Hochtaler in Quebec bears little relation to its Ontario counterpart since it is a blend of these two grapes with some added sweet reserve to give it a fruity Moselle-style taste.

For their reds they ship in either juice or refrigerated grapes of Ruby Cabernet, Petite Sirah and a little Zinfandel. These grapes make a full-bodied, richly flavoured product called La Souvenance, which is given some barrel age.

Andres' young winemaker, Jean-Yves Plamandon, studied his craft at the agricultural college in St. Hyacinthe and subsequently in France.

Storage capacity: 1,000,000 gallons.

LES VINS BRIGHTS, St. Joseph-du-lac, Quebec.

LES VINS LA SALLE, St. Hyacinthe, Quebec.

Brights was the first Canadian winery to establish itself in Quebec. In 1933 the company purchased the original Dow Brewery in Lachine, built in 1870, and set up 450,000 gallons of cooperage made of BC fir to store its sherries and ports.

In 1972, taking advantage of the new legislation in the province, they created a subsidiary company on the premises of an old tractor factory in St. Hyacinthe called Les Vins La Salle. The company was named after the seventeenth-century explorer of the Great Lakes, Robert Cavalier de La Salle. The intention was to produce wines specifically for the Quebec market and for export to the New England states.

When the Quebec government permitted grocery-store wine sales, Brights purchased the land, buildings and assets of La Cidrerie Deux-Montagnes at St. Joseph-du-lac—a plant of some 22,000 square feet—to meet the burgeoning demand in the province for table wines.

They now market their products under two labels—(Brights and La Salle), sharing the company's popular national brands between them. LiebesHeim, for instance, is sold under the La Salle label in Quebec, as is Brights' red and white House Wine (known in Quebec as Notre Vin Maison.) The white version is the top-selling Canadian white wine in the province. Brights still maintains control if its traditional sherries and ports, since it is well entrenched in this segment of the Quebec market with such products as Vin St. Georges (sherry) and 74 Port.

While the Lachine plant is used mainly for storage (it has no bottling line), the two wineries east and west of the island of Montreal buy in grape juice for fermentation from various parts of Europe (depending on the going price) and from California. They truck in juice, too, from Ontario (Maréchal Foch, Villard Noir, Seyval Blanc and Elvira) and in 1981 they purchased a half a million gallons of De Chaunac from the Ontario government to ease a surplus in Niagara. Consequently, La Salle now offers a varietal De Chaunac. But as with Andres, their national brands have a completely different taste profile from the same wines in Ontario.

Both companies produce sparkling wines but Brights President Champagne and its Brut version are the only two products marketed in Quebec that are made and bottled in Ontario. Because of the Quebec law they cannot use the name "champagne" on their label. Here they are styled President Grande Reserve Vine Mousseux; but the marketing men have found a way to get the message across that the wines are made in the traditional French style by including the term *"Méthode Champenoise."*

Situated as it is in the heart of apple-growing country, Brights' facility at St. Joseph-du-lac also produces a strong and a light cider by the Charmat process as well as apple vermouths.

Brights and La Salle between them produce 1,700,000 gallons of wine, sherry, port and vermouth under some sixty labels.

La Salle storage capacity: 1,000,000 gallons
Lachine storage capacity: 850,000 gallons
Brights' St.-Joseph-du-lac storage capacity: 100,000 gallons

LES VINS CORELLI, Ville Ste-Catherine, Montreal, Quebec.

The newest of Quebec's eleven wineries received its licence in 1980 and is housed in an ultra-modern building the style of which can only be described as Baghdad contemporary. The spare lines of the brick façade are punctuated with tall arched windows. The left side of the plant is dominated by gigantic white-painted outdoor storage tanks which extend above the level of the roof.

The winery was conceived and created by a dynamic and innovative Italian entrepreneur named Giovanni Miucci who emigrated to Canada from Apulia in 1956 with $10 in his pocket. He had come to Canada to make wine—the way his family had done since the eighteenth century. Nine years later he began to import Californian grapes for his fellow immigrants.

In 1975 he bought a state-of-the-art desulphiting machine from Italy to extract the sulphur from treated juice; but it took him five years before the Quebec government would grant him a licence to manufacture wines. Once secured, Miucci built his winery from scratch, including the placement and welding of five 45,000-gallon fermenting tanks. The investment with his partner, Vincenzo Morena, totalled $2.5 million. And Giovanni Miucci—an opera singer manqué—named the winery after his friend and favourite Italian tenor, Franco Corelli.

Like Vincent Geloso, Miucci imports his grapes from Italy, purchasing them himself in his native province at the heel of the country and from Piedmont in the north. In 1982 he brought over 200 tons of fresh grapes in refrigerated containers from the port of Naples. The varieties he favours are Primitivo, Montepulciano, Raboso, Malvesia and Verduzzo. Some 20% of freshly crushed grapes go into his single red wine, Castelnovo, named after a villa in the Piedmont region; the rest is from fermented juice. The company would like to vintage date this wine since it is made from the grapes of a single harvest, but under Quebec law this is not permitted.

Currently Corelli has three products in Quebec: Castelnovo, a Barolo-style red aged in steel tanks with added oak chips; a crisp white called Entre-deux-Pays (made from the Verduzzo grape), and a sparkling wine called Gran Mousseux (Pinot Blanc) whose label could easily be mistaken for Mumm's Cordon Rouge (but it stays this side of plagiarism since the red diagonal stripe goes the other way). Miucci also vinifies a naturally sparkling rosé for the American market and has plans for a semi-sweet German-style *vin nouveau* and a dry red called, operatically, La Réserve de la Bohème.

Corelli has at present 350,000 gallons in fermentation.

Storage capacity: 1,000,000 gallons.

eight

Other Provinces

"In ten years the Gaspereau Valley is going to look like the Moselle. Those slopes will be covered with vines."

(Roger Dial, owner of Grand Pré Wines, Wolfville, N.S.)

Although Ontario and B.C. are the largest wine-producing provinces, facilities have also been established in Alberta and Nova Scotia.

Alberta is the fastest growing wine market in Canada and to take advantage of this growth, three of the major wineries have facilities there. All three are situated on the outskirts of Calgary, close enough to California for that state to supply large quantities of grapes.

Leif Ericsson may have considered Nova Scotia to be Vineland nearly one thousand years ago but there is very little evidence that wine was grown there until a few years ago. Yet Nova Scotia may well turn out to be a substantial wine-producing region if the vision of one man, Roger Dial, owner of Grand Pré Winery, is realised. Dial has proved that hybrids and vinifera will grow and flourish in the Annapolis Valley and he has 25 acres of vines to prove it, as well as some very interesting wines vinified from these grapes.

ALBERTA

The oldest established winery in the province is Andres, built in 1964. Andres' highly automated plant sells over one million gallons, particularly in large format, heavily blended with Californian material.

Chateau-Gai's Stoneycroft Cellars facility was acquired in 1980. National brands such as Alpenweiss are made here (60% Californian) from BC and Ontario juice.

Jordan purchased Chalet Wines' seven-year-old plant in 1973 and now ferments wines from concentrates and juices trucked in from Ontario, BC and California.

There is also one cottage winery in Alberta which is unique in Canada— Andrew Wolf Cellars—an operation which deserves special mention.

ANDREW WOLF WINE CELLARS,
Cochrane, Alberta

Andrew Wolf is the maverick of the Canadian wine industry. A brewer and vintner with over 35 years' experience, he likes to project the image of himself alternately as the little old European winemaker or a prophet crying in the wilderness—a pioneer who read the signs for the need of better table wines at a time no one would listen.

In 1963 Wolf worked for his uncle, Andrew Peller, at Andres' Port Moody plant and ran the Calgary facility for the company until 1965 when he left to create his own business, Chalet Wines. Andrew will tell you that it was he who created "Baby Duck" for Andres. And certainly he knew the secret because his fellow directors at Chalet demanded that he produce a similar candy-flavoured beverage to compete with the Duck's phenomenal success. "So I came up with Luv-a-Duck", recalls Wolf. "It was exactly the same wine."

Today Andrew Wolf speaks disparagingly of such sweet, low alcohol drinks, calling them "kickapoo juice". While he acknowledges their importance to the trade in weaning the young off Coke and Pepsi and introducing them to wine, he believed that growing consumer sophistication demanded better wines from better grapes. In the early 1970s he watched the dramatic rise in sales of imported wines and concluded that the wineries should be competing against them rather than calling on their provincial governments to legislate them off the shelves.

In 1976, with an investment of $250,000, plus a $65,000 grant from the Department of Regional Economic Expansion, he opened his own winery. Set "in the heart of the Big Hill Country", 25 miles northwest of Calgary in the town of Cochrane, Andrew Wolf Cellars is an unprepossessing grey-brick warehouse opposite a sawmill. Inside, the space is packed floor to ceiling with oak puncheons and fermentation barrels. Here Andrew Wolf makes a range of varietal wines from premium Californian grapes *flash-frozen* in the fields. His original piece of equipment was a wine press he bought at an Italian supermarket.

In 1979, his first year of operations, he produced 50 cases of Chenin Blanc and Cabernet—he called them his "vin ordinaire". By 1982 Wolf was producing 5,000 cases under 16 labels.

The wines are aged in small oak casks (French and American)—two years for whites, four for reds. True to his philosophy of creating an "old country" winery, he ferments on the skins, both whites and reds, and since he uses frozen grapes (they arrive at the winery in plastic drums) he can vinify all year round and in the amounts he can handle.

The grapes currently come from the San Joachim Valley and are stored in a freezer plant in Calgary until he needs them. Wolf plans to buy additional European and Chilean grapes in future.

He also talks of using Okanagan-grown grapes and in 1982 he purchased some Gewurztraminer in Washington State.

Andrew Wolf Cellars' 1982 list was equally divided between reds and whites. Most of them appeared as single variety wines such as Zinfandel, Gamay Beaujolais, Pinot Chardonnay and Chenin Blanc (including light versions of three whites). All the uninspired labels are identical for reds and whites apart from the name of the wine. The products, vinified from the frozen grapes, have good varietal character although they all tend to be shy on the nose. Their long stay in casks gives the whites a big oaky taste, sometimes overpoweringly so.

In 1984 Wolf plans to open his new winery on the Bow River, south of Cochrane. The architect's design shows a Bordeaux-style chateau, complete with wrought-iron gates and twin towers. This $2.5 million project will increase his capacity to 200,000 gallons. As matters stand, the cellars are operated by a tiny staff of four who, under the benign control of the white-haired winemaker himself, do the entire operation by hand, down to the bottling, labelling, packaging and selling.

The small facility has its own retail outlet and a tasting area among the racked barrels. The whole rustic enterprise has the feeling of clutter and easygoing bonhomie. As Andrew Wolf says, "People enjoy the idea that here's someone getting out of the factory and going back to making good hand-made shoes that last for a long time. Not all this plastic you see around nowadays."

Eighteen Andrew Wolf wines are sold through the ALCB, although private customers can have special labels bearing their name if they buy in two-case lots from his winery store. Some limited bottlings are only available here.

Storage capacity: 30,000 gallons.

NOVA SCOTIA

At present there are only two wineries in the province: the massive Andres plant at Truro and the miniscule Grand Pré, near Wolfville. There is absolutely no competition between the two concerns because they serve very different tastes: Andres has cornered the market on 7% sparkling pop wines, such as Baby Duck and Moody Blue, and is heavy into sherry and port, while Roger Dial's operation concentrates on quality red varietals in small quantities for the palates of discerning Nova Scotians.

The taste preference in the province—and the Maritimes generally—lags behind the rest of the country. The white wine boom has yet to happen here; Nova Scotia's wine drinkers still favour the sweet labrusca taste in both sparkling and dessert wines.

ANDRES WINES (ATLANTIC), Truro, NS

A Peller family connection in the province was responsible for the creation of the winery in 1964, at the time when Andres had just opened its Calgary plant. Joe Peller's sister-in-law was married to the manager of the CBC Television station in Halifax, Lloyd McGuinness. At his suggestion, the company looked into the possibility of creating a facility in the unlikely location of Truro, where grapes were nonexistent and the inhabitants had little appreciation of wine. McGuinness gathered a group of investors together with a Truro businessman named Harold Goodspeed to help form Abbey Wines Ltd. The company set up for business in 1965 in a 10,000-square-foot plant.

The winery shipped in virtually all its grapes from California and was left to its own devices to create a market for its products. In its first year of operations, Abbey bottled 100 cases a day but sold only 700 gallons. The company limped along financially for a few years to a chorus of closure threats from the Nova Scotia Liquor Commission. Undeterred, Andres' head office poured more capital into the enterprise and thanks to Baby Duck the company began to turn around in the early 1970s. After two expansions it is now over twice its original size.

What began as a shoestring operation with "one-and-a-half employees" in 1965 supported a staff of 40 by 1982 and had a balance sheet that was the envy of wineries across the country—thanks to a former drug salesman from Montreal, Ralph Logan, who took over as manager and subsequently became vice-president of Andres Atlantic.

Today Andres accounts for a whopping 38% of NS Liquor Commission wine sales, mainly due to its sparkling wines. In this category the company has a vise-like grip on 65% of Maritime sales and is very strong in fortified dessert wines.

Apart from shipping in Concord for Baby Duck, the winery has little use for Ontario grapes for its still and sparkling wines. They prefer to ship them in from California since there are no import restrictions in the province.

The bland Thompson Seedless is extensively used, top-noted with more flavoursome grapes, such as Muscat of Alexandria, French Colombard, Chenin Blanc and some Rhine Riesling for its whites. The red wines are De Chaunac based, although the company does bring in some Cabernet Sauvignon from California.

Andres' answer to Schloss Laderheim in Nova Scotia is Schloss Wilhelm, a rather flabby latecomer to the field, although the company's lighter style Old Home Summer '82 (used by the Ministry of Tourism in the province) is a credit to its winemaker.

Storage capacity: 700,000 gallons

GRAND PRÉ WINES, Grand Pré, NS

The term "cottage winery" might have been coined for Roger Dial's operation at Grand Pré. The fermenting cellar is the size of a four-car garage, stocked with oak casks and three small stainless steel tanks. Above it is the retail shop (for table grapes only), the galley-sized laboratory and a storage attic. The upper part of the cellar was built in 1982 to complement the neoclassical style of the 1819 farmhouse. The farm itself was originally settled in the 1680s by Acadians who migrated north from Samuel de Champlain's first colony in the southern Annapolis Valley.

From Roger Dial's study window you can see five acres of vines and beyond them the Bay of Fundy, the soft rolling hills of the valley and the body of water which provides an ideal microclimate for grape growing. Twenty-two miles away, Dial has a further 20 acres planted on a southern slope of North Mountain at Billtown. On this combined acreage he grows 60 hybrid and vinifera vines, including such exotic varieties as Michurnitz, Severnyi, Tajoznyt Izumund, Zaria Siewiera and Oraniensteiner.

The 41-year-old owner of Grand Pré divides his time between his responsibilities as a professor of political science at Dalhousie University and the company's winemaker. An expatriate Californian, Dial came to Nova Scotia in 1969 after working with the Davis Bynum winery in Sonoma. A home winemaker of many years' experience, he continued his hobby in his adopted province, buying grapes from a university colleague, Dr. Norman Morse, who owned the vineyard Dial subsequently purchased. In 1977 he persuaded Morse to plant wine instead of table grapes, including the first viniferas in eastern Canada.

Part of the vineyard already contained two Russian Amurensis varieties

A view of Grand Pré Wines in Grand Pré, Nova Scotia. This "cottage winery" produces some of the most distinctive wines being made in Canada today. Courtesy: Grand Pré Wines Ltd.

(red, naturally), called Michurnitz and Severnyi. The strains arrived in Canada as a result of a barter deal with the Soviets—Nova Scotian raspberries for Russian vines. The cuttings were originally planted at the Summerland Agricultural Research Station in BC and some were eventually traded to Nova Scotia for blueberries. A couple of rows of vines ended up in Morse's vineyard on an experimental basis. Roger Dial bought some of the Russian grapes and vinified them. Excited by the results, he persuaded Morse to plant more. Today, these two varieties (with Maréchal Foch) are the mainstay of Grand Pré's red wine production. "The Amurensis varieties could be the Cabernet Sauvignon and the Pinot Noir of Nova Scotia," he says. "They're very complex with lots of tannins, enormous colour and big esters."

As a winemaker, Roger Dial is nothing if not traditional. He ferments his reds (which make up 60 percent of his grape production) in open 400-gallon fibreglass tanks. These tanks were designed for salting cod but he is quick to assure the visitor that they have never been used for that purpose! The wines are aged in Yugoslavian oak barrels and bottled with the minimum of filtration. The first white wine produced by the company was vinified from a French America hybrid developed at Vineland in Ontario, V-53261. As befits the Nova Scotian image, he named it L'Acadie Blanc, although in future, when his vinifera vines mature, he will be able to call upon such noble grapes as Chardonnay, Gewurztraminer and Riesling.

Grand Pré's first wines were offered to the public through the NS Liquor Commission in 1980—90 cases of Maréchal Foch. The shelves were empty within weeks. In 1982, the winery produced 300 cases, adding the varietal Severnyi 1981; and in the spring of 1983 it released two bread-and-butter blends, L'Acadie Blanc and L'Acadie Rouge (a blend of De Chaunac from 1980 and 1981). In the summer he brought out Cuvée d'Amur 1980. This wine ("The best I've made in Canada", says Dial), is a varietal Michurnitz although to label it as such might engender some consumer resistance. The name, with its association of love, comes from the Amur river valley in the far east of Russia where the grape was originally grown (hence Amurensis). Cuvée d'Amur, with its deep ruby colour and fruity sandalwood nose, resembles a Californian Zinfandel in style.

By 1985 Roger Dial predicts his company will be producing 6,000 to 8,000 cases but he is reluctant to let it grow much bigger if he is to concentrate on his craftsman-like wines and produce small amounts from a variety of premium grapes. "In another culture," he says, "I would find the best of my 60 planted varieties and go with that like Bordeaux. But we're trying to create a wine culture here in Nova Scotia as well as running a business, so we have to make a range of different wines."

The style of Grand Pré is based on big, strapping wines with a full-bodied, oaky taste. The natural flavour of the grape is enhanced by lengthy skin

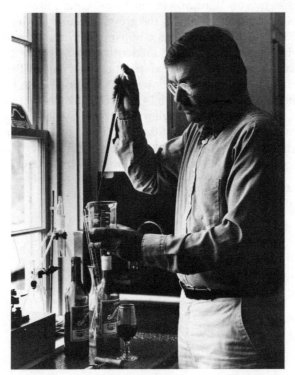

Roger Dial, owner and winemaker of Grand Pré Wines, concentrates on producing a few wines from a variety of premium grapes.
Courtesy: Grand Pré Wines Ltd.

contact with the must during fermentation and long aging in wood. Some of the reds I find overly oaky but they are among the most distinctive wines being made in Canada today and bear the unmistakable signature of the winemaker.

Roger Dial's vision of Nova Scotian wines made exclusively from locally grown grapes extends beyond the boundaries of his own property. He has a small nursery operation for propogating vines for other growers and he looks to the day when the slopes of the Annapolis Valley will be covered with grapes.

Why, one is tempted to ask, has no one exploited this area for viticulture before? Dial himself has no answer but before he and his partners invested $500,000 in the extraordinary idea of producing quality wines in the Annapolis Valley, he did months of research on soil and climatic conditions. Thanks to the warming effect of the Bay of Fundy, his vineyards enjoy a longer fall growing season than the Niagara Peninsula. Early spring frosts do not affect his vines because the water temperature holds down the soil temperature, preventing early budding.

In a paper written for the *Vinifera Wine Growers' Journal* (Fall 1979) entitled "Perspective on Winegrowing in Nova Scotia", Roger Dial showed that the average temperature during the growing season for the past decade produced 1736 heat units, a figure comparable to the Moselle; and the province's winters are considerably milder than many of the world's most prestigious wine-growing areas, not to mention the Niagara Peninsula.

If the future of a cottage wine industry in Nova Scotia is to be judged on the quality and style of Grand Pré wines, then Canadian consumers will be in for a pleasant surprise. In his pioneering efforts Roger Dial has done much to generate excitement and given confidence to those with the temerity—and the cash—to follow in his footsteps. As he himself confesses, "At present we sell the winery business in Nova Scotia more than we sell our wines."

Storage capacity: 10,000 gallons

nine

Canadian Wines—The Future

"If we continued to drape our products in the Canadian flag the consumer would never have bought them."

(David Ringler, Director of Marketing, Andres Wines.)

By virtue of provincial liquor boards, the Canadian consumer has the opportunity to taste the wines of the world cheek by jowl with our domestic products. Selection invites comparison and our national wine industry will only come of age when it realises that it cannot hide behind the skirts of government to protect indigenous products. Preferential treatment through mark-ups that discriminate against foreign imports is not going to improve Canadian wines. It may make them more attractive to budget-minded consumers in the short run but eventually our wines will have to compete on a level of quality.

The wine trade is international and like it or not our wineries will have to make products that can stand unblushing in the marketplace against those of Europe and the United States, and every other region that exports to our market. While our producers can continue to perfect the wines they make from hybrid grapes like Baco Noir, Maréchal Foch, Seyval Blanc and Vidal, they will only be taken seriously beyond our borders by the quality of the vinifera wines they make, like Chardonnay, Riesling and Gewurztraminer. The commercial wineries will argue that this is a mere 3% of the wines vinified in Canada but these are the best ambassadors since they act as a yardstick of the winemaker's art and speak to the quality of the lesser products. The benchmark for such wines has already been set by some 2,000 years of vinicultural practice in Europe. Wine-producing countries like Australia, South Africa, United States and Chile measure their best Cabernets, Pinot Noirs and Chardonnays against those of Bordeaux and Burgundy and eventually this is what the Canadian industry will have to do.

To say we don't have the climate to produce great wines begs the question. The answer lies in the selection of the best clonal varieties grafted onto the proper root stock and planted in the soil and microclimates suitable for them. The research is underway at government stations and winery vineyards and it is not beyond the realm of possibility that within a decade Canada will be taken seriously as a wine-growing country.

It is a truism to say the best grapes make the best wine and the future of the industry rests on the quality of the vines in the ground. Vineyard renewal is an expensive business and not one that growers would willingly undertake without financial assistance. The liquor boards could play a part in assisting farmers to uproot labruscas—and to some extent De Chaunac—if they were to plough back some of their vast profits into the industry. Provincial governments would not lose tax revenue if they were to add a 5¢ or 10¢ surcharge to all Canadian wines. The money raised could be used to subsidize the expense of planting preferred varieties in the interest of producing better wines for the consumer.

Efforts by companies like Jordan to remove the "foxy" aroma and taste from labrusca-based products by technological methods, such as the use of juice concentrators to remove unwanted flavour esters, while laudable in themselves, merely delay the process. There will always be consumers who enjoy the sweet grapey flavour of Concord and Elvira, but as wine drinkers in Canada become more sophisticated in their tastes they will eventually turn their backs on these wines in favour of more complex and elegant European products.

David Ringler, marketing director at Andres, voices the unspoken thoughts of his more reticent colleagues when he says, "My belief is that the consumer out there would not buy a bottle of Canadian wine if their life depended on it." The commercial wineries may bemoan the fact that the public takes a kind of perverse pride in dismissing Canadian wines, but they are not without some share of the blame. Up until the early 1970s wine lovers would not have been amused by the presumption of the domestic product. Instead of leading public taste, the wineries merely followed it and as soon as one of them had a commercial success with a Baby Duck or a Schloss Laderheim the rest leapt into their vats with both feet to come up with an identical product. The net result was—until the cottage wineries showed that there was a demand for wines of an individual character—that all-Canadian products tended to look and taste alike.

The success of companies like Inniskillin, Chateau des Charmes and Charal in Ontario, and Gray Monk, Sumac Ridge and Mission Hill in BC, coupled with the burgeoning growth of foreign imports, has polarized the domestic industry. On the one hand are the small producers—the cottage or farm wineries—dedicated to the production of labour-intensive wines in limited quantities, and on the other are the major companies whose initial concern is profit—the bottom line. While both arms of the industry are profit-motivated (wine for wine's sake is a luxury no one can afford), the small wineries flourish because of the individuality of their products. They may struggle financially and cut corners to stay in business but the fact that four licences for cottage wineries were applied for in 1982 in Ontario alone shows that there are enough entrepreneurs with faith in the future of Canadian winemaking to take the plunge.

Small is not necessarily beautiful, however, and cottage wineries can make as many dogs as their commercial colleagues; but the perception is that artisan wines made by traditional methods are more acceptable to a public whose knowledge and appreciation of wine is increasing every year. And perception—or image—is 90% of the battle when it comes to competing for consumer favour.

The problem for the small producers is that they tend to be underfinanced and have to release their wines as soon as they conscionably can rather than holding them to mature for the extra year that would make all the difference to the taste. While they could indicate on a back label that the wine will improve immeasurably with cellar age, they understand that the consumer buys a bottle to have with dinner and, apart from a small number of aficionados, is not willing to wait. Just as with the great Bordeaux wines, the best hybrids, like Maréchal Foch and Baco Noir, and viniferas, like Chardonnay and Gewurztraminer, are being drunk far too early. Even the large companies that ought to be able to hold their wines are too ready to rush them to the marketplace for a quick return on capital.

Lacking funds, the cottage wineries cannot produce a consistent blended product since they cannot afford to keep stocks to ensure a recognizable house style. The result is that the wines vary from year to year depending on the quality of the grapes they work with.

The gap between the wines produced by the cottage industry and those manufactured by the large wineries seems to be widening. The "Big Four", along with Barnes, London, Calona and Casabello, are moving more and more into the branded wine field. While they continue to vinify limited quantities of vinifera wines as flagships for their company (and to keep wine writers quiet) the financial dictates of the balance sheet make these quality products a luxury they may consider too expensive to indulge in for much longer. As they see imported wines taking a great share of the market the instinct is to imitate the taste and look of inexpensive European blends which are not necessarily any better than those they could produce from grapes currently at their disposal.

One of the great failings of the industry is that the marketing men have taken over from the winemakers. Packaging has become more important than the product. One executive told me bluntly that his company was in the marketing business: "You put the wine in a bottle and market the hell out of it.

Forget the mystique." This credo seems to prevail in an industry where companies vie with each other to get as many labels on the shelves as they can—rather like washing detergent manufacturers who believe that sheer volume will overpower the competition. But wine is a living organism and every vintage will be subtly different from the last. From a marketing man's perspective, the grape is a pain in the neck since it refuses to make a consistent product every year; the industry will only be "perfected" when that troublesome little berry has been conquered in the laboratory.

Coming from industries where "brand loyalty" is a hallowed concept, advertisers were confused by the caprices of the wine-drinking public, which prefers variety. The idea that a consumer will become attached to a product and then move up to another of the company's better wines, as a Ford driver might aspire to a Lincoln, has proved to be mere wishful thinking. Sales are the only index of success in this economy of ours and packaging and advertising seem to be the only methods of moving the product. The fact that Spumante Bambino outsells Baby Duck says more about the power of television advertising than it does about the relative merits of either "wine".

The old adage that you don't sell a book by its cover has been forgotten. Research has shown that 60% of wines in Canada are now bought by women. This fact has imprinted itself on the marketing men, who have instructed their art directors and designers accordingly. (Canadian wine labels have been generally more in line with mortuary ads than invitations to a pleasurable tasting experience.) The latest market research in the United States tells them that wine drinking is associated with romance. Quebec labels have long reflected this fact but the major Ontario companies have belatedly cottoned on to it. Witness Jordan's new label for its white blend called Interlude—brown and gold with a stylized rose; it looks like a box of chocolates. No doubt the trend in branded wines will be toward the Harlequin Romance school of label design in future.

The idea of making a wine that should taste light and fresh and look as if it's been around for a hundred years was finally put to rest by Chateau-Gai with their excellent label for Capistro—a wistful landscape in dreamy pastel colours.

The fact that worries the major companies most is that they are losing ground to foreign competition. If their market share is diminishing they want a piece of the action for all wine sales. Andres was the first company to buy two import agencies—Superior Wines and Watleys in 1982.

Right now the problem for the industry is how to deal with the flood of cheap Italian wine into our market. But the biggest threat to Canadian wineries will come not from Europe but from California. The Golden State produces vast quantities of good quality table wines which it is eager to export. Canada is the largest importer, taking some 50% of all Californian wines leaving the state. Bulk wines can be purchased there at a price which makes our own wineries quiver with envy. Ontario and BC companies could be bottling Californian jug wines cheaper than they can produce domestic varieties. With a change in provincial regulations our companies could become bottlers of Californian wine. As far as the Ontario Grape Growers are concerned, according to past president Ron Moyer, "If that brings down winery costs then they should be able to put a bottle of *our* wine on the table more cheaply." But this may be whistling in the dark.

There is a case to be made for Canadian companies to become brokers for Californian wine—they bring in enough of it already to perk up their blends. This would allow the farm wineries of Ontario and BC to concentrate on producing 100% Canadian wines. As matters stand, any regulation to exclude Californian wines from blended products would radically alter the taste profiles of many top-selling brands that bear a Canadian label, and would be fought tooth and nail by the big producers.

Unlike other food products, a bottle of wine does not tell us the contents in terms of percentage of blend and grape varieties. What we need is some sort of appellation system for Canadian wines, whether produced by large concerns or cottage wineries or at the very least an indication of origin. Sugar and acid standards should be instituted for all domestically grown grapes to improve the raw material. Those currently in force in BC and the De Chaunac sugar standard in Ontario are charitably low, favouring traditional grape-growing techniques. Most of the best grape-growing areas in Canada have already been located. The question remains, what are the best grapes to plant there? It all boils down to microclimates. As Edward Mason wrote in *Wine Tidings Magazine* (July 1982), "The opposite ends of the Okanagan Valley offer different microclimates. Essex and Kent counties in Ontario have rather softer wines than the Niagara region and that region subdivides at least into a western section between Hamilton and Vineland and the more intensive vineyard acreage around St. Davids and Niagara-on-the-Lake." To this I would add the Annapolis Valley since Grand Pré will not be alone in producing Nova Scotia-grown wines in future.

Surely it is not beyond the collective wit of the wine producers to institute the most basic of industry controls, an acknowledged practice in virtually all other wine-producing countries. In France and Germany, for instance, regulations govern the number of vines per acre, the methods of pruning, the yield per acre, soil types, and vinification methods. Canadian wine labels have yet to offer consumers a hint of where the wines come from.

But California wines are not the only source of competition facing our producers. The Quebec government announced the intention to allow its eleven wineries to import bulk wines from Europe for bottling in the province. This move will have a profound effect on the industry as a whole. Quebec wineries cannot compete successfully with the SAQ, which brings in bulk wines from Europe, bottles them and sells them through its own outlets as well as the grocery stores.

Other non grape-growing provinces will no doubt watch this experiment with great interest as a possible means to raise tax revenue in the future. If Manitoba and New Brunswick, for example, were to go into the wine bottling business themselves it could put intolerable pressure on Ontario and BC. With a flood of inexpensive wines entering Canada from Europe, South America, California, Australia and South Africa, the local industry could not compete on a cost basis. It could only survive if the companies were given the opportunity to sell Canadian wines in grocery stores or supermarkets. This would mean breaking the Liquor Board stranglehold on the sale of wine.°

In Quebec 35% of all wines are purchased in corner grocery stores. Products from Europe bottled by the SAQ stand shoulder to shoulder with those made by the local industry (fermented from imported juice) as well as national brands from Brights and Andres who have facilities in the province. But distributing the wine to the 10,000-odd grocery stores is expensive and the SAQ has no way of telling if they are losing or making money on the enterprise—in spite of computers. In addition, there is no control over how these wines are stored (generally badly by shopkeepers who don't understand the product) and how long they remain on the shelves.

These are problems which have to be addressed because the future health of domestic wineries depends upon readier accessibility as well as public acceptance of their products. Shackled by outmoded laws, beset by a plethora of contradictory provincial regulations, the Canadian wine industry hobbles along unsure of itself and defensive against aggressive competition from abroad. The result is a kind of fortress mentality. The only way to convince the public they have products worth drinking is to get out and beat the drum for them. Eugene Whalen, the Minister of Agriculture, who has championed the cause of Canadian wines for years, is their best salesman. He's not above being photographed in his green cowboy hat with his head stuck through an Ontario vine or demanding to see the "Canadian wine list" when he visits a restaurant. The problem is that few members of the industry itself follow his lead. When wine becomes a corporate concern where the balance sheet determines the priorities, it loses its magic and becomes just another highly packaged item like baked beans or Brillo pads.

Less than 20% of the adult population in Canada is estimated to be drinking wine regularly. The opportunities to expand are tremendous. Every year more Canadians are becoming wine drinkers and it is up to the local industry to compete with quality products for consumer favour—not to join the competition by buying into it. But it is one thing to make good wine and quite another to get the message across to the public. Government-controlled Liquor Boards, while enjoying the revenues they receive from the sale of

---

°A report in the *Globe and Mail* (November 9, 1982) by the Management Resource Group of Toronto stated that "The domestic industry in Ontario and British Columbia will need grocery store distribution to survive and flourish as more low-cost foreign wines enter the Canadian market." (Ironically, it is the large wineries themselves that stand in the way of this concept being realised. They all have hefty investments in their own company stores which sell their brands exclusively.)

wines, hinder the producers at every step in their attempts to inform and educate us about their wines.

The fact that the Baby Duck craze has given way to the Schloss Laderheim boom is perhaps the most cheering pointer of all: it shows that the wineries themselves are moving towards *authenticity* in their products—away from alcoholically flavoured sugar water to wines in which the grape predominates. We have only to look at a precedent created south of the border to see how far we can go. The giant Gallo winery created the American wine revolution in the early 1960s. They began with pop wines and upgraded their quality once they had created the taste and then the demand for better wines. Encouraged by enlightened Californian law, Gallo, the world's largest wine company, now produces a whole range of inexpensive, well-made products. Our own industry could well take note; what we have in Canada is not a beverage revolution but a wine revolution, sparked by an appreciation of wines from outside our shores. After 150 years of experimentation the Canadian wine industry is on the threshold of its most exciting period. With consumer support and less hypocrisy on the part of provincial governments, we could soon be drinking the wines we deserve. We have the grapes; we have the knowhow; we have the demand. It just takes imagination and flair to put the three elements together.

The Winewood Room at Brights Wines is a reception area made from two 68,000-gallon casks formerly used in winemaking. More than 50,000 visitors pass through this room annually.

Courtesy: Brights Wines Ltd.

ten

Tasting Notes

*"A manufacturer of Ontario wines may sell and deliver
only Ontario wine that (a) is (i) of a colour satisfactory to
the Board, (ii) of natural and pleasing odour, flavour and
bouquet, and (iii) free from sediment, turbidity, or foreign
matter ..."*

(Liquor Control Act, 1975)

In preparing this book I have tasted literally hundreds of Canadian wines, from ten-year-old bottles to experimental batches made in demi-johns. The bulk of the tasting was carried out from October 1982 to May 1983 so that my notes reflect the wines generally available during this period; that is to say, wines made from 1980 to 1982. Where possible I sampled wines of the same grape type side by side to see which winery made the best product. The styles of vinification I found varied considerably; the taste of a Riesling, for example, can change enormously depending on how the winemaker treated the fermentation and aging as well as what other wine was blended in (in Ontario a varietal wine can contain up to 25% of something else bearing the name of a grape type on the label.)

The tasting notes that follow are broken down by province and winery. Given the kind of protectionism practised by Ontario, BC and Quebec, the wines listed are, for the most part, available only in the province stated unless they are national brands from the large wineries. There are no farm winery products from BC available in Ontario and only Inniskillin is represented in BC's specialty shops.

I have not tasted every single Canadian wine on the market because many of them are the same blends under different labels. My focus has been on table wines (9 to 14% alcohol) although I have noted several 7% pop wines, as well as sherries, ports, vermouths, sparkling and crackling wines. Apart from an assessment of each wine I have noted (where available) the grape types from which the wine was made and what wines were blended in and in what proportions. This information is not easy to come by, because the wineries for reasons of competition would rather keep it secret. *But these grape types and percentages are merely an indication of how the wine is made since they will vary from year to year depending on the quality of the harvest and availability of grapes, particularly for brand name wines.* These blended wines will vary subtly—and some not so subtly—from year to year, especially from small producers who cannot afford to keep large stocks of wine. And even in a given year I have found variance of quality from one bottle to the next of the same wine depending on which vat it came from or when it was bottled.

Canadian wines are not generally long-lasting. Even the best reds have a life span of four or five years, with one or two exceptions. Most of them ought to be consumed within two years of production (for whites) and three for reds. Since the companies release them after one year the wines are bought and drunk too early. Newark's Gewurztraminer 1980, for example, is, at the time of writing, coming into its own and Inniskillin's Maréchal Foch 1980 has a good year or two before it will reach its peak.

Vintage dating, as our wines improve in quality, is becoming more important. To the consumer a year on the bottle carries a certain cachet, even if blended wines are sometimes superior since the whole can be better than the parts, as French champagne-makers well know; so a vintage date is not necessarily a sign of a superior wine. In Ontario, where spring and summer weather is less reliable and consistent than BC's, 1980 was a very good year; 1981 was poor. In terms of quality 1982 promises to be even better than 1980. The wines that will be release from the 1982 vintage ought to be the best yet made in Canada. (BC had a cooler summer, which affected the development of flavour and aroma in the grapes). The vinifera and hybrid vines of the cottage wineries and the growers who supply the big companies have matured; the winemakers have the technique and the public is demanding a superior product. If the industry cannot produce some excellent Canadian wines in 1982, then it should follow the example of Quebec. Give up the conceit of producing indigenous wine at all and ship it all in from countries who have the climate and commitment to make it well. For Canadian wineries, 1982 will be the watershed vintage. And from what I have tasted from the barrel, it looks as though Canadian wines have a bright future.

✲   ✲   ✲   ✲

Tasting is a highly subjective business, but there are certain criteria that tasters bring to bear on a wine to assess it even though they might not necessarily like the particular style. Is the wine well made? Does it have a pleasant bouquet? Are the fruit and acidity in balance? How does it feel in the mouth? Does it finish well with a lingering taste?

In evaluating each wine I have looked at four basic points: colour, bouquet, flavour and overall impression. I have noted the alcohol content and—where available—the grape varieties, unless this is implicit in the name on the label (e.g., Johannisberg Riesling). I have also had the temerity to recommend wines which I consider to be well-made examples of their kind. Those I like I have allotted one asterisk and those I consider to be in a class by themselves I have given two asterisks.

Label Language

Estate Bottled: Wine made from grapes grown under the control of a winery, generally from its own property or a single vineyard.

Vintage: Wine of a single, outstanding year.

Nonvintage: A blend of wine of various years.

Blanc de Blancs: Wine made from white grapes only.

Blanc de Noirs: White wine made from the juice of red grapes.

Rosé: Pink wine either vinified to the requisite colour from red grapes or a colour blend of red and white wines.

Crémant: French for "creamy"; a wine with a touch of sparkle.

Brut: Bone-dry sparkling wine.

Extra Dry: Dry (also called Extra Sec).

Sec: Slightly sweet.

Demi-sec: Sweet.

Doux: Very sweet.

Sekt: German term for sparkling wine (also Schaumwein).

Spumante: Italian term for sparkling wine.

ONTARIO WINERIES

In all LCBO stores the wines on the shelves and racks are codified by the amount of residual sugar. This is a rough guide of how sweet the wine is. Zero on the LCBO scale means a wine which contains up to .49 grams of residual sugar per 100 ml of wine. One on the scale represents those wines in the range of .5 grams and 1.49 grams of residual sugar. Two equals 1.5 to 2.49 grams; three is 2.5 to 3.49 and so on up. A sugar code of 1 can mean a wine with as little as .6 grams of residual sugar or as much as 1.48 grams—a considerable difference in apparent sweetness.

ANDRES

RED

★ **Auberge Red**
COLOUR: ruby   BOUQUET: not much on the nose
FLAVOUR: soft, perfumed, medium-weight, good flavour in Pinot style, dry finish. Simple, unassuming. A well-priced *vin de table*. Sugar code 1. (11.5%; screwtop, litre)

Botticelli Red   *(De Chaunac, Vincent, Foch)*
COLOUR: inky ruby   BOUQUET: sweet, aged strawberry
FLAVOUR: sweet grapey, *spritzig*, short. Sugar code 7. (9%; screwtop, litre)

Cellar Cask Dry Red
COLOUR: good polished ruby colour   BOUQUET: synthetic fruit nose
FLAVOUR: thin fruit taste, perfumed De Chaunac, giving way to a final bitterness. Sugar code 1. (11%; bag-in-box)

Cellar Cask Medium Dry Red
COLOUR: ruby   BOUQUET: pronounced grapey character
FLAVOUR: sweet, alcoholic grape juice. Sugar code 4. (11%; bag-in-box)

★ **Domaine d'Or Red**   *(De Chaunac, Foch, Le Commandant and some vinifera)*
COLOUR: light ruby   BOUQUET: shaggy, perfumed nose
FLAVOUR: light, soft fruit character, Beaujolais style; dry, short finish. Sugar code 1. (11.5%)

Dinner Wine Red   *(De Chaunac, Le Commandant, Foch, Concord)*
COLOUR: ruby   BOUQUET: warm, perfumed, grapey
FLAVOUR: grapey taste, sweetish, unstructured. Sugar code 3. (11.5%; screwtop, litre)

Eagle Ridge Mountain Red *(De Chaunac, Foch, Chelois with some Concord)*
COLOUR: pale garnet   BOUQUET: jammy nose with a hint of rubber
FLAVOUR: light, perfumed taste with a citrus finish. Undistinguished. Sugar code 2. (11.5%; screwtop, litre)

Fiorino Red *(De Chaunac, Foch, Le Commandant, President, decolourised De Chaunac)*
COLOUR: aged ruby   BOUQUET: tired fruit
FLAVOUR: perfumed De Chaunac taste which dries out immediately. Thin, unprepossessing. Sharp finish. Sugar code 1. (11.5%; screwtop, litre)

Lake Country Red *(De Chaunac, Vincent, Le Commandant, President, Foch)*
COLOUR: pale ruby   BOUQUET: perfumed De Chaunac nose
FLAVOUR: soft, light perfumed taste; sugar masks the acidity. Apricot-like finish. Sugar code 2. (11.5%; litre)

Red Wine *(no-name wine, probably De Chaunac)*
COLOUR: cherry   BOUQUET: powerful grapey aroma
FLAVOUR: very perfumed in the mouth, light in character but not much substance. Unstructured. Sugar code 2. (11.5%; screwtop)

Other reds: Galante

ROSÉ

Dinner, Cellar Cask, Auberge.

WHITE

★**Auberge White**
COLOUR: straw   BOUQUET: hint of labrusca
FLAVOUR: grapey taste; medium-weight with a touch of sweetness; clean and well-balanced. Sugar code 3. (11.5%; screwtop, litre)

Botticelli Estate *(Elvira, Catawba, decolourised De Chaunac, Niagara, Californian Dry White)*
COLOUR: gold   BOUQUET: sulfur
FLAVOUR: sweet, soft, grapey, *spritzig*. Sugar code 5. (9%; screwtop)

Cellar Cask White
COLOUR: straw   BOUQUET: sweet, faintly labrusca nose
FLAVOUR: sweet grapefruit taste, some residual sugar, short but clean. An inoffensive quaffing wine. Sugar Code 3. (11%, bag-in-box. The Cellar Cask Reserve is slightly drier (1) and stronger at 11.5%)

★**De Chaunac Blanc 1980**   *(Richelieu label)*
COLOUR: gold   BOUQUET: appley nose
FLAVOUR: substantial, faintly perfumed, viscous, touch of sugar; reminiscent of a hot country white. Powerful, well-made. Sugar code 2. (11.5%)

★★**Domaine d'Or White**   *(Aurore, Seyval and some vinifera)*
COLOUR: straw   BOUQUET: fruity, hint of labrusca
FLAVOUR: full in the mouth, well-made with a touch of sweetness; clean finish. A Rhône-style white. Good value. Sugar code 1. (11.5%)

Fiorino White   *(Elvira, Catawba, decolourised De Chaunac, Californian Dry White)*
COLOUR: straw   BOUQUET: synthetic
FLAVOUR: dry, unattractive, woody finish. Sugar code 1. (11.5%; screwtop, litre)

Franciscan Canadian Chablis
COLOUR: straw   BOUQUET: lemon crystal nose
FLAVOUR: perfumed taste, touch of sweetness, somewhat unbalanced and fat. Sugar code 1. (11.5%)

Franciscan Light   *(Johannisberg Riesling, Okanagan Riesling, Siegfried, Aurore, Seyval, Vidal, Dutchess, Delaware, Elvira, Californian Dry White)*
COLOUR: water white   BOUQUET: green apple
FLAVOUR: soft grapey taste, plump middle with a touch of residual sugar; innocuous. Short acidic finish. Sugar code 1. (9%)

★**Franciscan Light**   *(Alberta version—100% Californian grapes)*
COLOUR: pale straw   BOUQUET: fruity, sweet
FLAVOUR: altogether more personality than Ontario's version; round, well-balanced, good fruit and length of finish. A stylish product. (9%)

Hochtaler
COLOUR: straw   BOUQUET: pronounced sweet floral labrusca nose
FLAVOUR: full in the mouth, aggressive fruitiness, sweetish Rhine style but well-balanced; in the end the labrusca comes through. Sugar code 2. (11%)

★**Hochtaler**   *(Alberta version)*
COLOUR: straw   BOUQUET: soft, fruity
FLAVOUR: softer and more subtle than the Ontario version; less aggressive and more complex. More stylish and better acidity, less sweet. (11%)

★**Johannisberg Riesling 1980**   *(Richelieu label)*
COLOUR: straw   BOUQUET: sweet floral
FLAVOUR: soft, well-balanced, touch of sweetness, good length of finish. Sugar code 2. (11.5%)

Lake Country White *(Elvira, Niagara, Catawba, decolourised De Chaunac, decolourised Le Commandant, Californian Dry White)*
COLOUR: pale straw   BOUQUET: fresh, fruity
FLAVOUR: soft, perfumed, almond character; some residual sugar. Quite weighty in the mouth. Sugar code 2. (11.5%; litre)

Pinot Chardonnay 1980 *(Richelieu label)*
COLOUR: straw   BOUQUET: appley nose
FLAVOUR: light, dry fruit character; finishes dry with a slight mustiness in the finish. Sugar code 1. (11.5%)

Regency Extra Dry *(Elvira, Niagara, Catawaba, decolourised De Chaunac, decolourised Le Commandant, California Dry White)*
COLOUR: pale straw   BOUQUET: fruity, perfumed
FLAVOUR: dry, hybrid taste. Finishes well, but not much character. Sugar code 1. (11.5%; screwtop bottle)

Rhinekeller
COLOUR: pale straw   BOUQUET: sweet grapey
FLAVOUR: soft, round, sweet but light. Could use a touch more acid for a cleaner finish. A worthwhile commercial blend. Sugar code 2. (11.5%; screwtop, litre)

Similkameen Superior
COLOUR: pale straw   BOUQUET: spicy Okanagan Riesling nose
FLAVOUR: round, sweet taste, heavy in the mouth, lots of glycerine; finishes almost dry but could do with more acidity to lengthen the finish. Sugar code 2. (11.5%)

Souvenance Blanc de Blancs
COLOUR: almost water-white   BOUQUET: grassy with a hint of sweetness
FLAVOUR: initial sweetness gives way to a dry, slightly woody finish. Sugar code 1. (11.5%)

★**Wintergarten**
COLOUR: pale gold   BOUQUET: fresh, clean
FLAVOUR: soft, gently sweet, fruity; round with a good finish. A well-made wine. Easy-drinking Moselle-style. Sugar code 3. (11.5%)

Other whites: White Dinner (sugar code 4)

SPARKLING

Baby Canadian Champagne
COLOUR: water-white   BOUQUET: fresh, faintly grapey
FLAVOUR: lively, good fruit character for a 7% wine without the labrusca showing through. Surprisingly good. Sugar code 4. (7%)

Baby Duck   *(70% red labrusca, 30% white labrusca)*
COLOUR: strawberry   BOUQUET: sweet
FLAVOUR: What do you say about a legend? Sweet, Concord-grapey taste, good length of finish; the first and best of its pop genre. Not my cup of tea but Andres can sulk all the way to the bank over any wine writer's criticism of this fun product that introduced millions of Canadians to the world of wine. Sugar code 5. (7%)

Cordoba Blanca
COLOUR: pale straw   BOUQUET: not much of anything
FLAVOUR: dry, not much flavour, lacklustre. Sugar code 3. (7%)

Kurhauser Trocken Sekt
COLOUR: pale straw   BOUQUET: grapey
FLAVOUR: light, grapey taste, good mousse; dries out to a slightly gluey finish. Sugar code 2. (9%)

★**Richelieu Canadian Champagne**   *(Aurore, Seyval, Dutchess, Delaware, Elvira, Californian Dry White)*
COLOUR: straw   BOUQUET: fresh fruity
FLAVOUR: quite heavy, good fruit character, slightly peppery finish. Well-made. Sugar code 2. (11.5%)

Richelieu Canadian Light Champagne
COLOUR: water-white   BOUQUET: clean, fresh, hint of grape
FLAVOUR: dry, delicate taste, watery finish. Sugar code 2. (7%)

★**Richelieu Canadian Pink Champagne** *(Aurore, Seyval, Dutchess, Delaware, Elvira, Californian Dry White, Concord, Vincent)*
COLOUR: pink-gold   BOUQUET: candied fruit nose
FLAVOUR: perfumed taste, dry cherries and chocolate; full in the mouth. Interesting. Sugar code 2. (11.5%)

Other sparklers: Sangria, Baby Bubbly White, Chanté Blanc, Rouge and Rosé, Baby Duck White, Moody Blue, Spumante and Spumante Cristallo. Crackling wines include Vin Blanc and Vin Rosé (all 7%).

CRACKLING

Rosé
COLOUR: burnt orange   BOUQUET: labrusca
FLAVOUR: sweet, grapey, lingering. Good of its style. Sugar code 4. (11.5%)

SHERRY

Richelieu Golden Cream
COLOUR: red-chestnut   BOUQUET: alcoholic, shy
FLAVOUR: sweet, somewhat sharp, hot taste and finish. Sugar code 14. (19%)

Other sherries: Almond and Coffee Cream (both sugar code 24), Club House Gold (7), Medium Dry (6).

BARNES

RED

★**Beauvoir** *(De Chaunac plus Californian Petite Sirah)*
COLOUR: purple   BOUQUET: earthy, peppery
FLAVOUR: full-bodied, lots of fruit thanks to the Petite Sirah, good spicy finish. Good value. Sugar code 0. (12%)

Heritage Estates Canadian Burgundy *(De Chaunac plus some vinifera)*
COLOUR: deep ruby   BOUQUET: sappy nose
FLAVOUR: aged fruit taste, somewhat plummy, dry, a little thin on the finish with some astringency. Sugar code 0. (12%)

★**Heritage Estates Canadian Claret**   *(Foch with some vinifera)*
COLOUR: good ruby   BOUQUET: vegetal nose
FLAVOUR: full in the mouth, good dry fruit character, a touch green on
   the finish. Well-priced. Sugar code 0. (12%)

Ontario Country Red   *(De Chaunac and Foch)*
COLOUR: inky red, light in appearance   BOUQUET: dry fruit
FLAVOUR: light, hint of sweetness, inoffensive. Attractive homespun label.
   Sugar code 1. (11%; screwtop, litre)

Rubiwein   *(De Chaunac and Foch)*
COLOUR: deep ruby   BOUQUET: sweet
FLAVOUR: sweet, grapey. Sugar code 3. (12%)

ROSÉ

Heritage Estates Canadian Rosé   *(De Chaunac)*
COLOUR: deep pink   BOUQUET: synthetic, waxy, sweet nose
FLAVOUR: full, grapey taste; soft, short, unctuous. Sugar code 3. (12%)

. Barnes also does a Still Cold Duck rosé from labrusca grapes.

WHITE

Bon Appetit   *(Elvira and Niagara)*
COLOUR: pale straw   BOUQUET: sweet, grapey
FLAVOUR: soft, unstructured. Sugar code 2. (9.5%; screwtop, litre)

Heritage Estates Canadian Chablis   *(Seyval, Ventura with some vinifera)*
COLOUR: straw   BOUQUET: soft citrus
FLAVOUR: grapefruit quality, crisp, dry and rather tart on the finish. Sugar
   code 0. (12%)

Heritage Estates Canadian Rhine
COLOUR: pale straw   BOUQUET: clean, fruity
FLAVOUR: soft, inoffensive, an edge of sweetness, uninspiring. Sugar code
   2. (9.5%)

★★**Johannisberg Riesling 1982**   *(Limited Edition)*
COLOUR: straw   BOUQUET: floral fruity
FLAVOUR: good fruit and acidity, fat, lots of sugar; well-made. Sugar code
   2. (11.5%)

★**Ontario Country White**   *(Elvira, Seyval and Ventura)*
COLOUR: straw   BOUQUET: sweet, floral lubrusca character
FLAVOUR: soft, well-balanced, finishes well. Sugar code 1. (11%; screwtop,
   litre)

Seyval Blanc 1981 *(Limited Edition)*
COLOUR: deep straw BOUQUET: faint licorice
FLAVOUR: dry, medium-weight, alcoholic. Somewhat dull, lacking in character. Sugar code 0. (12%)

Weinfest *(Elvira, Seyval plus California Emerald Riesling)*
COLOUR: straw BOUQUET: sweet, faintly labrusca character
FLAVOUR: sweetish, fruity, well-balanced, clean finish. Sugar code 2. (11%)

Barnes also makes a sweet Sauterne from 95% Niagara grapes. Sugar code 4.

SPARKLING

Spumante Bianco *(New York Muscat)*
COLOUR: pale straw BOUQUET: grapey
FLAVOUR: light, sweet but well-balanced. Sugar code 5. (7%)

Other sparklers: a sweet white and pink "Champagne" under the Grand Celebration label. Barnes also makes an even sweeter Crackling Wild Duck and a Sangria Red.

SHERRY

Heritage Cream (mahogany colour; baked taste; good finish). Sugar code 12. Heritage Dry (well-balanced; winey finish). Sugar code 3. Heritage Very Pale Dry (foxy taste; light and dry). Sugar code 1.

Other sherries: Heritage Golden and Catawba. Sugar code 8 and 6.

OTHER PRODUCTS

Concord Port (sugar code 9) and a syrupy Hostess Sweet Red with a
sugar code of 16.

BRIGHTS

RED

★★ Baco Noir (1980)
COLOUR: deep purple   BOUQUET: rich raisiny
FLAVOUR: full-bodied, generous fruit; smoky blackberry taste.
Harmonious, dry finish. Sugar code 0. (12%)
(In 1982 Brights produced a Late Vintage Baco which promises to be
first-rate.)

Dry House
COLOUR: intense ruby   BOUQUET: vegetal
FLAVOUR: very dry, somewhat astringent, initial softness suggests more
fruit than there is. Powerful alcoholic finish. Sugar code 0. (12%; litre)

Entre-Lacs Red
COLOUR: ruby   BOUQUET: vegetal
FLAVOUR: dry, acidic; a nervous wine with a somewhat stemmy finish.
Sugar code 0. (12%)

House Red
COLOUR: ruby   BOUQUET: oily-sweet
FLAVOUR: soft, fruit character, gentle, slightly sweet. A neophyte's dry
red. Sugar code 2. (10%; litre)

Manor St. Davids Dry   *(Foch, De Chaunac, Chelois)*
COLOUR: light ruby   BOUQUET: sweet, grapey nose
FLAVOUR: soft, mellow, round with a touch of sweetness. Hot finish.
Sugar code 0. (12%; screwtop bottle)

Maréchal Foch
COLOUR: aged ruby   BOUQUET: woody-fruity
FLAVOUR: dry, austere, short on flavour. Sugar code 0. (12%)

Papa Carlo Red
COLOUR: deep ruby   BOUQUET: raspberry jam
FLAVOUR: soft, round, touch of sweetness; dry finish with good length. A
good commercial blend. Sugar code 0. (12%; screwtop, litre)

President Burgundy
COLOUR: tawny-ruby   BOUQUET: alcohol, little else
FLAVOUR: dry, Burgundy-style, somewhat burnt, raisiny finish. Sugar code
1. (12%)

Riuscita
COLOUR: garnet   BOUQUET: vegetal
FLAVOUR: sweet, light, grapey, *spritzig*. Short finish. A pop wine. Sugar
code 5. (9%; screwtop bottle)

Other reds: Mazel Tov (sugar code 17), Cresta Roja (6), Still Cold Duck
(5); all labrusca-based.

ROSÉ

House Rosé and Dubarry Still

WHITE

Baron Ludwig
COLOUR: pale straw   BOUQUET: fruity, straw-like nose
FLAVOUR: soft, sweetish, Germanic-style. Light, fruity taste. Clean finish.
(Club Spritz without the carbonated spring water.) Sugar code 2.
(10.5%; screwtop bottle)

★Dry House
COLOUR: pale straw   BOUQUET: fresh, clean, grassy
FLAVOUR: light, crisp, dry; clean finish. Good value. Sugar code 0. (11%;
litre)

★★Entre-Lacs White
COLOUR: pale straw   BOUQUET: appley nose
FLAVOUR: clean, fresh, crisp, dry finish with nice length. Well-made.
Sugar code 0. Good value (11%)

★Gewurztraminer 1981
COLOUR: pale gold   BOUQUET: medicinal, closed
FLAVOUR: closed, spicy fruit. Good acidity; lacks the concentration of
fruit the excellent 1980 had on the nose and palate but will develop
well. More acidity than 1980. Sugar code 0. (11%)

House White
COLOUR: straw   BOUQUET: grapey, hybrid quality
FLAVOUR: soft, round, medium-weight; a touch sweet. Finishes well.
White Bordeaux-style. Sugar code 2. (9%; litre)

★**Johannisberg Riesling 1980**
COLOUR: golden   BOUQUET: appley, floral nose
FLAVOUR: apple taste, soft, well-balanced. Good fruit character. Finishes
   cleanly. Sugar code 2. (11%)

LiebesHeim
COLOUR: straw yellow   BOUQUET: floral, stony
FLAVOUR: full, sweet grapefruit taste; medium-weight. Finishes dry.
   Sugar code 2. (11%)

★**Papa Carlo White**
COLOUR: palest straw   BOUQUET: grassy citrus
FLAVOUR: grassy, fresh, very dry; crisp finish. Like a dry Californian
   Chablis. Good value. Sugar code 1. (11%; screwtop, litre)

★**Pinot Chardonnay 1981**
COLOUR: deep straw   BOUQUET: fresh, concentrated fruit
FLAVOUR: lively, fresh, good Chardonnay character. Good depth and
   weight; austere, dry finish. Sugar code 0. (11%)
The 1980 was better on the nose and had more fruit.

Riuscita White
COLOUR: pale gold   BOUQUET: aged fruit
FLAVOUR: sweet labrusca character; *spritzig*. Dry, woody finish. Sugar
   code 5.(9%; screwtop bottle)

Seyval Blanc 1981
COLOUR: straw yellow   BOUQUET: big, floral
FLAVOUR: overblown, aggressive, steely; lacks charm, like a hot country
   white. Grapefruit taste. Dry, acidic finish. Sugar code 1. (11%)

WarnerHof
COLOUR: gold   BOUQUET: appley
FLAVOUR: oxidized, aged fruit taste. Sugar code 1. (11%; litre)

Other whites: Manor St. Davids Medium Dry (5), President Extra Dry (0)
the base wine for the champagne, President Sauterne (5), Vino Di Casa
(2), and Brights White (1).

SPARKLING

★★Pinot Champagne (Chardonnay)
COLOUR: straw gold   BOUQUET: hazel nuts
FLAVOUR: nutty, full-bodied Chardonnay taste, good balance and finish
   with a hint of sweetness in the end. A terrific Canadian "champagne".
   Sugar code 3. (12.5%)

★President Brut Champagne
COLOUR: pale straw   BOUQUET: fresh, clean
FLAVOUR: dry, well-balanced, hint of labrusca in the middle taste, but
   finishes clean. Sugar code 1. (12.5%)

President Champagne Dry
COLOUR: straw   BOUQUET: grapey
FLAVOUR: flabby with a residual sweetness. Sugar code 3. (12.5%)

Other sparkling wines: President Pink (sugar code 4), Club Spritz (5%
with spring water added), Cold Duck, three spumantes and various 7%
pop wines, such as Pussy Cat, Champers, Dubarry Vin Rosé.

SHERRY

President
COLOUR: gold-copper   BOUQUET: alcoholic, woody
FLAVOUR: rich, sweet, but hot on the finish. Sugar code 10. (19%)

Other sherries: Cream (sugar code 12), Dry (4), Hermit (9), Napoleon (9),
St. Georges Vin Blanc (7), "67" (7), and "74" (10).

PORT

★**President Port**
COLOUR: good deep ruby   BOUQUET: flinty-sweet
FLAVOUR: rich, full, sweet, generous, long finish. A creditable port. Sugar
   code 14. (19%)

OTHER PRODUCTS

Red and White Vermouth, Durouget.

CHARAL

RED

★**Baco Noir**
COLOUR: aged ruby   BOUQUET: vanilla, oaky nose
FLAVOUR: soft, oaky-fruity taste, hint of sweetness; good weight in the
   mouth with a long, lemony finish. Sugar code 0. (11.5%)

★**Chandelle Rouge**   *(De Chaunac with Villard Noir)*
COLOUR: ruby   BOUQUET: touch of oak
FLAVOUR: sappy taste of young oak, sprightly, hint of sweetness. Well-
   made. Sugar code 2. (11%)

★**Maréchal Foch**
COLOUR: ruby   BOUQUET: tobacco, minty nose
FLAVOUR: sweet, full-bodied, rich soft fruit, but ultimately lacks acid to
   give it staying power. Sugar code 0. (11.5%)

★**Première Rouge**   *(De Chaunac with some Foch)*
COLOUR: deep ruby   BOUQUET: meaty nose
FLAVOUR: perfumed fruity taste, medium-weight, soft velvety quality.
   Finishes dry with lingering taste. Sugar code 1. (11%)

ROSÉ

Chandelle Rosé   *(New York Muscat with De Chaunac)*
COLOUR: tawny-garnet   BOUQUET: touch of labrusca, fruity
FLAVOUR: full fruit with some sweetness, quite heavy grapey taste; acidic
   finish. Sugar code 3. (11%)

CHARAL

MARÉCHAL
FOCH

12% alc./vol. 750 mL.

A dry varietal Canadian burgundy wine grown from
the Maréchal Foch vinifera hybrid grape.

Vin bourgogne canadien sec, fait de raisins vinifers de
l'hybride Maréchal Foch.

Product of Canada — Produit du Canada
Charal Winery and Vineyards Inc.
Blenheim, Ontario, Canada

WHITE

Chandelle Blanc *(Aurore with 30% Californian French Colombard)*
COLOUR: yellow gold BOUQUET: heavy, sweet, grassy nose
FLAVOUR: full, fruity, somewhat ponderous in the mouth, sweet, flabby.
Sugar code 2. (10.5%)

★**Chardonnay 1980**
COLOUR: straw BOUQUET: flowery nose
FLAVOUR: dry, full-bodied with good fruit flavour. Finishes crisp with
good acidity if somewhat tart. Sugar code 0. (10.5%)

Cuvée Blanc *(Siegerrebe and Riesling)*
COLOUR: straw BOUQUET: crisp, fruity
FLAVOUR: starts off with a round floral fruitness which narrows out to a
dry, crisp finish. Rhine style although it comes in a Burgundy bottle.
Sugar code 0. (11%)

Dutchess
COLOUR: straw BOUQUET: spicy
FLAVOUR: soft, good fruit quality; round with a clean finish. Sugar code
1. (11%)

★**Riesling 1980**
COLOUR: pale straw BOUQUET: floral
FLAVOUR: full, round, well-balanced with a crisp dry finish. Stylish. Sugar
code 0. (10.5%)

Seyval Blanc
COLOUR: yellow straw BOUQUET: fruity, citrus nose
FLAVOUR: quite full but a dry, somewhat acidic taste. Touch of the filtre
at the end; a tart grapefruit aftertaste. Sugar code 1. (11%)

★**Vidal 1982**
COLOUR: bright straw   BOUQUET: round, sweet, warm
FLAVOUR: fat, rich, fruity. Will develop well. Sugar code 1. (10.5%)

SPARKLING

Light White Spumante   *(carbonated, labrusca; bottled by Brights)*
COLOUR: straw   BOUQUET: foxy
FLAVOUR: sweet, grapey, fades in the mouth. Sugar code 5. (7%)

FRUIT WINES

Vinacopia Red   *(strawberry and apple)*
COLOUR: orange-red   BOUQUET: intense strawberry
FLAVOUR: Strawberry, but finishes quite dry. Sugar code 3. (6.9%)

Vinacopia White   *(apple and pear)*
COLOUR: straw yellow   BOUQUET: sweet cidery
FLAVOUR: cidery, but dries out. Sugar code 3. (6.9%)

CHATEAU DES CHARMES

RED

Cabernet (Franc) 1982
COLOUR: ruby with blue highlights   BOUQUET: nose of wet bark
FLAVOUR: light Cabernet style, dry elderberry taste. No threat to Château
   Lafite but an encouraging effort that displays the characteristics of this
   difficult grape. Tannic and acidic backbone but lacking in fruit
   concentration. Sugar code 0. (11.5%)

Cour Rouge   *(De Chaunac with Californian Petite Sirah)*
COLOUR: ruby   BOUQUET: fruity-plummy
FLAVOUR: soft, perfumed fruity taste. Easy-drinking. Sugar code 0. (10%)

★**Gamay Beaujolais Nouveau 1982**   *(tasted when released in November
   1982)*
COLOUR: deep ruby—good depth of colour   BOUQUET: perfumed
   cherries
FLAVOUR: soft, fruity with a peppery finish. A fine effort. Sugar code 0.
   (11.5%)

★Pinot Noir 1982
COLOUR: light ruby   BOUQUET: fruity Pinot nose
FLAVOUR: initially soft with a pronounced Burgundy flavour. Attractive, with surprisingly good fruit and acidity but green on the finish. The first Pinot Noir I've tasted in Ontario which promises better things for the future (if the vines can survive some more winters). Sugar code 01. (12%)

Primeur Rouge 1982   *(Gamay and Villard Noir, plus 10% Pinot Noir)*
COLOUR: ruby-purple   BOUQUET: not much on the nose
FLAVOUR: fresh, full-bodied, fruity Rhône style, vaguely perfumed taste. Very dry finish. Well-made (carbonic masceration). (Sugar code 0. (11.5%)

Sentinel Rouge 1979   *(Foch, Chancellor, Chelois, Villard Noir with some Californian Petite Sirah)*
COLOUR: aged ruby   BOUQUET: pruney
FLAVOUR: aged fruit taste, dry. More Italian than French in style. Sugar code 0. (11.5%)

WHITE

★Aligoté 1980
COLOUR: straw   BOUQUET: crisp nose with some fruit
FLAVOUR: good clean taste, fresh, crisp, with good balance. Sugar code 0. (11%)

The first Aligoté made in Canada. None about unfortunately: only 30 cases were made. (The 1982 vintage is a rounder, more generous wine with more fruit).

Auxerrois 1981
COLOUR: straw   BOUQUET: gunflint nose
FLAVOUR: austere, dry, well-balanced, slightly salty finish. Sugar code 0. (11%)

★★**Chardonnay 1980 Estate**   *(black label)*
COLOUR: yellow straw   BOUQUET: hazel nuts
FLAVOUR: round, full-bodied with a touch of vanilla sweetness from three months in Limousin oak. Good fruit character and finesse. Finishes well, everything in balance. Sugar code 0. (12%)

★**Chardonnay 1980 Nokara Estate**   *(gold label)*
COLOUR: straw   BOUQUET: good varietal nose
FLAVOUR: dry, flinty with a soft fruit finish; reminiscent of a Chablis. Sugar code 0. (12%)

Chardonnay 1981   *(white label)*
COLOUR: pale gold   BOUQUET: fresh, youthful
FLAVOUR: locked in with an austere, dry woody finish. Will develop though some bottles vary. Sugar code 0. (11.5%)

Chardonnay 1981 Estate   *(black label)*
COLOUR: gold   BOUQUET: touch of sulfur (and fining?)
FLAVOUR: soft, round taste; mellow with a hint of sweetness but some off flavours, particularly in the finish. Sugar code 0. (12%)

★★**Chardonnay 1981 Nokara Estate**   *(gold label)*
COLOUR: good, light gold   BOUQUET: nutty quality
FLAVOUR: buttery taste, good fruit; well-balanced in Burgundy style. Sugar code 0 (12%)

(Watch out for Paul Bosc's 1982 Chardonnays. I tasted some 20 clonal varieties grown in various soils, treated with different oak; the results should be magnificent in the future.)

★**Cour Blanc**   *(Elvira plus some decolourised red varieties with some Californian Dry White in the blend)*
COLOUR: pale straw   BOUQUET: fruity
FLAVOUR: soft, found, fruity taste; good clean finish. Sugar code 3. (10%; litre)
("Based on the old Alpenweiss recipe," says the winemaker, Paul Bosc.)

Gamay Beaujolais Blanc 1981   *(from black grapes)*
COLOUR: straw with a hint of pink   BOUQUET: warm, earthy nose
FLAVOUR: full-bodied, dry fruit with a tart finish and a slight prickle. The
1980 is altogether more generous in the mouth, rounder with a better
balance and a kinder finish. Sugar code 0. (11.5%)

Pinot Noir Blanc 1981
COLOUR: straw   BOUQUET: dumb
FLAVOUR: surprisingly good fruit with a nutty, dry character, but falls
short. A good attempt to make a white wine from difficult red grapes.
Sugar code 0. (11%)

★**Riesling 1980 Nokara Estate**   *(gold label)*
COLOUR: straw   BOUQUET: fruity, floral nose
FLAVOUR: full in the mouth, well-balanced with some Riesling character
in the taste; attractive, a touch of residual sugar. Finishes cleanly. Sugar
code 2. (10.5%)

Riesling 1981   *(white label)*
COLOUR: straw   BOUQUET: musty
FLAVOUR: fruity, some residual sugar in spite of its zero sugar code, fuller
than the Estate bottling. (10.5%)

Riesling 1981 Nokara Estate   *(gold label)*
COLOUR: straw   BOUQUET: gunflint nose
FLAVOUR: austere, stony with a tart finish but elegant. Sugar code 0. (11%)

★★**Sentinel Blanc 1982**   *(Seyval plus Californian Chenin Blanc and some
Vidal, Rosette with some Villard cross)*
COLOUR: straw   BOUQUET: flint and fruit
FLAVOUR: soft in the mouth, good flavour, dry with a roundness in the
middle taste. Fresh and well-made. A first-rate blend. Sugar code 1.
(11.5%)

★**Seyval Blanc 1982**
COLOUR: pale straw   BOUQUET: flinty, fresh
FLAVOUR: dry, light, well-balanced with a clean finish. Sugar code 0.
(11.5%)

CHATEAU-GAI

RED

Alpenweiss Red   *(Foch, De Chaunac of different vintages, plus 5-15%
Californian Carnelian)*
COLOUR: tawny-ruby   BOUQUET: intense De Chaunac nose
FLAVOUR: Soft, plummy taste, some residual sugar; medium-weight
   Easy-drinking. Chill to cut down the sugar. Good value. Sugar code 1.
   (10.5%; litre bottle)

★**Beau de Joie**   *(100% Foch)*
COLOUR: orange-garnet   BOUQUET: fresh, fruity nose
FLAVOUR: soft, fruit perfumed taste, light-bodied, good finish. Hint of
   sweetness. Good value. Sugar code 1. (11.5%)

Burgonay   *(Le Commandant, Foch)*
COLOUR: aged ruby   BOUQUET: full, fruity nose, touch of labrusca
FLAVOUR: dry, perfumed fruit taste; ordinary. Sugar code 1. (11.5%)

Capistro Red   *(Foch plus Californian Red)*
COLOUR: pale garnet   BOUQUET: jammy nose
FLAVOUR: light, perfumed taste, good weight for an 8% wine. Touch of
   sweetness. Sugar code 1.

Cassini Robusco
COLOUR: tawny-ruby   BOUQUET: perfumey labrusca nose
FLAVOUR: light, Valpolicella style; pronounced hybrid taste. Dry raisiny
   finish. Sugar code 1. (11.5%)

★**Cavallo Rosso**   *(De Chaunac)*
COLOUR: ruby   BOUQUET: oaky nose
FLAVOUR: soft, dry, somewhat austere taste; well-made. Lemony finish.
   Good value. Sugar code 1. (10.5%; litre)

Cavallo Rosso *(Alberta version)*
COLOUR: tawny-amber   BOUQUET: not much on the nose
FLAVOUR: soft, light, fruity character, hint of sweetness, peppery finish.

Chianno Rosso   *(Foch and De Chaunac)*
COLOUR: light ruby   BOUQUET: wood, fruit
FLAVOUR: dry, perfumed De Chaunac taste, somewhat green on the
   middle and final taste. Sugar code 1. (10.5%; screwtop, litre)

Chianno Rosso *(Alberta version)*
COLOUR: strawberry colour   BOUQUET: aged strawberry jam nose
FLAVOUR: soft, good fruit with a hint of tannin. Dry finish.

House Wine Red *(Foch, Le Commandant, De Chaunac)*
COLOUR: light ruby   BOUQUET: minty nose
FLAVOUR: hint of sweetness, grapefruit quality; soft, somewhat flabby.
   Sugar code 2. (10.5%; screwtop, litre)

Maréchal Foch
COLOUR: tawny-ruby   BOUQUET: alcoholic, fruity nose
FLAVOUR: thin fruit character; dry cherry-like; hot, woody finish. Sugar
   code 0. (12%)

★**Merlot 1980**   *(Lincoln County series)*
COLOUR: light orange-ruby   BOUQUET: a nose of flint and raspberries
FLAVOUR: more Merlot flavour than the colour suggests. In the Italian
   rather than the Bordeaux style. Tannic, acidic; will last. Only trouble
   with it is the colour. Sugar code 0. (12%) ·

★**Princière Rouge**   *(Gamay, Villard Noir, Le Commandant)*
COLOUR: aged ruby   BOUQUET: minty nose
FLAVOUR: dry, minty taste; medium-weight. Well-made. Sugar code 0.
   (11.5%)

Red Table Wine   *(Concord, De Chaunac, a little Foch)*
COLOUR: light ruby   BOUQUET: woody nose
FLAVOUR: sweet, grapey, good balance and finish. Sugar code 5. (10.5%;
   screwtop bottle)

Regal Rouge   *(Concord, De Chaunac)*
COLOUR: garnet   BOUQUET: perfumed Concord-style nose
FLAVOUR: sweet, grapey, soft; lacks acidity. Sugar code 5. (10.5%;
   screwtop, litre)

Seibel   *(De Chaunac and Chelois)*
COLOUR: pale tawny-ruby   BOUQUET: not much
FLAVOUR: thin fruit, not much character, green aftertaste. Sugar code 1.
   (11.5%)

ROSÉ

★**Gamay Rosé 1980**   *(Lincoln County)*
COLOUR: tawny-orange   BOUQUET: fruity
FLAVOUR: well-balanced, medium-weight, dry, good length of finish with
   a touch of pepperiness. Sugar code 1. (10.5%)

Regal Rosé   *(Elvira, some Ventura and Agawam)*
COLOUR: deep amber   BOUQUET: sweet, grapey, medicinal
FLAVOUR: sweet with a cleansing touch of acidity. Good of its kind.
   Sugar code 5. (11.5%; screwtop, litre)

Rosé   *(Elvira, De Chaunac, some Ventura and Agawam)*
COLOUR: tawny orange-amber   BOUQUET: sweet, grapey, medicinal
FLAVOUR: sweet, syrupy, lots of glycerine; cough mixture taste. Labrusca
   finish. Sugar code 5. (12.5%; screwtop, litre)

WHITE

Alpenweiss   *(French hybrids, plus Ventura, Catawba and 30% Californian
   White)*
COLOUR: pale straw   BOUQUET: rubbery, grapey nose
FLAVOUR: sweet, soft taste, not much personality. Sugar code 2. (10.5%;
   litre)

(The BC and Alberta version has a 60% Californian base; water-white with
a nose of Okanagan Riesling; sweet, round, soft, with a crisper finish.)

Canadian Riesling   *(Elvira, Agawam, some N.Y. Muscat, Catawba)*
COLOUR: pale straw   BOUQUET: heavy labrusca nose
FLAVOUR: fat, heavy, sweet, grapey. Sugar code 3. (10.5%; screwtop, litre)

Canadian Sauternes   *(Elvira, Agawam, Niagara)*
COLOUR: palest straw   BOUQUET: strong labrusca-grapey nose
FLAVOUR: grapey taste, full, rich, sweet. Well-balanced. Good of its kind.
   Sugar code 4. (10.5%; screwtop bottle)

Capistro   *(Dutchess, Catawba, N.Y. Muscat)*
COLOUR: straw-white   BOUQUET: fresh with a touch of sulfur
FLAVOUR: light, appley taste; soft, finishes clean. Sugar code 2. (8%)

(Alberta version has a hint of sweetness and is made from Okanagan
Riesling and Muscat grapes with a labrusca variety.)

Cavallo Bianco   *(Elvira, Agawam, Catawba)*
COLOUR: light straw   BOUQUET: disagreeable
FLAVOUR: unstructured and acidic. Tart finish. Sugar code 1. (10.5%; litre)

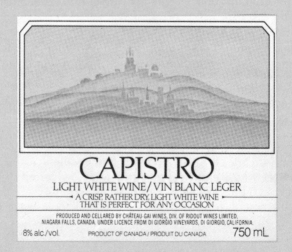

CAPISTRO
LIGHT WHITE WINE/ VIN BLANC LÉGER
A CRISP, RATHER DRY, LIGHT WHITE WINE
THAT IS PERFECT FOR ANY OCCASION

PRODUCED AND CELLARED BY CHÂTEAU-GAI WINES, DIV. OF RIDOUT WINES LIMITED,
NIAGARA FALLS, CANADA, UNDER LICENCE FROM DI GIORGIO VINEYARDS, DI GIORGIO, CALIFORNIA.
8% alc./vol.   PRODUCT OF CANADA / PRODUIT DU CANADA   750 mL

Chianno Bianco *(Californian White, N.Y. Muscat, Agawam, Elvira)*
COLOUR: pale straw   BOUQUET: aggressive grapiness
FLAVOUR: drier than expected, woody finish, acidic. Sugar code 1. (10.5%;
screwtop bottle)

Dry White Table Wine *(Catawba, Ventura)*
COLOUR: palest straw   BOUQUET: bubble gum nose
FLAVOUR: soft, touch of sweetness. Not much character. Sugar code 2.
(10.5%)

Edelwein *(Ventura, French Hybrids, Elvira, plus Californian White)*
COLOUR: light straw   BOUQUET: gasoline nose
FLAVOUR: soft, Rhine-style, tea-leaf taste. Round, lingering fruity finish.
Sugar code 2. (10.5%)
(Alberta version has hint of green in the pale straw colour; touch of
labrusca on the nose. Soft, bland, flabby.)

House Wine White *(Catawba, Venture, Some Agawam and a touch of
N.Y. Muscat)*
COLOUR: straw   BOUQUET: fruity, grapey nose
FLAVOUR: soft, sweet, somewhat flabby for want of acid. Sugar code 4.
(10.5%)

Johannisberg Riesling 1980 *(Lincoln County)*
COLOUR: straw   BOUQUET: peppermint
FLAVOUR: touch of sweetness; dull, flabby, little character. Sugar code 2.
(10.5%)

Julianne
COLOUR: straw-white   BOUQUET: hint of sweetness on the nose, with
evident sulfur.
FLAVOUR: fuller in the mouth than Capistro. Sweet, lemony finish. Sugar
code 1. (7%; screwtop bottle)

★**Pinot Chardonnay 1980** *(Lincoln County)*
COLOUR: straw   BOUQUET: fresh, light floral character
FLAVOUR: appley-grassy; more like a dry Chenin Blanc than a
Chardonnay. Medium-weight. Good dry finish if a little hot. Sugar
code 0. (10.5%)

★**Princière White** *(Chardonnay, French hybrids, plus Californian White)*
COLOUR: pale gold   BOUQUET: interesting grassy nose
FLAVOUR: dry grapefruit-like flavour, good length and finish. Well worth
the price. Sugar code 0. (10.5%)

Regal Sauterne *(Agawam and Elvira)*
COLOUR: palest straw   BOUQUET: grapey labrusca nose
FLAVOUR: soft, round, full sweet grapey taste. Cloying. Sugar code 5.
(10.5%; screwtop, litre)

SPARKLING

Imperial Canadian Champagne Brut *(Catawba and French hybrids)*
COLOUR: straw   BOUQUET: slightly metallic
FLAVOUR: dry, yeasty taste with a woody finish. Sugar code 2. (12%)

Imperial Canadian Champagne Dry *(Catawba and French hybrids)*
COLOUR: pale gold   BOUQUET: yeasty nose
FLAVOUR: soft, touch of sweetness, woody finish. Sugar code 3. (12%)

Imperial Canadian Champagne Pink *(Le Commandant, Foch,*
   Catawba)
COLOUR: orange-amber   BOUQUET: pruney nose
FLAVOUR: sweetish, dried fruit taste, oxidized quality, sour finish. Sugar
   code 5. (12%)

Sparkling Alpenweiss *(same as Alpenweiss but carbonated and a little*
   sweeter)
COLOUR: straw   BOUQUET: clean nose
FLAVOUR: sweetish, light, softer than still Alpenweiss; not much mousse
   visible. Sugar code 3. (10.5%)
(Alberta version is slightly sweeter than the Ontario.)

Cheventé Rosé *(same as regular rosé but carbonated)*
COLOUR: pink-amber   BOUQUET: alcohol and wood
FLAVOUR: medicinal, with a green finish. Sugar code 5. (11.5%)

★**Spumante Classico** *(N.Y. Muscat)*
COLOUR: pale straw   BOUQUET: pronounced Muscat nose
FLAVOUR: full Muscat taste. A good, inexpensive Spumante. Sugar code
   8. (8%)

Other sparkling products: Cheventé, a 7% labrusca pop wine in white,
rosé and red and a Cold Duck (6.7%) under the Chateau Cartier label.

CRACKLING

Castel Vecchio *(De Chaunac)*
COLOUR: garnet   BOUQUET: sweet, grapey
FLAVOUR: sweet strawberry taste, soft; well-made of its kind. Sugar code
   6. (7%)

Chateau Cartier Crackling Rosé *(same as regular rosé)*
COLOUR: pink-amber   BOUQUET: light De Chaunac nose
FLAVOUR: sweet, carbonated taste, foxy finish. Sugar code 5. (11.5%)

SHERRY

Canadian Sherry   *(Concord)*
COLOUR: copper   BOUQUET: oily sweet
FLAVOUR: the sweetness thins out to a burnt finish. Sugar code 7. (17%)

Cartier Cream   *(Concord)*
COLOUR: amber-copper   BOUQUET: alcohol
FLAVOUR: undistinguished labrusca taste. Sugar code 10. (18%)

Hallmark Cream   *(Agawam)*
COLOUR: copper brown   BOUQUET: alcohol
FLAVOUR: sweet, cloying. Sugar code 12. (18%)

Hallmark Dry   *(Agawam)*
COLOUR: old gold   BOUQUET: faint flor character
FLAVOUR: synthetic. Sugar code 3. (18%)

★**Hallmark Oloroso**   *(Agawam)*
COLOUR: golden copper   BOUQUET: oily nutty
FLAVOUR: sweetness at first, giving way to a nutty, alcoholic character.
   Sugar code 7. (18%)

Private Stock Canadian Sherry   *(Concord and Agawam)*
COLOUR: copper   BOUQUET: woody nose
FLAVOUR: sweet character, baked taste, nutty finish. Sugar code 9. (18%)

PORT

Canadian Port   *(Concord)*
COLOUR: ruby-chestnut   BOUQUET: alcoholic, raisiny nose
FLAVOUR: sweet sherry taste. Sugar code 10. (17.5%)

Private Stock Canadian Port   *(Concord)*
COLOUR: chestnut   BOUQUET: baked, chocolate nose
FLAVOUR: sweet nuts and raisins quality in the taste. Sugar code 12. (18%)

COLIO

RED

Fragolino *(100% Concord)*
COLOUR: pale rose   BOUQUET: sweet, grapey
FLAVOUR: strawberry; soft, sweet dessert wine. Very well-made crackling
  wine which does not exhibit the foxiness of labrusca grape. Sugar code
  5. (9%)

★**Maréchal Foch 1981**
COLOUR: deep purple   BOUQUET: fruity nose
FLAVOUR: sweet raspberry quality. Clean, medium-weight, stylish.
  Vinified in stainless steel for ready consumption; fresh and fruity.
  Sugar Code 0. (12%)

★★**Riserva Rosso Secco 1981** *(Foch, Chelois and 5% Californian Cabernet)*
COLOUR: purple   BOUQUET: fruity
FLAVOUR: soft, round, ample, lots of flavour. Medium-weight with a
  touch of sweetness; well-balanced. Fresh. Steel fermented. Sugar code
  1. (12.2%)

Rosso *(80% Foch, 20% De Chaunac)*
COLOUR: ruby   BOUQUET: sweet, soft nose
FLAVOUR: sweet, fruity, tends to fade in the mouth. Sugar code 1. (12%)

★**Rosso Secco** *(80% Foch, 20% De Chaunac)*
COLOUR: garnet   BOUQUET: lemony Foch nose
FLAVOUR: very soft, youthful but good fruit flavour with some acid on
  the finish. Similar to a young Bardolino. Sugar code 0. (12.2%)

Rubino *(85% Foch, 15% De Chaunac)*
COLOUR: purple   BOUQUET: fruity, perfumed
FLAVOUR: a cocktail wine with 2.5 grams residual sugar. Sweet, slightly
  crackling from secondary fermentation in bottle, fruity, perfumed
  taste. Sugar code 4. (11.5%)

ROSÉ

Rosato *(100% De Chaunac)*
COLOUR: tawny-orange   BOUQUET: not much
FLAVOUR: sweet, crackling; well-balanced with a good flavour and clean
  finish. Sugar code 2. (12%)

WHITE

★**Bianco Secco**   *(80% decolourised De Chaunac, 10% Aurore, 10% Seyval)*
COLOUR: pale straw   BOUQUET: shy, a hint of licorice
FLAVOUR: soft, grapey; medium-weight with some residual sugar. A little
flabby for want of acid but finishes cleanly enough. Sugar code 1.
(12%)

Bianco Semi-Dry   *(same blend as the Secco)*
COLOUR: straw   BOUQUET: sweet
FLAVOUR: rich, soft, apple taste. Sweet, little acidity. Sugar code 3. (12%)

★**Johannisberg Riesling 1982**
COLOUR: straw   BOUQUET: fresh varietal nose
FLAVOUR: fruity, barky taste; quite full in the mouth with some residual
sugar. Powerful. Good length of finish. Sugar code 1. (12½%)

Perla   *(100% Niagara grapes)*
COLOUR: pale straw   BOUQUET: grapey labrusca nose but not unpleasant
FLAVOUR: slightly sparkling, grapey flavour with 2.5 grams residual sugar.
A well-made labrusca. (11%)

★★**Riserva Bianco Secco**   *(60% Seyval Blanc, 20% De Chaunac, 20% Aurore)*
COLOUR: pale straw   BOUQUET: fresh, clean nose
FLAVOUR: soft, good fruit, well-balanced. Clean finish with a touch of
residual sugar. Sugar code 1. (12%)

★**Seyval Blanc 1982**
COLOUR: straw   BOUQUET: fresh, clean, grassy
FLAVOUR: almost dry, fruity taste, hint of sugar. Medium-weight, crisp
and lingering on the finish. In the style of an Italian Oriveto. A credit
to the winemaker. Sugar code 0. (12.5%)

HILLEBRAND ESTATES (Newark)

RED

Newark Chevalier Rouge 1981   *(90% Foch, 10% Seyve-Villard)*
COLOUR: ruby   BOUQUET: lemony, tobacco nose
FLAVOUR: lemony taste, medium-weight with thin fruit, dry, with a tart
finish. Sugar code 0. (12%)

ROSÉ

Newark Elizabeth Rosé 1981   *(75% decolourised De Chaunac, 25% Le
Commandant)*
COLOUR: pale garnet   BOUQUET: faintly alcoholic
FLAVOUR: dry, interesting woody taste but finishes green. Sugar code 1.
(12%)

WHITE

Newark Chardonnay 1980
COLOUR: straw   BOUQUET: fresh varietal nose, suggestion of almond
FLAVOUR: reminiscent of a white Bordeaux rather than a Burgundy. Fat,
hint of residual sugar, curiously unknit with a dry, woody finish. Sugar
code 0. (11.5%)

Newark Comtesse Blanche 1981   *(75% Dutchess, 15% Riesling, 10% Vidal)*
COLOUR: pale straw   BOUQUET: spicy citrus
FLAVOUR: dry, spicy grapefruit taste; finishes a trifle hot. Sugar code 0.
(12%)

★★**Newark Gewurztraminer 1980**
COLOUR: deep straw   BOUQUET: spicy, good varietal nose
FLAVOUR: light fruit character, dry style, well-balanced with a fine, clean
finish. But expensive. Sugar Code 0. (11.5%)

★**Newark Gewurztraminer 1981**
COLOUR: straw   BOUQUET: undeveloped
FLAVOUR: light, spicy but still closed. A delicate Gewurz, not as fruity as
1980. Sugar code 0. (11.5%)

Newark Johannisberg Riesling 1981
COLOUR: pale straw   BOUQUET: wet-dog nose
FLAVOUR: touch of sweetness, unknit; green, acidic finish. Sugar code 2.
(10.5%)

Newark Lady Ann 1981   *(90% decolourised Le Commandant with 10%*
Couderc Muscat)
COLOUR: almost water-white   BOUQUET: sweetish, cardboard nose
FLAVOUR: initial sweetness with an underlying chemical taste. Sugar code
3. (10%)

Newark Seyval Blanc 1981
COLOUR: pale straw   BOUQUET: herbaceous, citrus
FLAVOUR: good fruit and acidity balance; big in the mouth but somewhat
austere and dry. Sugar code 1. (12%)

★★**Schloss Hillebrand**   *(decolourised De Chaunac, Dutchess, Seyval with*
some Morio Muscat)
COLOUR: pale straw   BOUQUET: intense floral nose
FLAVOUR: sweet, Rhine-style, sound with good balance. A real
winemaker's wine and the best of the Canadian-German imitation
blends. Good length but a touch more acid needed for my taste. Good
value. Sugar code 3. (11%)

SHERRY

Newark Canadian Sherry   *(Agawam grapes)*
COLOUR: pale copper   BOUQUET: light, sweet toffee nose
FLAVOUR: sweet, not much depth of flavour; linear taste. Sugar code 3.
(18.5%)

Newark Canadian Cream Sherry   *(as above with added caramel)*
COLOUR: deep pinkish-copper   BOUQUET: toffee
FLAVOUR: full, rich, alcoholic but lighter than other Canadian Cream
sherries; ultimately short. Sugar code 5. (18.5%)

INNISKILLIN

★**Brae Rouge**   *(Foch, De Chaunac, Villard Noir, Chancellor and 12%*
Californian Dry Red)
COLOUR: ruby   BOUQUET: plums
FLAVOUR: good weight, well-made table blend, dry. Sugar code 0. (12%)

Chamburcin 1980   *(Limited Edition)*
COLOUR: light cherry   BOUQUET: faint fruit
FLAVOUR: soft, light cherry flavour, a summer wine, Beaujolais-style.
Sugar code 0. (12%)

Chelois 1981
COLOUR: garnet   BOUQUET: meaty
FLAVOUR: very dry, light, Beaujolais-style, a little tart on the finish. Sugar
code 0. (12%)

★**De Chaunac 1980**
COLOUR: good ruby   BOUQUET: fruity, perfumed
FLAVOUR: perfumed taste, medium-weight, soft, well-balanced with a
good lingering finish. Sugar code 0. (12%)

Gamay Noir 1980   *(Limited Edition)*
COLOUR: garnet   BOUQUET: fresh fruity
FLAVOUR: light Gamay character, dry; somewhat green on the finish.
Sugar code 0. (12%) (The 1982 Gamay, while still light in colour, shows
better fruit character than 1980.)

Leon Millot 1980   *(Limited Edition)*
COLOUR: deep, dense ruby   BOUQUET: fruity
FLAVOUR: big mouthfilling taste, similar to Maréchal Foch, but rather
two-dimensional. Very dry, lemony finish, inclining to tartness. Sugar
code 0. (12%)

★★**Maréchal Foch 1980**
COLOUR: deep ruby, almost purple   BOUQUET: sweet tobacco nose
FLAVOUR: to my mind the best red wine made in Canada. Great depth of
fruit with good acidity and a touch of tannin. Complex, dry, rich taste
with a long, lemony finish. Needs a year or two yet. Sugar code 0.
(12%)

★**Maréchal Foch 1981**
COLOUR: deep ruby   BOUQUET: sweet tobacco
FLAVOUR: not as full as 1980 but good flavour with tannin and acidity in
evidence, without the hint of sweetness in the 1980. A keeper. Sugar
code 0. (12%)

Merlot 1980 *(Puddicombe-Lenko Vineyards) (Limited Edition)*
COLOUR: pale garnet   BOUQUET: elderberry, wet woody nose
FLAVOUR: light, not much fruit, more North Italy than St. Emilion. The
taste is almost there, but woody on the finish. Sugar code 0. (12%)

★**Millot-Chamburcin 1980**   *(a mix of the two French hybrids) (Limited
Edition)*
COLOUR: purple   BOUQUET: shaggy, fruity
FLAVOUR: perfumed, fruity taste. Interesting lemony finish. Generous in
the mouth. Dry. Sugar code 0. (12%)

ROSÉ

★**Rosé 1980**   *(De Chaunac and Villard Noir)*
COLOUR: orange amber   BOUQUET: fresh nose
FLAVOUR: touch of sweetness, good balance, good weight in the mouth
with a faint prickle. Sophisticated, dry. Sugar code 1. (11.5%)

WHITE

★**Brae Blanc**   *(Verdelet, Dutchess, Seyval Blanc, "and several other blanc
de noir grape varieties")*
COLOUR: pale straw   BOUQUET: fresh, stony
FLAVOUR: crisp with thin fruit; an astringent, bitter almond finish. An
attractive blend in the Italian style of whites. Sugar code 1. (11%)

Chardonnay 1980   *(Seeger Vineyard) (Limited Edition)*
COLOUR: straw-gold   BOUQUET: neutral nose
FLAVOUR: dry, grapefruit taste, acidic, lacks middle fruit, with a prickle.
Short finish. Sugar code 0. (11.5%)

Chardonnay 1981
COLOUR: pale gold   BOUQUET: alcoholic, fresh nose
FLAVOUR: sappy, green taste with a tart finish. Sugar code 0. (11.5%)

(In 1982 winemaker Karl Kaiser made five styles of Chardonnay, two
each from the Seeger and Montague Vineyards, matured in either
Limousin or Nevers oak. The fifth style is a Chardonnay from grapes
brought in from other vineyards. The best of them is the Seeger Vineyard
matured in Nevers oak—a French-style Chardonnay with a nutty
character—much the best Chardonnay yet produced by Inniskillin. The
Seeger Vineyard aged in Limousin is coarser with a toasted quality on the
finish. The Montague wines are from younger vines and lack the
concentration of fruit as yet.)

★**Gamay Blanc 1980**   *(Limited Edition) (Rhine Bottle)*
COLOUR: pink-gold blush like an eye-of-the-swan rosé   BOUQUET:
grapefruit nose
FLAVOUR: crisp, acidic with some residual sugar in the middle taste.
Opens up in the mouth to a lingering grapefruit finish. Sweet reserve
added to give it a German rather than French style. Sugar code 0.
(11.5%)

Gewurztraminer 1980   *(Limited Edition)*
COLOUR: straw   BOUQUET: shy, soapy-spicy on the nose.
FLAVOUR: light, spicy, somewhat closed taste. A delicate Gewurz at best.
Sugar code 1. (11.5%)

★**Riesling 1980**   *(Limited Edition)*
COLOUR: straw   BOUQUET: light, fresh, floral nose
FLAVOUR: fruity taste, slightly *spritzig*, soft, a touch of sweetness, well-
balanced with a citrus finish. Sugar code 3. (11%)

Riesling 1981   *(curiously there are two versions of this wine available
under the same Limited Edition label. The only way to tell them apart
is the degree of alcohol.)*

★**10.5% alcohol**
COLOUR: bright straw   BOUQUET: not very pronounced
FLAVOUR: soft, fruity with some residual sugar, well-balanced; finishes
clean. Sweet reserve added. Sugar code 3.

11% alcohol
COLOUR: straw   BOUQUET: apple-aromatic with a touch of the filtre on
the nose.
FLAVOUR: dry, floral-peppery taste, austere hot finish of pepper. (The
1982 Riesling is showing excellent fruit quality.) Sugar code 1.

Seyval Blanc 1981
COLOUR: straw-lemon   BOUQUET: gluey, touch of the filter
FLAVOUR: dry, medium-weight, cardboard taste in the finish. Sugar code
1. (12%)

★**Seyval Blanc 1982**
COLOUR: almost water-white   BOUQUET: concentrated fruity-acidic nose
FLAVOUR: big, lots of fruit, sugar and acidity; grapefruit taste. Will
develop into an excellent wine. Fifty percent of this wine was aged for
a short time in oak. Sugar code 1. (11.7%)

★★Vidal 1981 *(Limited Edition)*
COLOUR: pale straw, almost white BOUQUET: fresh, peachy nose
FLAVOUR: medium-weight, stony grapefruit taste, round and soft, well-balanced with a good long clean finish. Slightly *spritzig*. Much better than the 1980 version, which was somewhat fat and flabby. Sugar code 2. (10.5%)

★Vidal 1982
COLOUR: water-white BOUQUET: fresh, clean
FLAVOUR: light Moselle-style, floral character. Well-balanced with a clean, dry finish. Sugar code 0. (11%)

★★Vidal 1982 Late Harvest Brae Burn Estate *(Limited Edition)*
COLOUR: pale straw BOUQUET: peachy, grassy nose
FLAVOUR: rich, concentrated fruit, rich sweet floral taste; good balance with a long lingering finish. Will develop into a luscious dessert-style wine. (Sweet reserve added) Sugar code 4. (12%)

(Inniskillin's Limited Edition labels are produced in small quantities and are only available at the winery or at the company's Toronto Boutique in First Canadian Place or its St. Catharines' outlet.)

JORDAN

RED

Canadian Claret   *(De Chaunac and Foch)*
COLOUR: tawny-cherry   BOUQUET: alcoholic
FLAVOUR: dry, lightweight, anaemic, not much flavour. Sugar code 0
  (11%; screwtop, litre)

★**Grande Cuvée**   *(De Chaunac, Bacchus, Baco Noir)*
COLOUR: tawny-ruby   BOUQUET: blackberry
FLAVOUR: light, dry, cherry taste; a simple, easy-drinking wine. No
  fireworks, but reliable. Sugar code 0. (11%)

Jordan Valley Canadian Burgundy   *(De Chaunac and Foch)*
COLOUR: ruby   BOUQUET: woody, medicinal
FLAVOUR: dry, medium-weight, ordinary. Medicinal taste. Sugar code 0.
  (11%)

Maréchal Foch   *(Maîtres Vignerons neck label)*
COLOUR: garnet   BOUQUET: unpleasant
FLAVOUR: thin, watery, lacklustre. Sugar code 0. (11%)

Maria Christina   *(De Chaunac and Foch)*
COLOUR: tawny garnet   BOUQUET: neutral
FLAVOUR: sweetish taste of dried fruit; perfumed finish. Sugar code 3.
  (11%; screwtop, litre)

Rubi-Rouge   *(labrusca)*
COLOUR: orange-cherry   BOUQUET: grapey
FLAVOUR: soft, sweet but not aggressively foxy. Well-made of its kind.
  Sugar code 5. (11%; screwtop bottle)

Toscano Red   *(De Chaunac and Foch)*
COLOUR: orange-ruby   BOUQUET: hybrid nose
FLAVOUR: dry, linear taste with a woody finish. Sugar code 0. (11%;
  screwtop, litre)

Other reds: Menorah (sugar code 16).

ROSÉ

Jordan Valley Crackling
COLOUR: pink-amber   BOUQUET: perfumed De Chaunac
FLAVOUR: sweet, grapey, good length. Good of its kind. Sugar code 5.
  (10.5%; screwtop bottle)

Other rosés: Jordan Valley Still (a little less sweet, with a sugar code of 4),
Maria Christina Rosé.

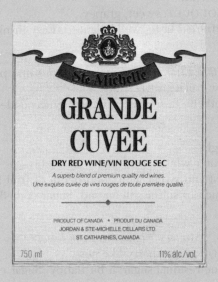

Ste-Michelle

GRANDE CUVÉE

DRY RED WINE/VIN ROUGE SEC

A superb blend of premium quality red wines.
Une exquise cuvée de vins rouges de toute première qualité.

PRODUCT OF CANADA • PRODUIT DU CANADA
JORDAN & STE-MICHELLE CELLARS LTD.
ST. CATHARINES, CANADA

750 ml   11% alc./vol.

WHITE

Autumn Harvest
COLOUR: almost water-white   BOUQUET: grapey, sweet
FLAVOUR: soft, grapey, sweet but finishes dry. Sugar code 3. (11%; screwtop bottle)

Canadian Sauterne
COLOUR: palest straw   BOUQUET: foxy
FLAVOUR: sweet, grapey, undistinguished. Sugar code 5. (11%; screwtop, litre)

★**Dutchess**   *(Maîtres Vignerons neck label)*
COLOUR: palest straw   BOUQUET: sweet, vaguely floral nose
FLAVOUR: soft, well-balanced, sweet grapefruit taste. Clean finish. Well-made. Sugar code 2. (10.5%)

Falkenburg   *(Elvira)*
COLOUR: straw   BOUQUET: faint labrusca nose
FLAVOUR: soft, light, inoffensive, Germanic style. Touch of sweetness. Sugar code 2. (10.5%)

★**Grande Cuvée White**
COLOUR: straw   BOUQUET: grassy, appley
FLAVOUR: dry, well-balanced, appealing taste, reminiscent of white Bordeaux. Sugar code 1. (10.5%)

Jordan Valley Dry White
COLOUR: straw   BOUQUET: sweet, grapey
FLAVOUR: dry, perfumed taste, well-balanced. Easy-drinking. Sugar code
1. (10.5%)

Maria Christina   *(60% Elvira with Catawba, Delaware, plus Californian)*
COLOUR: pale straw   BOUQUET: fruity
FLAVOUR: soft, synthetic taste; sweet, flabby. Sugar code 3. (10.5%;
screwtop, litre)

Maria Christina Light
COLOUR: almost water-white   BOUQUET: faint labrusca
FLAVOUR: soft, light and sweet with good depth of fruit for a light wine.
Crisp finish. Touch of sulfur still on end. Sugar code 3. (7.9%;
screwtop, litre)

Pinot Chardonnay   *(Maîtres Vignerons neck label)*
COLOUR: straw   BOUQUET: sherry-like nose
FLAVOUR: soft, some residual sugar; a bit flabby. Sugar code 2. (10.5%)

★**Pinot-Muscato**   *(blend of Chardonnay and Couderc Muscat; Maîtres
Vignerons)*
COLOUR: pale straw   BOUQUET: sweet, alcoholic
FLAVOUR: rich, honey, peachy taste with a cleansing acidity on the finish.
A good dessert wine. Sugar code 4. (10.5%)

Rhine Castle
COLOUR: straw   BOUQUET: vegetal, fruity
FLAVOUR: soft, initial sweetness gives way to a long, acidic finish. Short
fruit, long acid. Sugar code 3. (10.5%)

Selected Riesling   *(Maîtres Vignerons)*
COLOUR: straw   BOUQUET: oily-appley
FLAVOUR: thin, ungenerous. Lacks fruit. Dry with a woody green finish.
Sugar code 2. (10.5%)
(1981 version was back-blended with 1980 which was much better.)

Seyval Blanc   *(Maîtres Vignerons)*
COLOUR: pale straw, almost white   BOUQUET: sweet citrus nose
FLAVOUR: well-balanced with a touch of sweetness. Citrus quality in the
taste. Finishes dry with good length. Sugar code 2. (11%)

Toscano   *(Elvira and Catawba)*
COLOUR: pale straw   BOUQUET: hybrid nose
FLAVOUR: dry grapefruit quality. Metallic aftertaste. Sugar code 1. (10.5%;
screwtop, litre)

Vidal   *(Maîtres Vignerons)*
COLOUR: palest straw   BOUQUET: honeyed apple
FLAVOUR: full in the mouth, lots of glycerine; sweet citrus taste. Good
   acidity although a touch too sweet. Sugar code 1. (11%)

Other whites: Cask Medium Dry (Sugar code 3.)

SPARKLING

Gold Seal Canadian Champagne Dry   *(Catawba and Delaware)*
COLOUR: straw   BOUQUET: musky-grapey
FLAVOUR: heavy, touch of sugar; not much visible mousse. Sugar code 3.
   (12%)

Other sparkling wines: Gold Seal Pink Champagne. 7% sparkling wines based
on Elvira and Ventura include Prince de Mousseaux Red and White and Rosé,
Spumante Bambino, Luv-a-Duck, Baby Bear, Sno-Bird, Baby Deer, Sangria,
Cold Turkey, Lonesome Charlie.

CRACKLING

Perle Blanche, Cold Duck.

SHERRY

(Concord and Agawam)

Branvin
COLOUR: orange-copper   BOUQUET: light labrusca nose
FLAVOUR: varnish; sweet, no depth, grapey finish. Sugar code 7. (16.5%)

★**Classic Cream**
COLOUR: red-chestnut   BOUQUET: deep, sweet nose
FLAVOUR: mouth-filling, sweet, round with good weight and finish.
   Raisiny taste. Sugar code 12. (19.5%)

★**Patina Dry**
COLOUR: aged gold   BOUQUET: biscuity
FLAVOUR: good nutty taste, some alcoholic burn on the finish. Sugar code
   1. (19%)

★**Royal Crest**
COLOUR: orange-copper   BOUQUET: alcohol and wood
FLAVOUR: faintly medicinal first taste but opens up with a sweet nutty
   character. Soft. Sugar code 10. (18%)

Other sherries: 4 Aces (7), Sippin' (6).

PORT
Branvin (9)

VERMOUTHS
Milano Extra Dry, Milano Sweet.

LONDON

RED
Baco Noir 1981
COLOUR: deep ruby   BOUQUET: old nose, aged fruit
FLAVOUR: medicinal taste, dry. Sugar code 1. (11.5%)

Bellavista De Chaunac 1981
COLOUR: deep ruby   BOUQUET: foxy, medicinal (some labrusca in the
   blend?)
FLAVOUR: dry, aggressive green taste, short, lacks fruit. Sugar code 0.
   (11.5%; litre)

Dinner Red   *(De Chaunac, Foch, Chelois)*
COLOUR: ruby   BOUQUET: pruney nose
FLAVOUR: sweet Burgundy, finishes dry (6 months in oak). Sugar code 3.
   (12%)

Londini Castini Rosso 1981 *(Foch, De Chaunac with some Chelois)*
COLOUR: thin ruby   BOUQUET: alcoholic, oxidized fruit
FLAVOUR: thin, synthetic, insipid taste. Sugar code 2. (10%; screwtop)

Maréchal Foch 1981
COLOUR: bright ruby   BOUQUET: alcoholic, minty
FLAVOUR: thin fruit, mustiness in the taste. Sugar code 2. (11.5%)

OTHER PRODUCTS

London also makes a communion wine called Red St. Augustine which
was originally produced by the J.S. Hamilton Company in the latter
part of the last century.

WHITE

Bellavista Delaware 1981 *(100% Delaware)*
COLOUR: pale straw   BOUQUET: appley labrusca nose
FLAVOUR: soft grapey taste with a dry lingering finish. A well-made
labrusca. Sugar code 1. (11.5%)

Blanc de Blancs *(Elvira, Ventura, Dutchess with Californian base white)*
COLOUR: pale straw   BOUQUET: grapey nose
FLAVOUR: very soft and round with a hint of sweetness in the perfumed
taste. Sugar code 3. (10.5%)

Londini Castini Bianco 1981 *(Elvira, Niagara, Ventura with Californian
base white)*
COLOUR: palest straw   BOUQUET: bubble gum nose
FLAVOUR: sweet, grapey taste, flabby. Sugar code 2. (10%; screwtop)

★**Chablis** *(Elvira, Delaware, some Ventura with Californian Chenin
Blanc)*
COLOUR: pale straw   BOUQUET: gentle fruity nose, touch of sulfur
FLAVOUR: soft, fruity grapefruit taste, tart dry salty finish. Sugar code 1.
(11.5%)

★**Chenin Blanc** *(Californian Chenin plus Delaware and Elvira)*
COLOUR: pale straw   BOUQUET: fruity nose
FLAVOUR: very little acid, textured, good finish. Sugar code 1. (10.5%)

Dinner White Medium Dry Canadian Sauterne *(Delaware, Elvira, some
Niagara)*
COLOUR: pale straw   BOUQUET: sweet, grapey, labrusca nose
FLAVOUR: medium sweet labrusca taste, lingers—an old-style Canadian
wine. (Comes in a collectable bottle). Sugar code 5. (11%)

Other whites: Buffet Sauterne (Elvira, Ventura, some Niagara), Vinroi
White (virtually the same blend), Bellevinta White (Delaware, Elvira with
Californian base white).

SPARKLING

Bella Spumante *(Elvira and Niagara, carbonated)*
COLOUR: pale straw BOUQUET: sweet, fresh, labrusca nose
FLAVOUR: London's answer to Andres Chanté. Spumante suggests the
muscat grape. Here we have labrusca. Sugar code 4. (7%)

Other sparklers: Pink Flamingo (a little De Chaunac, Elvira and Niagara;
7%), Jubilee Champagne (Dutchess with a little Delaware; 12.5%), Pink
Jubilee (the same, coloured with De Chaunac), Londini Spumante (Elvira
and Niagara), Crackling Burgundy (De Chaunac with some Foch).

SHERRY

London Candlelight Medium Dry
COLOUR: copper BOUQUET: sweet
FLAVOUR: sweet concentrated taste, lightly baked, better in the palate
than the nose. Alcoholic finish. Sugar code 9. (18%)

★**London Cream**
COLOUR: mahogany with red highlights BOUQUET: toasty nose with
alcohol
FLAVOUR: baked quality; rich, full, sweet taste with a lingering finish.
Sugar code 12. (18%; Glass decanter with glass stopper)

London Dry Flor
COLOUR: old gold BOUQUET: synthetic, tobacco nose
FLAVOUR: faintly metallic taste, raw alcoholic finish. Sugar code 4. (18%)

Other sherries: Westminster (7), XXX (7), Supreme (9), Creme d'Or (13).

HONEY WINES

Ancient Mead Golden Honey Wine *(fancy bottle)*
COLOUR: old gold BOUQUET: like the inside of an old suitcase
FLAVOUR: honey but surprisingly light, somewhat artificial aftertaste.
Sugar code 12. (16%)

PORT

410 Canadian Port
COLOUR: Ruby BOUQUET: baked labrusca
FLAVOUR: medium sweet fruitcake taste which fades. Produced by the
company in the same blend since 1927. Sugar code 9. (16%)

XXX Canadian Port
COLOUR: ruby   BOUQUET: as above
FLAVOUR: as above, but more intensity and length because of extra
  alcohol. Sugar code 9. (18%)

PODAMER (MONTRAVIN CELLARS)

CHAMPAGNE

(in order of dryness)

★★**Brut Blanc de Blancs**   *(100% Chardonnay)*
COLOUR: pale straw   BOUQUET: fresh, clean, yeasty
FLAVOUR: crisp, with a faintly almond flavour, soft in the mouth with a
  dry finish. Excellent mousse. Sugar code 1. (12%)

Brut   *(Seyval Blanc, Aurore with some Riesling and Chardonnay)*
COLOUR: pale straw   BOUQUET: yeasty
FLAVOUR: dry, crisp with a slightly irony taste. Sugar code 2. (12%)

★**Extra Dry/Très Sec**   *(Seyval Blanc and Dutchess)*
COLOUR: pale straw   BOUQUET: grapey
FLAVOUR: fruity with a touch of sweetness, well-balanced with a
  lingering finish. Sugar code 2. (12%)

Cuvée Speciale/Special Reserve   *(same blend as Très Sec)*
COLOUR: straw   BOUQUET: sweet nose
FLAVOUR: full in the mouth with an aged sweet taste, but good length of
   finish. Sugar code 3. (12%)

RED

De Chaunac
COLOUR: light ruby   BOUQUET: alcoholic
FLAVOUR: aged fruit taste, very dry, thin, Italianate-style; austere, stemmy
   finish. Sugar code 0. (12%)

Maréchal Foch
COLOUR: ruby   BOUQUET: aged fruit, alcohol
FLAVOUR: oxidized taste. Sugar code 0. (12%)

Concerto
COLOUR: ruby   BOUQUET: plummy
FLAVOUR: oxidized fruit taste, sharp finish, disappointing. Sugar code 1.
   (12%; screwtop)

WHITE

Concerto
COLOUR: pale gold   BOUQUET: clean, warm, fruit nose
FLAVOUR: round, somewhat bland and short; with a green apple, acidic
   finish. Sugar code 1. (12%; screwtop)

Seyval Blanc
COLOUR: straw   BOUQUET: faint sherry nose
FLAVOUR: dry, aged taste rather like a Portuguese white; attractive if you
   like that style. Sugar code 1. (11.5%)

BC WINERIES

ANDRES

RED *(Viniferas)*

(Richelieu Label)

★**Cabernet Sauvignon 1979** *(Monterey County, California)*
COLOUR: purple-ruby BOUQUET: oaky, herbal nose
FLAVOUR: intense young fruit, still closed in and will need to age two to
three years. (I tasted the 1976 vintage of this wine made from the first
commercial cropping of these Californian wines. Ruby in colour, the
wine was light, woody and still tannic. The 1979 version promises
much more.)

★★**Petite Sirah 1979** *(Monterey County, California)*
COLOUR: big deep purple BOUQUET: herbaceous, generous
FLAVOUR: a very big, full-bodied, chewy wine given three months of
wood. Lemony finish. Needs two years to age. Will be first-rate. (13%)

OTHER PRODUCTS

Also under this label are Zinfandel and Gamay Beaujolais from
Californian grapes.

WHITE

(Richelieu Label)

Auxerrois 1981
COLOUR: pale straw BOUQUET: yeasty nose
FLAVOUR: a crisp, dry, well-balanced wine with a flinty grapefruit
quality. A little dusty on the finish.

Ehrenfelser 1980
COLOUR: pale gold BOUQUET: shy
FLAVOUR: soft, round, full-bodied dried apricot taste. Lacks acidity.

★**Gewurztraminer 1979** *(Monterey County, California)*
COLOUR: pale gold BOUQUET: spicy, oily nose
FLAVOUR: floral in the mouth but finishes dry—a wine of character.

Johannisberg Riesling 1980 *(Imkameep Vineyards)*
COLOUR: pale straw BOUQUET: closed
FLAVOUR: light, dry, fruit character, slightly barky taste in the finish. The
vines were only four years old for this vintage. 1982 should provide a
more stylish wine. (10.5%)

RED

★**Domaine D'Or**   *(70% Foch and De Chaunac, with Californian Petite Sirah and Ruby Cabernet)*
COLOUR: ruby   BOUQUET: light, fruity nose
FLAVOUR: soft raspberry taste, well-balanced, good tannin for backbone.
   (11.5%)

★**Similkameen Superior**   *(95% De Chaunac, 5% Foch)*
COLOUR: ruby   BOUQUET: perfumed
FLAVOUR: youthful, fresh, flavourful. (When it was first brought out in
   1968 it was called Canadian Beaujolais, which best describes its style.)
   (11.5%)

OTHER PRODUCTS

(Andres produces a variety of red wines based on hybrid grapes: Lake
Country Red, Cellar Cask, Auberge Red, Regency Red Dry, Eagle
Ridge, Pacific Coast Cellars, House Wine and a lacklustre utility wine
to get rid of De Chaunac stocks called simply Red Wine, a no-name
type of product.)

WHITE

Domaine D'Or   *(100% Californian French Colombard and Chenin Blanc)*
COLOUR: straw   BOUQUET: freshly cut grass
FLAVOUR: big grassy taste, dry at first with at touch of residual sugar.
   Buxom but unstructured. (11.5%)

Eagle Ridge   *(70% Okanagan Riesling, 10% Muscat, Verdelet and
   Californian French Colombard)*
COLOUR: straw   BOUQUET: spicy
FLAVOUR: grapey, with a soft spicy taste and residual sugar, medium dry.
   (11.5%)

Hochtaler   *(35% each of French Colombard and Chenin Blanc from
   California, 20% Verdelet and 10% Muscat)*
COLOUR: pale straw   BOUQUET: lightly perfumed
FLAVOUR: dry, well-balanced, clean. A well-blended wine. (The original
   blend had Californian Semillion instead of the Verdelet and Muscat).
   (11%)
(Wintergarten is a slight sweeter version.)

House Wine White   *(Diamond, Okanagan Riesling and Thompson
   Seedless)*
COLOUR: pale straw   BOUQUET: papery, labrusca nose
FLAVOUR: full grapiness in the mouth but flabby. (11.5%)
(Called Dinner Wine in Ontario.)

Okanagan Riesling
COLOUR: pale straw   BOUQUET: wet-dog nose, rather Muscat-like
FLAVOUR: aggressive fruit, not much acid but finishes well. A triumph of
the winemaker to make it so well. (11.5%)

Similkameen Superior White   *(40% Okanagan Riesling, 20% Verdelet, 15%
Californian Sémillion and 25% Thompson Seedless)*
COLOUR: very pale, almost water-white   BOUQUET: spicy nose
FLAVOUR: innocuous, some residual sugar, not much acid. Apple-like
finish. (11.5%)

★**Souvenance Blanc de Blancs**   *(Californian Sémillion)*
COLOUR: pale straw   BOUQUET: flinty nose
FLAVOUR: reminiscent of a French Sauvignon Blanc (modelled on St.
Jovian).

Other whites: Regency Extra Dry, Lake Country White, Auberge White,
Cellar Cask White, Franciscan Chablis, Rhinemesiter and the sweet
Botticelli and White Dinner.

SPARKLING

Richelieu Canadian Champagne   *(90% French Colombard)*
COLOUR: pale straw   BOUQUET: clean, yeasty nose
FLAVOUR: crisp, Sekt character with a slight sweetness on the finish.
(11.5%).
(Andres also makes a light version at 9% alcohol and a sweeter pink
product.)

SHERRY

(Richelieu Golden Cream Sherry won a silver medal in its class at the 1982
Septober Wine Festival.) The company also produces a Pale Dry, a Medium
Dry and a Select Sherry.

BRIGHTS

RED

Dry House Red   *(Foch and De Chaunac)*
COLOUR: ruby   BOUQUET: soft fruit
FLAVOUR: smooth, gentle, good fruit taste, tends to fade in the mouth.
(12%)

Papa Carlo   *(mainly Foch with some De Chaunac)*
COLOUR: ruby   BOUQUET: shaggy
FLAVOUR: fresh, young; a spaghetti wine for knocking back. Acidic finish.
   (11%)

Other reds: Entre Montagnes Rouge Sec (12%).

WHITE

★Dry House Wine   *(Chenin Blanc with decolourised De Chaunac picked early)*
COLOUR: straw   BOUQUET: fresh
FLAVOUR: light, uncomplicated, hint of sweetness. Well-balanced. (11%)

★Entre Montagnes Blanc Sec   *(Chenin Blanc with Okanagan Riesling)*
COLOUR: straw   BOUQUET: fresh, fruity
FLAVOUR: soft, light, good fruit character, some residual sugar. Easy-
   drinking. (11%)

House Wine   *(Diamond and Okanagan Riesling with a base of Thompson Seedless)*
COLOUR: pale straw   BOUQUET: a touch foxy
FLAVOUR: sweet, short, innoffensive. (11%)

CALONA WINES

RED

★Chancellor 1981
COLOUR: deep ruby   BOUQUET: thin fruit
FLAVOUR: dusty, dry, austere, good fruit acidity. (12%)

★Haut Villages   *(Californian Gamay, Petite Sirah and BC Rosette)*
COLOUR: bright ruby-garnet   BOUQUET: grapey nose
FLAVOUR: light Burgundy-style, fruity, soft with a dry, peppery finish.
   (11.5%)
(Silver medal winner at Septober Wine Festival 1982.) (Available in
Ontario.)

★★Maréchal Foch 1978   *(Winemasters' Selection)*
COLOUR: warm ruby   BOUQUET: raisiny nose with oaky overtones
FLAVOUR: dry, majestic, like an old Barolo, though lighter in the mouth.
   A full-blooded wine. (11.5%)
(Gold medal winner at Septober Wine Festival 1982.)

Rougeon 1981
COLOUR: light, aged look   BOUQUET: lemon crystals
FLAVOUR: perfumed, complex, evidence of tannin and acidity. (12.5%)

Sommet Rouge   *(predominantly De Chaunac with some Rougeon and Maréchal Foch, coloured and strengthened with Californian Ruby Cabernet and Petite Sirah).*
COLOUR: ruby   BOUQUET: plummy, alcoholic nose
FLAVOUR: soft, velvety, slightly perfumed with a dry, astringent finish. (12.5%).
(Available in Ontario.)

Other reds: Mountain Red (available in Ontario), Monashee Estate Red (blend of Mountain Red and San Pietro), Palazzo Reale Red (low alcohol, marked sweetness), Red Dry (bag-in-box style, mild blend, fruity with a touch of labrusca), Royal Red (similar blend to Red Dry and could be called Red Sweet), San Pietro (fruity, Chianti style red, quite mellow; available in Ontario), Rich Red (sweet, high alcohol with labrusca predominating).

WHITE

★★**Chenin Blanc 1981**   *(50th anniversary bottling)*
COLOUR: pale straw   BOUQUET: full, fruity nose
FLAVOUR: good fruit, well-balanced, harmonious, with a crisp spicy taste. Fine finish. (11.5%)
(This is one of five anniversary bottlings of varietals brought in from Washington State. The others are Gewurztraminer, Fumé Blanc, Johannisberg Riesling and Chardonnay.)

Festspiel   *(a blend of five wines including Okanagan and Californian Riesling, three of those from Schloss Laderheim)*
COLOUR: pale straw   BOUQUET: sweet, straw-like
FLAVOUR: pleasant, light wine with good acidity and clean finish. A younger, slightly dryer sister to Schloss Laderheim. (10.5%)

★**Haut Villages White**   *(40% Californian Chenin Blanc, 20% Californian French Colombard; the rest Aurore)*
COLOUR: pale straw   BOUQUET: flowery, grapy nose
FLAVOUR: medium-weight with a touch of residual sugar. More in the style of a Californian Chablis than a white Burgundy, which it is dressed up to be. But a good wine for all that. (11.5%)
(Available in Ontario.)

Mountain Riesling   *(Okanagan Riesling)*
COLOUR: pale gold   BOUQUET: hint of labrusca
FLAVOUR: quite weighty, slightly soapy taste with a dry, acidic finish. (12.5%)

Schloss Laderheim *(Californian Johannisberg Riesling, Aurore and Delaware)*
COLOUR: pale straw   BOUQUET: sweet
FLAVOUR: soft, round, somewhat flabby, a professional wine, easy-drinking. (11.5%)

Sommet Blanc *(Verdelet with six other grapes including American Riesling, Sémillon, French Colombard and Chenin Blanc)*
COLOUR: pale straw   BOUQUET: sweet
FLAVOUR: soft, round, somewhat flabby. A professional wine, easy-drinking. Sugar code 2. (11.5%)
(Available in Ontario.)

Other whites: Palazzo Reale White (made from the Californian Muscat of Alexandria grape; sweet) Royal White (local labrusca grapes, particularly Diamond; very sweet) San Pietro White (Okanagan Riesling and Californian base white. Calona says this wine will be made drier in future in Italian style. Available in Ontario) White Dry (similar to Royal White but considerably drier).

SPARKLING

★**Cuvée Blanc** *(Okanagan Riesling with Californian Muscat)*
COLOUR: palest straw   BOUQUET: muscat on the nose
FLAVOUR: light, perfumed dry muscat taste on the palate; crisp finish.
  Good mousse. (7%).
(Available in Ontario.)

Other sparklers: Strawberry Angel, Fontana Bianco (spumante) and the
sweet, muscat-flavoured La Scala Spumante which had honourable
mention at September Wine Festival 1982 (all 7%).

DESSERT WINES

Muscatel, Port, and three sherries: medium dry '35 Sherry, dry Cocktail
  Sherry, sweet Cream Sherry.

FRUIT WINES

Berry Jack (blackberry and blueberry, 14%), Black Jack (blackberry, 14%),
Double Jack (apple).

CASABELLO

RED

(Estate Selection label)
★**Canadian Burgundy** *(Californian Carignane plus De Chaunac, Foch and
  Chancellor)*
COLOUR: cherry   BOUQUET: warm, earthy nose
FLAVOUR: meaty wine with good body and a dry finish. Slight tannic
  edge. (11.5%)
(Gold medal winner at September Wine Festival 1982.)

Pinot Noir 1978 *(Washington grapes)*
COLOUR: pale ruby   BOUQUET: cough medicine
FLAVOUR: light, more rosé in character, thin fruit; acidic, tannic finish.
  (11%)

(Also under the Estate label are Gamay Beaujolais and Zinfandel from
California.)

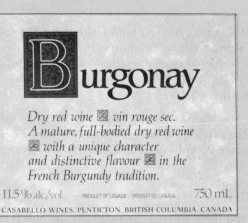

Burgonay *(De Chaunac, Foch, Rougeon with Washington grapes)*
COLOUR: ruby   BOUQUET: woody, aged fruit
FLAVOUR: thin, ungenerous with a dry rasping finish. (11%)

★**Osoyoos Select** *(100% BC De Chaunac and Foch)*
COLOUR: cherry   BOUQUET: not much on the nose
FLAVOUR: pleasant, dry, with good fruit flavour and a decent finish. (11%)

Other reds: Dinner Wine (hybrids, medium dry), Burgon (De Chaunac
and Foch, sold in carafes) and a range of inexpensive keg wines under
the Gala and Casavino labels.

WHITE

(Estate Selection label)
★**Chenin Blanc 1978**   *(Okanagan Valley grapes)*
COLOUR: palest straw   BOUQUET: grassy, apple nose
FLAVOUR: viscous, round in the mouth, apple-like flavour, hint of
  sweetness. Good balance with a crisp, clean finish. (11%)
(Silver and Bronze medal winner at Septober Wine Festival 1982.)

Fleur de Blanc   *(Okanagan Riesling blend plus Californian French
  Colombard)*
COLOUR: pale, almost water-white   BOUQUET: floral
FLAVOUR: slightly sweet, candy-like finish. A good commercial product.
  (11%)

★Gewurztraminer 1978 *(Okanagan Valley)*
COLOUR: pale straw   BOUQUET: spicy, melon
FLAVOUR: rich fruit flavour, touch of sweetness that thins out to a
somewhat watery, flabby end. Lacks acidity. A great pity that the
promise on the nose and first taste do not follow through. (11%)

Johannisberg Riesling 1978 *(Okanagan)*
COLOUR: straw   BOUQUET: candy nose
FLAVOUR: floral taste with some residual sweetness; burnt sugar in the
end taste. (11%)

Pinot Chardonnay 1978 *(Washington grapes)*
COLOUR: pale straw   BOUQUET: grassy quality
FLAVOUR: soft, round, a little flabby and unstructured. (11%)
(Also under the Estate Selection label are a Grey Riesling and a Sémillion,
both from Washington State.)

Alpenweiss *(Californian Thompson Seedless, Chenin Blanc, French
Colombard, Late Sweet Muscat, 20% Okanagan Riesling)*
COLOUR: pale straw   BOUQUET: sweet, sappy nose
FLAVOUR: round in the mouth, sweet, cloying, lingering French
Colombard taste. Needs acid to clean the palate. (10.5%)

Canadian Chablis Blanc *(40% basic Californian white blend with 20%
Muscat of Alexandria with Okanagan Riesling).*
COLOUR: pale yellow   BOUQUET: sweet
FLAVOUR: Muscat sweetness, almost a licorice character; fruity, light
finish. A commercial blend. (10.9%; sold in carafes)

★Edelwein *(20% Okanagan Riesling, the rest California Dry White)*
COLOUR: pale straw   BOUQUET: assertive fruit
FLAVOUR: well-made, good balance, dry finish to this Rhine-style wine.
(10.9%)

Rhinegarten *(Okanagan Riesling and Muscat of Alexandria)*
COLOUR: palest straw   BOUQUET: not much
FLAVOUR: slightly sweet, soft, little character, but finishes well. (10.9%)

Summerland Riesling *(Okanagan)*
COLOUR: pale straw   BOUQUET: undistinguished
FLAVOUR: light Okanagan Riesling character, soft finish, somewhat fat.
(10.5%)

Other whites: Osoyoos Select, Capistro and keg wines under the Gala and
Casovino labels.

Gala Keg Dry White   *(second-run ameliorated product blended half and half with Californian white)*
COLOUR: pale straw   BOUQUET: stemmy nose, assertive Okanagan Riesling
FLAVOUR: grapey taste, watery finish.

Gala Keg Dry Medium   *(as above)*
Fermented dry and cane sugar added to sweeten the wine to a sugar code reading of 4.

CLAREMONT

RED

★**Maréchal Foch 1979**
COLOUR: dense purple   BOUQUET: herbal nose
FLAVOUR: medicinal taste, somewhat oaky and austere. Very dry and powerful like a young Californian Cabernet. Needs time. (12.5%).
(The 1980 version of this wine is not as heavy and will in time be more gracious.)

Rougeon 1979
COLOUR: intense purple   BOUQUET: acetone nose
FLAVOUR: green berry taste, tannic but good fruit acidity. An aggressive wine. (12%)
(In future Claremont hopes to release a Pinot Noir and a Merlot.)

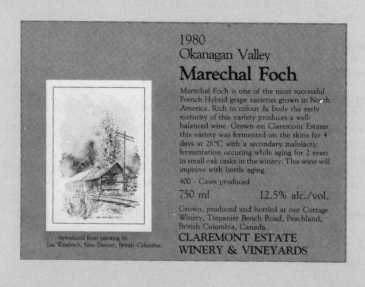

1980
Okanagan Valley
Marechal Foch

Marechal Foch is one of the most successful French Hybrid grape varieties grown in North America. Rich in colour & body the early maturity of this variety produces a well-balanced wine. Grown on Claremont Estates this variety was fermented on the skins for 4 days at 26°C with a secondary malolactic fermentation occuring while aging for 2 years in small oak casks in the winery. This wine will improve with bottle aging.

400 - Cases produced

750 ml   12.5% alc./vol.

Grown, produced and bottled at our Cottage Winery, Trepanier Bench Road, Peachland, British Columbia, Canada.
**CLAREMONT ESTATE
WINERY & VINEYARDS**

... reproduced from painting by Les Weisbrich, New Denver, British Columbia.

WHITE

Muscat Reisling 1980 *(in a blend of 45-55% Alexander Muscat to Okanagan Riesling)*
COLOUR: straw   BOUQUET: pleasing Muscat nose
FLAVOUR: viscous, aggressive Muscat perfumed taste; a big, vigorous wine somewhat green on the finish. (11.5%)

★**Pinot Blanc 1981**
COLOUR: pale gold   BOUQUET: peach-like nose
FLAVOUR: assertive, viscous with a hint of sweetness but well-balanced. (11%)

Riesling 1980 *(Okanagan Riesling)*
COLOUR: pale straw   BOUQUET: shaggy, spicey
FLAVOUR: the nose is confirmed on the palate. Dry with a good acidic finish. (11.5%)

★**Vin Blanc 1980** *(Vedelet, Chenin Blanc and Sémillion)*
COLOUR: pale gold   BOUQUET: astringent nose
FLAVOUR: bone dry, rather tart with a green apple aftertaste. (11.5%)

OTHER PRODUCTS

Claremont also produces limited editions of Gewurztraminer and Sauvignon Blanc Fumé 1981. Future releases include a Johannisberg Riesling.

GRAY MONK

WHITE

Johannisberg Riesling 1981
COLOUR: water-white   BOUQUET: delicate Riesling character
FLAVOUR: light, young, a little green, with a citrus finish. (11%)

★**Kerner 1981**
COLOUR: water-white   BOUQUET: shaggy Riesling nose with floral overtones
FLAVOUR: racy floral taste with long, delicate follow through. Fascinating wine. (11%)

★★**Pinot Auxerrois 1981 Kabinett**
COLOUR: water-white   BOUQUET: appley nose
FLAVOUR: full in the mouth, round with enough acid to clean the palate. Beautifully made. (10.8%)

★Pinot Gris 1981 Kabinett
COLOUR: water-white with a pinkish tinge   BOUQUET: aromatic,
    perfumed nose
FLAVOUR: soft and round in the mouth. Delicate, mellow, viscous. Great
    finish. (9.5%)

★Pinot Gris 1980   *(Late Harvest)*
COLOUR: water-white   BOUQUET: rhubarb with a hint of botrytis.
FLAVOUR: sweet rhubarb taste, enhanced by sweet reserve. (10.8%)

OTHER PRODUCTS

Gray Monk also make Gewurztraminer which won the Consumers'
Gold Medal in its class at the 1982 Septober Wine Festival and two
rarities—a Bacchus and a Rotberger, one of three true rosés in the
world.

JORDAN & STE.-MICHELLE

RED

Rougelais   *(Maréchal Foch)*
COLOUR: deep rose   BOUQUET: meaty quality on the nose
FLAVOUR: initial sweetness gives way to a woodiness. Thin, ungenerous
    with an acidic finish. (12%; screwcap)

Toscano Rosso   *(80% Foch with De Chaunac)*
COLOUR: deep rose   BOUQUET: thin, rubbery nose
FLAVOUR: short, stubby wine with a sweet port quality that dries quickly
    to an acidic finish. (11.5%; screwcap)

Zinfandel   *(100% Californian)*
COLOUR: tawny-cherry   BOUQUET: hot, roasted nose
FLAVOUR: light, acidic with a dry barky quality on the finish. (12%)

Other reds: Ruby Cabernet and Cabernet Sauvignon from California,
Maréchal Foch, Chateau Rouge, and a variety of labrusca wines under the
Beau Sejour label as well as the sentimental Slingers Grape and Villa Red Dry
(sugar code 6).

WHITE

★Chenin Blanc   *(100% Californian)*
COLOUR: pale straw   BOUQUET: fresh clean, fruity
FLAVOUR: medium-weight, soft fruit character, slightly harsh on the finish
    but fine length. (11%)

Falkenberg   *(30% Chenin Blanc with Verdelet and other hybrids)*
COLOUR: almost water-white   BOUQUET: sweet, grassy nose
FLAVOUR: burnt sweetness on the palate, unstructured; tart acidic finish.
(10.5%)

★**Johannisberg Riesling**   *(Okanagan Valley—Maîtres Vignerons neck label)*
COLOUR: straw   BOUQUET: fresh, faintly varietal nose
FLAVOUR: good Riesling character on the palate but ultimately the fruit
overpowers since it lacks balancing acidity. Finishes rather clumsily.
(9.5%)

★**Johannisberg Riesling 1981 Special Reserve**   *(single vineyard—Maîtres
Vignerons label)*
COLOUR: pale straw, brilliant   BOUQUET: fresh, crisp with a hint of
sweetness
FLAVOUR: lots of fruit and acid. Spätlese in quality, a good Rhine-style
Riesling. The balance was not there when I tasted it a year after it was
made but a little bottle age will make this a rich, mouthfilling wine.
(This wine won a gold and a bronze medal at the Septober Wine Festival
in 1982.)

★**Rhine Castle**   *(Californian Thompson Seedless, French Colombard, with
25% Okanagan Muscat)*
COLOUR: straw   BOUQUET: Muscat nose
FLAVOUR: Muscat taste, perfumed and very soft with a sweet floral
finish. (11%)

Toscano Bianco   *(Thompson Seedless, Okanagan Riesling, Chenin Blanc)*
COLOUR: pale straw   BOUQUET: undistinguished
FLAVOUR: soft, fruity quality, somewhat flabby with a grapey finish. (11%;
screwtop)

750 ml   11% alc./vol.

Canadian
Rhine Castle

White Wine / Vin Blanc
PRODUCT OF CANADA   PRODUIT DU CANADA
JORDAN & STE-MICHELLE CELLARS LTD., SURREY, CANADA

Toscano Light
COLOUR: water-white   BOUQUET: sweet
FLAVOUR: sweet with an acidic finish, not much character. (7.9%)

Other whites: Sémillion from California, Auxerrois, Maria Christina, Sauterne, the Beau Sejour labels, Bon White and Slingers White.

MISSION HILL

RED

(Private Reserve Label)

★**Cabernet Sauvignon 1981**   *(Washington grapes)*
COLOUR: deep purple   BOUQUET: vanilla, oaky nose
FLAVOUR: young oak taste which overpowers the fruit, a locked-in taste
  that finishes with a hint of tobacco. An earthy wine that needs three or
  four years to show its quality. (12%)

★**Pinot Noir 1981**   *(Washington)*
COLOUR: purple   BOUQUET: rich, sweet vanilla-oak nose
FLAVOUR: woody fruit taste (oak chips). Robust, building to a tannic,
  acidic finish. Very deep colour for an American Pinot Noir. The tannin
  will allow it to age well and release the full fruit flavour. (12%)

WHITE

(Private Reserve Label)

Chenin Blanc 1981   *(60% Washington grapes blended with Californian bulk white)*
COLOUR: pale gold, hint of lime   BOUQUET: tea leaf and grass nose
FLAVOUR: full in the mouth, alcoholic, melon-like taste. Hot finish. (11%)

★**Gewurztraminer 1981**   *(Okanagan grapes)*
COLOUR: palest straw   BOUQUET: youthful, spicy nose
FLAVOUR: full Gewurtz spice and flowers taste. Could do with a touch more acid to clean off the palate. Very round and soft. Not fully knit yet but will develop with a year of bottle age to be first-rate. (11%)

★**Johannisberg Riesling 1981**   *(Okanagan grapes)*
COLOUR: pale straw   BOUQUET: youthful Riesling nose
FLAVOUR: good fruit character, slightly *spritzig*. Green finish with a touch of sulfur but age will ameliorate these deficiencies. (11%)

(Mission Ridge Label)

Premium Dry Red
COLOUR: tawny ruby   BOUQUET: sweet, fruity nose
FLAVOUR: soft, fruity tobacco taste, very round, slightly medicinal. Touch of sweetness and tannin in the finish. Could do with a touch more acidity. (11%)

★**Premium Dry White**
COLOUR: pale straw   BOUQUET: fresh, clean nose
FLAVOUR: grassy taste, soft with good acidity, though a little hot on the finish. (11%)

(Caves Chauvignon Label)

★**Chauvignon Rouge**
COLOUR: ruby   BOUQUET: alcoholic, sappy nose
FLAVOUR: medium body, soft fruit-raisiny quality, good finish with a tannic bite. (11%)
(Bronze medal winner at Septober Wine Festival of 1982.)

Reserve Speciale Blanc
COLOUR: pale straw   BOUQUET: sweet, marshmallow nose
FLAVOUR: little fruit character, acidic finish. (11%).
(Also under this label: Chauvignon Blanc (11%))

★**Reserve Speciale Rouge**
COLOUR: ruby   BOUQUET: aged fruit
FLAVOUR: stylish full-bodied fruity blend, good character and balance. A
year in the bottle should soften the tannin. (11%)

(Klosterberg Cellars Label)
Schloss Weinberg Trocken
COLOUR: pale straw   BOUQUET: Okanagan Riesling, slightly green on the
nose
FLAVOUR: viscous, unstructured, flabby, undistinguished. (11%)

Tollerkranz
COLOUR: pale straw   BOUQUET: alcohol, faint Riesling
FLAVOUR: sweetish taste, soft, lacklustre, unctuous. (11%)

(Honourable mention at Septober Wine Festival 1982.)

(Also under this label: Sonnenwein, a sweeter version of Schloss
Weinberg. (11%))

(Golden Valley Label—Hybrid Varietals; to be renamed Pandosy Cellars)
De Chaunac
COLOUR: aged tawny ruby   BOUQUET: stemmy, musty nose
FLAVOUR: thin fruit, astringent with a tart finish. (12%)

★**Maréchal Foch (1976/77)**
COLOUR: deep ruby, hint of mahogany   BOUQUET: woody nose
FLAVOUR: good fruit, aged taste, well-balanced with a generous feel. Dry,
slightly tannic finish. (11%)

(Silver medal winner at Septober Wine Festival 1982.)

SPARKLING

Spumante
COLOUR: pale straw   BOUQUET: muscat nose
FLAVOUR: light, pleasant, grapey taste; not much character. Sweet.

PORT

★**Mission Hill Port**   *(33% 1968 vintage, 15% 1974 vintage, 52% 1977 vintage)*
COLOUR: ruby-chestnut   BOUQUET: plummy
FLAVOUR: sweet oaky-chocolate taste, well-balanced; in the style of a
Tawny. Good length. The best Canadian port I've tasted. (18%)

SHERRY

★★**Mission Hill Sherry** *(90% 1974 vintage, 10% 1980 vintage)*
COLOUR: old gold BOUQUET: sweet, nutty, alcoholic
FLAVOUR: full winey taste, medium dry with great length and style.
Surprisingly good. (18%)

SUMAC RIDGE

RED

★**Chancellor 1980**
COLOUR: deep ruby BOUQUET: light, fruity nose
FLAVOUR: strawberry taste, soft, needs time. (11.5)

★**Chancellor 1981**
COLOUR: bright ruby BOUQUET: lemony overtones and green pepper
FLAVOUR: light, fresh, acidic, like a young Beaujolais in style. Tart finish.
(11.5%)

ROSÉ

Summerland Rosé *(Okanagan Riesling and Chancellor blend)*
COLOUR: deep pink BOUQUET: shaggy
FLAVOUR: sweetness on the palate, soft, gentle, well-made for such a
blend. Finishes well with a fine dryness. (10.9%)

WHITE

★**Chenin Blanc 1981**
COLOUR: lemon BOUQUET: grassy nose
FLAVOUR: full fruit, very dry with a good acidity but well-balanced and
clean. (10.9%)

Gewurztraminer 1981
COLOUR: pale straw BOUQUET: gentle, spicy nose
FLAVOUR: round, perfumed taste, good balance but lacking
concentration. An odd cidery flavour in the end taste. Perhaps this will
disappear with a little bottle age. (10.9%)

★Okanagan Riesling 1981
COLOUR: pale, almost water-white   BOUQUET: fresh, delicately perfumed
   nose
FLAVOUR: light, well-balanced, a sappy-sweetness in the middle taste.
   Finishes crisp and clean. More harmonious and discreet than the 1980
   vintage which was made for Sumac at Casabello. (10.9%)

Verdelet 1980
COLOUR: pale straw   BOUQUET: fresh, sweet grassiness on the nose
FLAVOUR: the promise of the nose is dissipated on the palate. Slightly
   oxidized, gluey finish. Ultimately disappointing. One hopes the 1981
   will be better. (11.5%)

UNIACKE ESTATE WINES

RED

★Merlot 1981   *(Special Reserve)*
COLOUR: pale ruby   BOUQUET: baked apples
FLAVOUR: light Merlot fruit character, soft, dry, well-balanced. A little
   green; will improve with age. (10.5%)

Pinot Noir 1981
COLOUR: deep rose   BOUQUET: youthful, closed, hint of sweetness
FLAVOUR: light, grapefruit-like taste, tart with a green finish. (10.5%)

WHITE

Chasselas 1981
COLOUR: straw, hint of green   BOUQUET: fresh, with a touch of spice
FLAVOUR: dry, good fruit quality but a stalky, acidic finish. (10%)

★Chenin Blanc 1981
COLOUR: pale straw   BOUQUET: toasty, spicy nose
FLAVOUR: good fruit character, grassy, acidic with a woodiness in the
   finish. (10%)

Gewurztraminer 1981
COLOUR: straw   BOUQUET: viscous, vaguely lychee nose
FLAVOUR: initial softness gives way to a stemmy, acidic finish. Short on
   fruit. (10%)

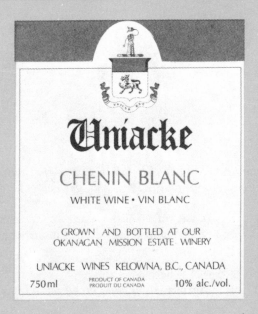

★**Johannisberg Riesling 1981**
COLOUR: straw   BOUQUET: viscous, floral nose
FLAVOUR: good soft, floral fruit quality, well-made but ultimately let
down by a green finish. Otherwise first-rate. (10%)

★**Okanagan Riesling 1981**
COLOUR: yellow straw   BOUQUET: sweet floral with a hybrid quality
FLAVOUR: instant fat sweetness, initially flabby before the acidity asserts
itself. The initial full fruit flavour thins out. (10.5%). (This wine won a
(This wine won a gold medal in its class at the 1982 Septober Wine
Festival.)

QUEBEC WINERIES

LES ENTREPRISES VERDI

RED

Cuvée des Moines de l'Abbaye   *(blend of five or six Californian grapes. The base is the same for all the reds, only the percentage of blend changes.)*
COLOUR: garnet   BOUQUET: soft, fruity
FLAVOUR: aged fruit taste, some residual sugar, somewhat apathetic. (10%)

La Nuit d'Amour
COLOUR: garnet   BOUQUET: herbal
FLAVOUR: light, soft and fruity, somewhat green on the finish. (11%)

Portneuf (1978)
COLOUR: ruby-mahogany   BOUQUET: pruney nose
FLAVOUR: aged taste, somewhat oxidized. (11%)

★**Le Vieux Manoir**
COLOUR: ruby   BOUQUET: aged Burgundy nose
FLAVOUR: generous fruit with a peppery finish, full-bodied and complex. Reminiscent of a Côte du Rhone. (11%)

Other reds: Le Cachet, VinBec.

WHITE

★**Kineret Blanc** *(Kosher)*
COLOUR: yellow straw BOUQUET: fresh, reminiscent of Sauvignon Blanc
grapes
FLAVOUR: dry with a hint of sweetness, well-made. (11%)

★**Tourbillon d'automne** *(Ugni Blanc grapes)*
COLOUR: straw BOUQUET: floral quality on the nose
FLAVOUR: crisp and dry with a touch of rersidual sugar, but thanks to a
good acid balance it finishes cleanly. (12%)

Other whites: from the Ugni Blanc grapes, Le Cachet and VinBec as well
as a range of four 11% kosher wines under the Kineret labels.

JULAC INC.

WHITE

★**Cuvéé Val-Jalbert**
COLOUR: yellow straw BOUQUET: pebbly-papery nose
FLAVOUR: dry fruity taste, with an appealing aged middle flavour
reminiscent of southern Italian whites. Good finish. Good value. (11%)

LUBEC INC.

RED

Cellier des Châtelains *("20% Rioja, 20% Cabernet from Argentina and
house wine", according to the winemaker)*
COLOUR: good ruby BOUQUET: closed
FLAVOUR: austere, good balance of acid and tannin, peppery finish.

La Nuit Volage *("20% Rioja with house wine")*
COLOUR: plum BOUQUET: closed
FLAVOUR: light Burgundy-style, dry, medium-weight, alcoholic finish.
(11%)

The St-Antoine-Abbé red I tasted was oxidized. The other dry offered is
Tourne Fête (11%)

Lubec Inc.,
St-Antoine
Abbé,
Québec,
Canada.

Servir
froid

Vin blanc
sec

11% alc./vol.
750 ml

Serve
chilled

Dry white
wine

LA **N**UIT **V**OLAGE

Blanc de Blanc

WHITE

★★**La Nuit Volage**   *(Greek)*
COLOUR: bright pale straw   BOUQUET: crisp, fresh
FLAVOUR: well-balanced with good acidity, clean finish. A well-made
   wine. (11%)

Other whites: Tourne Joie (11%) and Cuvée Ste. Clothilde (11%).

APERITIFS

Aperossimo   *(red; apple-based vermouth)*
COLOUR: brown-red   BOUQUET: sugar
FLAVOUR: sweet, herbal, not very well-knit. (16%)

Aperossimo   *(white)*
COLOUR: water-white   BOUQUET: undistinguished
FLAVOUR: overly flavoured with herbs, sweetish finish. (16%)

★**Aperossimo Moitié**
COLOUR: amber, touch of orange   BOUQUET: acceptable
FLAVOUR: better balanced, less sweet than Aperossimo, harmonious. (16%)

★★**Mundial**   *(Vermouth Cassis)*
A good black currant flavour well-blended into the cider base. An
interesting aperitif. (16%)

LA MAISON SECRESTAT LTEE

RED

Abbey Cellar *(Ruby Red Californian concentrate with 30% Cabernet Sauvignon with a further 30% blending wine)*
Company description—"a light bodied dry red table wine" (not tasted.)

Chambord
COLOUR: ruby, dull   BOUQUET: meaty nose
FLAVOUR: thick, substantial in the mouth, a nutty quality but soapy on the finish. (12%; litre carafon)

★**Servino**   *(similar blend to Abbey Cellar)*
COLOUR: light ruby   BOUQUET: a nose of wet branches, suggestive of Cabernet
FLAVOUR: a taste of elderberries but assertive acidity in the finish. A wine of some character, though. (11.5%)

WHITE

Chantilly   *(30% Californian French Colombard added to basic concentrate)*
COLOUR: yellow   BOUQUET: grassy nose
FLAVOUR: soft, bland, inoffensive; the nose promises more than the taste delivers. Tart finish. (12%; litre carafon)

Servino   *(30% Muscat-Riesling to the concentrate)*
COLOUR: straw   BOUQUET: sulfur on the nose, otherwise soft and neutral
FLAVOUR: not much; some residual acidity. (11.5%; litre)

ROSÉ

Pica   *(a blend of red and white wines carbonated to two atmospheres)*
COLOUR: attractive pink   BOUQUET: fresh, wholesome
FLAVOUR: slightly sweet, *petillant*, soft and plaint in the mouth, but finishes with alarming acidity. Basically synthetic and unstructured. (12%)

VERMOUTH

San Mareno   *(Extra Sec)*
A nose like Christmas pudding—tastes like it too, including the alcoholic burn in the finish. (16.5%)

San Mareno   *(Red)*
Sweet, burnt medicinal flavour. Unappealing. (16.5%)

Secrestat also makes a Sangria and a medium sweet sherry called
Granada.

LES VIGNOBLES CHANTECLER

RED

Cuvée Table Ronde
COLOUR: ruby   BOUQUET: meaty, spearmint nose
FLAVOUR: soft, overly sweet, lacks acid and tannin for backbone. (10%;
   litre)

★**Rossini**   *(Californian Ruby Cabernet, Italian Merlot plus filler from*
   Argentina)
COLOUR: ruby   BOUQUET: aged fruit
FLAVOUR: soft, rich, some residual sugar. Lacks the vitality of a Chianti
   which it tries to emulate. (11%; comes in a litre Chianti straw flask)
(Plaisir d'Amour is the same blend of grapes in a less prepossessing
combination.)

Other reds: La Belle Cour, Charlesbourg, Gargantua, Sillery and Le Bon Fut
(in 37 litre casks).

WHITE

Cuvée Table Ronde
COLOUR: straw   BOUQUET: sweet
FLAVOUR: fat, flabby, sweet, forgettable. (10%; litre)

Rêve d'Été
COLOUR: pale straw   BOUQUET: sulfur on the nose
FLAVOUR: sweet, light, little character, sulfur on the finish, too. (9%)

Other whites: Marée Haute, La Belle Cour, Le Bon Fut.

APERITIFS

Bellini   *(apple-based vermouth)*
COLOUR: tawny-brown   BOUQUET: herbal, sweet
FLAVOUR: sweet, syrupy, medicinal. (15.5%)
(Bellini Moitie-Moitie is less sweet and slightly more palatable. Chantecler makes this vermouth in red and white as well as a Cassis-flavoured beverage called 5 à 7.)

LES VIGNOBLES DU QUEBEC

RED

Petit Prince   *(Ruby Cabernet)*
COLOUR: light ruby   BOUQUET: perfumed cherry
FLAVOUR: soft, lightweight, hint of sweetness with some residual tannin.
   (11.5%)

Seigneur de Beaujeu
COLOUR: light ruby   BOUQUET: perfumed nose reminiscent of
   pomegranate
FLAVOUR: perfumed taste which lingers and cloys, lacking acidity and
   tannin to give it structure. (11.5%; screwtop, litre)

WHITE

★Petit Prince   *(French Colombard)*
COLOUR: pale gold   BOUQUET: grassy nose
FLAVOUR: full-bodied taste in the Californian Chablis mould, finishes
   well. (11%)

VIN GELOSO INC.

RED

Beausoleil
COLOUR: light inky ruby   BOUQUET: pomegranate
FLAVOUR: pugnacious, austere with a green finish. Surprisingly
   characterful for a wine of such light colour. Probably from young
   vines. (11%)

★★La Réserve à Vincent
COLOUR: brilliant ruby   BOUQUET: aged fruit and oak
FLAVOUR: soft, woody, dry with an elegant peppery finish. Very
   Italianate. (This wine is aged from 3 to 5 years in oak. The bottles are
   numbered.)

La Romaine
COLOUR: ruby   BOUQUET: spicy, dry
FLAVOUR: tough, tannic, green finish. (12%)

Other reds: Cuvée Rouge, Caberneaux, Haut Ste-Françoise, Réserve du
Patrimoine, La Bonne Carafe and Cuvée Village Rouge.

WHITE

Cuvée Blanc   *(Trebbiano grapes)*
COLOUR: straw   BOUQUET: closed sappy nose
FLAVOUR: dry and unyielding; a pursed-lipped, ungenerous wine with a
   tart finish. (11%)

★Entre deux Poissons
COLOUR: pale straw   BOUQUET: light, leafy nose
FLAVOUR: astringent, very crisp and dry with a volcanic quality of a
   Soave. (12%)

Lafleurie
COLOUR: deep straw   BOUQUET: unpleasant
FLAVOUR: unbalanced, semi-sweet. (12%)

★**Orfée Blanc**
COLOUR: straw   BOUQUET: fresh nose, crisp
FLAVOUR: well-balanced, light, green apple acidity in the finish. (11%)

Other whites: La Romaine, La Bonne Carafe and Cuvée Village Blanc.

SPARKLING

★**Brutus**   *(Charmat process)*
Dry, faintly metallic taste, good light flavour with some residual sugar and a clean finish. (9%)

Other sparklers: Gran Delizia (Asti Spumante-style Muscat), Baron Dry and Baron Brut (all Charmat method).

OTHER PRODUCTS

Fontanel Rosé and two Vermouths—Amoroso Rouge and Rosé.

LES VINS ANDRES DU QUEBEC LTEE

RED

★**Cuvée Vieux Marché**   *(Petite Sirah from California plus Ontario hybrids)*
COLOUR: purple   BOUQUET: dry grapiness on the nose
FLAVOUR: full-bodied, fruity, somewhat alcoholic. (11.5%)

Moulin Rouge   *(Californian Ruby Cabernet and De Chaunac)*
COLOUR: ruby-purple   BOUQUET: dried apricot nose
FLAVOUR: dry fruit taste, austere, touch of tannin in the finish. (11.5%)

★★**La Souvenance**   *(all Californian—Ruby Cabernet and Petite Sirah)*
COLOUR: purple, good depth   BOUQUET: fruity, intense
FLAVOUR: rich, full taste with a touch of tannin. (11.5%)

Other reds: Réserve de L'Aubergiste (litre bottles) and Auberge for the restaurant trade in 20-litre casks.

WHITE

Cuvée Vieux Marché   *(Californian French Colombard)*
COLOUR: pale straw   BOUQUET: sweet, candy-like
FLAVOUR: hint of red licorice in the taste; some acidity—more would be
   desirable. (11.5%)

Hochtaler   *(Californian French Colombard, Chenin Blanc with sweet
   reserve)*
COLOUR: almost water-white   BOUQUET: sweet floral
FLAVOUR: soft, fruity, grapey taste; lacks acidity. (11%)

★**Moulin Blanc**
COLOUR: straw   BOUQUET: faintly sweet, fruity
FLAVOUR: soft, gently fruity, easy-drinking. Could use more acid to
   balance the wine. (11%)

Other whites: like the reds—Réserve de L'Aubergiste (litres) and Auberge in
20-litre casks.

SPARKLING

Baby Duck   *(Ontario labruscas)*
COLOUR: orange-rose   BOUQUET: nebulous, hint of the pad filter used to
   polish and clarify
FLAVOUR: sweet, carbonated. (7%)

★**Chanté Blanc**   *(virtually all Ontario labruscas)*
COLOUR: water-white   BOUQUET: sweet, grapey
FLAVOUR: sweet labrusca, but honest and refreshing. (7%)

Richelieu Brut   *(100% Californian grapes—carbonated product)*
COLOUR: pale straw   BOUQUET: cardboard
FLAVOUR: thin with a dry, woody finish. (11%)

Other sparklers: Chanté Rosé, Sangria and Moody Blue in the 7%
sparkling wine category.

LES VINS BRIGHTS
LES VINS LASALLE

RED

L'Entre-Côte
COLOUR: light ruby   BOUQUET: very little
FLAVOUR: enough body and dry fruit flavour to lift it above the uninspiring. (11%)

Mon Village
COLOUR: garnet   BOUQUET: jammy nose
FLAVOUR: aged fruit taste, dry, interesting. (11%)

Notre Vin Maison
COLOUR: raspberry   BOUQUET: sweet nose
FLAVOUR: candied fruit, medium-weight, little behind the sweetness. A cunningly made wine, very soft and easy. (10%)

Papa Carlo
COLOUR: ruby   BOUQUET: dry old fruit with a hint of labrusca
FLAVOUR: heavy in the mouth, dry with a touch of residual sugar, acidic finish. Unknit. (12%)

Plaisir Divin
COLOUR: ruby   BOUQUET: aged fruit nose, oxidized
FLAVOUR: perfumed, slightly burnt taste, finishes short. (11%)

La Récolte de Chaunac
COLOUR: garnet   BOUQUET: raspberry jam
FLAVOUR: raspberry jam, linear taste, no highs, no lows. (11%)

Other reds: Griffon Rouge, Nouvelle France.

WHITE

★Baron Ludwig
COLOUR: straw   BOUQUET: clean, fruity nose
FLAVOUR: soft, full taste, clean finish, balanced. Sweetish Liebfraumilch style. Good value. (10.5%; screwtop)

L'Entre-Côte
COLOUR: straw   BOUQUET: touch of labrusca
FLAVOUR: dry, not much character, dull. (11%)

LiebesHeim
COLOUR: pale straw   BOUQUET: sweet acidic nose
FLAVOUR: bubble gum taste, soft, inoffensive, nothing to write home about. (11%)

Manoir St. David
COLOUR: straw   BOUQUET: labrusca nose
FLAVOUR: sweet rich grape and honey taste, heavy in the mouth. Almost
  a dessert wine but well-made, doesn't cloy. (11%; screwtop).

Mon Village
COLOUR: pale straw   BOUQUET: horse blanket nose
FLAVOUR: tart, thin, little fruit. Bland. (11%)

★**Notre Vin Maison**
COLOUR: pale straw   BOUQUET: French Colombard nose
FLAVOUR: slightly sweet, soft and round with a touch of acidity. A good
  commercial product. (10%)

Other whites: Sève d'Or, Griffon Blanc, Nouvelle France.

SPARKLING

Cresta Blanc Spumante Extra
COLOUR: pale straw   BOUQUET: labrusca nose
FLAVOUR: frothy, sweet, perfumed taste which fades quickly. (6.5%)

Dubarry Rosé D'Amour
COLOUR: pretty pink   BOUQUET: labrusca nose
FLAVOUR: medium dry Concord taste, carbonated. (6.5%)

LES VINS CORELLI

RED

★★**Castelnovo**   *(Montepulciano, Rabozza plus 5% Cabernet—all from
    Italy)*
COLOUR: ruby   BOUQUET: sappy
FLAVOUR: soft, fruity with an appealing acidity; Barolo in style. (11%)

WHITE

★**Entre Deux Pays**   *(Verduzzo grapes)*
COLOUR: pale straw   BOUQUET: crisp, stony
FLAVOUR: dry, Soave style, slightly smoky finish with a touch of sulfur.
    (11%)

SPARKLING

Gran Mousseux   *(Pinot Bianco grapes; Charmat process)*
COLOUR: straw   BOUQUET: yeasty, coarse
FLAVOUR: dry, slightly metallic. (11.5%)

OTHER PRODUCTS

Corelli also makes a rosé called Giovini from Italian grapes which is fresh and *petillant*.

ALBERTA

ANDREW WOLF WINE CELLARS

RED

Cabernet   *(Ruby Cabernet and Cabernet Sauvignon flash-frozen grapes)*
COLOUR: ruby   BOUQUET: acetone
FLAVOUR: medium-weight, soft with residual sugar, alcoholic finish.

Canadian Burgundy   *(Royalty, Cabernet and Gamay; four-year-old blend)*
COLOUR: ruby   BOUQUET: shy on the nose
FLAVOUR: baked taste, slight mustiness with a port-like finish.

Canadian Claret   *(Cabernet, Pinot Noir and Zinfandel; two-year-old blend)*
COLOUR: pale orange-ruby   BOUQUET: closed
FLAVOUR: light, dry, easy-drinking. Pleasant. (10%)

Gamay Beaujolais
COLOUR: ruby with a halo of mahogany   BOUQUET: shy
FLAVOUR: aged, very soft and round. Mature fruit taste, touch of sugar, well-balanced.

★Pinot Noir
COLOUR: good ruby   BOUQUET: tentative
FLAVOUR: soft with good fruit character and admirable length of finish. (10%)

Royalty   *(the port grape of California)*
COLOUR: rich ruby   BOUQUET: shy
FLAVOUR: fruity with a sweet porty taste. (10%)

Zinfandel
COLOUR: deep ruby   BOUQUET: alcohol
FLAVOUR: soft on the palate at first, with some residual sugar. It grows in the mouth to a tannic bite at the end. Somewhat clumsy. (11%)

ROSÉ

Grenache Rosé
COLOUR: pale pink   BOUQUET: a touch of sulfur
FLAVOUR: full, rich and soft. A big oaky, sweet rosé with a good acidic finish to clean it off. (10%)

WHITE

Canadian Chablis *(Chenin Blanc, Chasselas, Chardonnay)*
COLOUR: pale gold   BOUQUET: touch of sulfur
FLAVOUR: candy-like quality on the palate, light and soft; it could do
with more acidity. Hot finish. (11%)

Canadian Sauterne *(Riesling with 25% Chenin Blanc and 25%
Chardonnay)*
COLOUR: pale gold   BOUQUET: sweet
FLAVOUR: rich, full, medium sweet; rather flabby. Needs acidity for
backbone. (11%)

Chasselas
COLOUR: light gold   BOUQUET: closed
FLAVOUR: light character, slightly sawdust in taste. (10%)

Chenin Blanc
COLOUR: golden yellow   BOUQUET: earthy, oaky
FLAVOUR: good fruit and acid balance. Touch of residual sugar, soft on
the palate. (11%)

French Colombard
COLOUR: gold   BOUQUET: assertive floral nose
FLAVOUR: faintly oxidized, delicate with a good dry finish that keeps it
from cloying.

★**Golden Muscat**
COLOUR: gold   BOUQUET: delicate Muscat nose.
FLAVOUR: rich, full, perfumed in the mouth with lingering Muscat
   flavour, a touch of sweetness and a hint of oak. Well-made.

★**Pinot Chardonnay**
COLOUR: pale gold-straw   BOUQUET: delicate
FLAVOUR: good fruit character, soft and surprisingly fresh for three years
   in wood. Could do with a touch more acid for better balance.

Riesling
COLOUR: yellow gold   BOUQUET: fat Riesling nose
FLAVOUR: round somewhat flabby with residual sugar and noticeable
   alcohol in the finish. (11%)

Other whites: a light Chenin Blanc, Pinot Chardonnay and Riesling.

NOVA SCOTIA

GRAND PRÉ WINES

RED

*(These wines apart from the 1981 Maréchal Foch, were all tasted from
the barrel at the winery.)*

★★**Cuvée D'Amur 1980**   *(Michurnitz grape)*
COLOUR: deep ruby   BOUQUET: sandalwood and berries
FLAVOUR: big cedary taste, a flavour of strawberries, finishes dry with an
   appealing acidity. Like a Californian Zinfandel in character. Needs
   cellar age in bottle. (11.5%)

Cuvée D'Amur 1981   *(Michurnitz grape)*
COLOUR: dense, deep purple   BOUQUET: sappy, piney nose
FLAVOUR: big, oaky, full of tannin and acid. (12%)

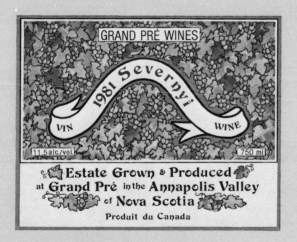

De Chaunac 1981
COLOUR: ruby   BOUQUET: good berry and oak nose
FLAVOUR: the fruit is overpowered by oak, high in acidity, touch of tannin. (11%)

Maréchal Foch 1980
COLOUR: deep ruby   BOUQUET: sappy, oaky nose
FLAVOUR: fruit character doesn't come through the oak, a woody taste with an acidic finish. Disappointing. (Aged 22 months in Slovanian oak.) (9.5%)

★Maréchal Foch 1981
COLOUR: deep purple   BOUQUET: sweet, oaky nose
FLAVOUR: medium-weight, light Foch character, oaky taste with a dry lemony finish. Again, the young Slovanian oak comes through to overpower the grape. (10.5%)

★Severnyi 1981
COLOUR: dense purple   BOUQUET: shaggy, black currant
FLAVOUR: low acidity but rich sweetness. A big, round woody wine, like a Zinfandel. Teeth-staining. (11.5%)

OTHER PRODUCTS

Grand Pré also markets L'Acadie Blanc and Rouge.

Glossary of Wine Tasting Terms

Over the years winemakers have developed a vocabulary of descriptive terms in an attempt to codify the highly subjective art of wine tasting. Trying to pin down and express to others the individual smell and flavour of a particular wine is perhaps the most difficult of all forms of communication: a bouquet that reminds someone of lychee nuts will smell like incense to someone else; or the odour of an old suitcase may translate itself in one person's smell-memory as the stink of a wet dog. However, there are certain terms which form the basis of all wine appreciation and I have listed them here. Sometimes it is impossible to express the olfactory sensation without reaching for an adjective which may seem odd. For instance, when I describe the nose of a wine as "shaggy", it has a particular meaning to me—slightly coarse or hairy but not necessarily offensive. For such flights of fancy I apologise, but in the end it is up to each taster to come to his or her own conclusions. If the language used to describe smell or taste means something to the taster, then that in the final analysis is enough. This glossary is merely a guide to your own enjoyment of wine.

ACETIC: A vinegary taste from acetic acid, usually denoting a wine that has begun to oxidize.

ACIDIC: A sharpness of taste from a preponderance of acidity. The right degree of acidity gives a wine freshness and crispness.

AFTERTASTE: The finish of a wine, what is left on the palate when you swallow. The best wines have a lingering taste if the sugars and acids are in balance.

AROMA: The scent of the grape in young wines as opposed to the bouquet, which is the smell of the wine.

ASTRINGENT: The sharp, strong tea taste left by undissolved tannins.

AUSTERE: Undeveloped, not showing its full character, especially on the nose.

BAKED: A hot taste, usually from red wines grown in hot climates where the grapes may become toasted in the sun.

BALANCE: A harmonious blend of all the elements in a wine—sugars, acids, tannins and alcohol—where no single element predominates.

BOUQUET: The fragrance of the wine once it has been fermented and begins to mature.

BODY: The weight of the wine in the mouth. A full-bodied wine has weight and substance and can be termed "chewy". The greater the alcohol the fuller the wine, particularly those grown in hot climates.

CHARACTER: As in people, a distinctive unmistakable quality as in the bouquet of Muscat or Gewurztraminer.

CLOYING: A sweetness that lingers on the palate because of an acid deficiency, making the wine heavy and unappealing.

CLEAN: Fresh and true without any off odours or flavours.

COMPLEX: A variety of perfumes and subtle taste changes found only in the best wines.

CORKED: A wine that has gone off, generally because of oxidation. Can also refer to the effect of a diseased cork which infects the taste of the wine and its bouquet. One sniff of the cork will tell you.

DRY: The absence of sugar, although a totally dry wine would be undrinkable. Dry refers to wines with less than 1% residual sugar.

EARTHY: The suggestion of the soil in which the grapes were grown.

FINESSE: Breeding, a certain elegance of style.

FINISH: The impression of taste left in the mouth. The best wines have a long finish.

FLINTY: A dry, stony taste—crisp, usually descriptive of young white wines, such as Chablis or Loire wines. The smell of flints struck together.

FLOWERY: The impression of flowers, as in Rieslings.

FRUITY: The fruit flavour you get from young wines when they are fresh.

FOXY: The aroma and bouquet of Labrusca varieties like Concord. A grape juice smell which pervades the flavour as well.

GRAPEY: The heavy grape smell from certain varieties like Muscat.

GREEN: The taste and bouquet of unripe grapes from unconverted acids.

HARD: A wine with undissolved tannins, most frequently in reds which need bottle age to soften up. Excess acidity can also be a factor.

LIGHT: A wine of low acidity that lacks body. Not necessarily a criticism unless the style of the wine suggests more generosity.

LUSCIOUS: For sweet dessert wines, a honeyed, rich, ripe quality.

MADERIZED: A flat, metallic taste in white wine that has begun to oxidize. The colour will suggest this taste (of Madeira) when it turns brownish.

MEATY: For red wines—full-bodied, powerful, chewy.

MUSTY: A mouldy or dusty nose or flavour which suggests unclean casks or rotten grapes.

OXIDIZED: The effect of too much air on a wine, prematurely aging it.

PETILLANT: The presence of some residual carbon dioxide in a wine giving it a faint sparkle that is detectable on the tongue.

RAISINY: The odour and taste of sun-dried grapes usually from hot climates.

RIPE: A wine at its peak of maturity, mellow and full-blown.

ROBUST: A big, full-bodied wine high in alcohol yet well-rounded.

RUBBERY: A fault evident on the nose—the smell of old tires.

SAPPY: A quality wines inherit from new oak barrels.

SHARP: A high degree of acidity which renders the wine tart.

SILKY: A softness of feel on the palate, especially evident in mature fine red Burgundy.

SOFT: Mellow, well-rounded. But could be a pejorative term for lack of backbone provided by alcohol and acidity.

SPICY: A predominating perfume and taste of herbs, especially from the Gewurztraminer grape.

SPRITZIG: The German term for a wine with a faint sparkle. The Italian equivalent is *frizzante*. The French is *petillant* (see).

STEMMY: The influence of stalks on the odour and taste of a wine, imparting a woodiness or green taste.

SWEET: The presence of unconverted sugars in wine, desirable for certain styles (i.e., dessert wines). Sweetness is only a virtue when it is well balanced with acidity and alcohol. Wines can be artificially sweetened by the addition of sweet reserve (unfermented grape juice).

TANNIN: An essential element in wine to give it long life. Tannins exist in the skins, pips and stalks of the grapes and can be introduced by fermenting or aging in oak barrels. Tannins in young red wines can be harsh and unpleasant but will soften out with bottle age. Old red wines precipitate their tannins as a deposit in the bottle and should be decanted.

TARTARIC ACID: One of four basic acids in grapes but the most important in its concentration and effect. It gives the wine a fresh, crisp taste. The other acids are malic, citric and ascorbic. Tartaric acid can precipitate as crystals if the wine is chilled too low but these do not affect its taste.

WELL-BALANCED: The best compliment one can pay a wine—all the elements are in harmony: fruit, tannins, alcohol and acidity.

WOODY: The taste of the barrel in which the wine has been aged. A detrimental flavour. Not to be confused with oaky which can be a virtue if not excessive.

YEASTY: The smell of fermented yeast in young wines which will disappear within a matter of months after fermentation. This smell is most noticeable in young champagnes once they have undergone a secondary fermentation.

Glossary of Terms

Auslese: German wine term meaning the selection of especially ripe grapes of high sugar content, designating a sweet wine.

Botrytis: A beneficial mould which attacks the skin of ripening grapes particularly in the Sauternes region of France and the Rhine Valley. The effect is to concentrate the sugars and flavour. The resulting dessert wine has a honeyed sweetness.

Brix: Scale used in North America to measure the approximate sugar content of grapes before fermentation. One degree Brix translates roughly to half a degree of alcohol after fermentation.

Carbonic Masceration: A winemaking technique by which the grapes are not crushed but are allowed to ferment in a closed vat without air inside their skins before a light pressing.

Champagne Method: The process by which a still wine is allowed to referment in a sealed bottle to become a sparkling wine. The secondary fermentation is achieved by the addition of sugar and yeast and the resulting carbon dioxide gas is trapped in the wine.

Charmat Process: A cheaper method of producing sparkling wine in bulk. The secondary fermentation takes place in large sealed stainless steel tanks. The wine is subsequently bottled under pressure; but it lacks the finesse of the Champagne Method (see). Also called Cuve close.

Continuous Still: A patent still invented in 1830 by Aeneas Coffey for the distillation of neutral spirits. The tall column rectifies the alcohol as it separates from water. Used in the production of gin and vodka. The copper pot still, with its distinctive goose neck, is used to distill cognac, some armagnacs and the better fruit brandies since it retains the aromas of the original liquid.

Cooperage: A term applied to a winery's wooden casks, vats or barrels, which are usually oak. The man who makes and maintains the barrels is called a cooper.

Crown Caps: Closures for carbonated drinks. Used in the production of champagne during the secondary fermentation in bottle before disgorging (see) after which a mushroom-shaped cork is inserted.

Cultivar: The basic stock of any grape variety.

Decolourization: The technique of producing white wine from red grapes. Only colourless juice is used and no skin contact allowed.

Disgorging: The act of removing the sediment from the secondary fermentation of sparkling wine in bottles. The dead yeast cells are collected on
the closure by a process known as riddling (see) and the unwanted
matter is ejected by the pressure in the bottle when the closure is
removed. The bottle is then topped up with fresh, sweetened wine and
corked.

Esters: The action of acids and alcohol form volatile and neutral esters which
have a sweet, fruity aroma and form part of the wine's bouquet.

Fermentation: The process by which grape sugar is converted into alcohol
and carbon dioxide by the action of yeast. Grape juice can be
fermented in wood, glass, stainless steel or concrete tanks. Fermentation is carried on until virtually all the sugars are converted into alcohol
unless a sweet wine is wanted. Modern wineries prefer stainless steel
because they can control the temperature of the fermentation and
ensure that no air gets into the must (that is, the juice or the crushed
grapes). A neutral container such as stainless steel, concrete or glass
retains the freshness and the fruitiness of the wine. Fermentation or
aging in wood imparts certain flavours and tannins, particularly to red
wines, softening the acids and rounding out the flavour.

Flor: A white yeasty film or "flower" that develops on the surface of certain
wines when exposed to air, particularly Spanish sherries. Its presence
ensures the wine will be very dry. Flor can be artificially inoculated to
create a fino or dry sherry.

Free Run Juice: The best juice for winemaking; it runs from grapes crushed
by their own weight or with a light pressing.

Hybrid: The grapes that develop when two varieties are genetically crossed
to incorporate the best qualities of different parent vines. Hybridization
is carried out to improve flavour, disease resistance and winter
hardiness. Hybrids are generally named after the person who developed them and bear a code number such as Vidal 256, created by J.L.
Vidal.

Labrusca: A native North American vine species whose grapes have a "foxy"
flavour and aroma. Very winter hardy and prolific. The best known are
Concord and Niagara.

Late Harvest: Grapes which have been left on the vine to accumulate the
maximum amount of sugar before being picked.

Millipore Filter: A membrane filtre invented in Germany and used in the
Second World War to purify water supplies. An American soldier
"liberated" one of the machines, brought it back to the States and went
into the business of manufacturing them for the wine industry. Before
this filter was available to prevent bacteria from getting into the bottles,
the shelf life of most grape fermented products was very limited.

Mousse: The French term for the bubbling action in sparkling wines.

Must: Freshly pressed juice or crushed grapes.

Oenologist: Oenology is the science of wine—its vinification and preservation. An oenologist is a technician who has studied the subject and gained a diploma in the discipline.

Residual Sugar: The amount of sugar left in a wine when the yeast is no longer powerful enough to convert it to alcohol or its action has been stopped by the addition of sulfur or grape spirit.

Riddling Process: The method used to clarify champagne. The dead yeast cells are collected in the neck of the bottle after secondary fermentation. The riddler gives each bottle a shake and a light turn daily, tilting it upwards in the rack over a period of three or four months. Eventually all the debris collects against the crown cap and will be removed by disgorging (see). The French call it *remuage*. An experienced *remueur* can turn, shake and tilt sixty bottles in a minute. This labour-intensive action is slowly being taken over by machines in the large sparkling wine houses.

Secondary Fermentation: The natural process which gives the wine its sparkle since the carbon dioxide cannot escape and is dissolved into the wine.

Solera System: A method developed in Spain for the progressive maturation and blending of fortified wines. The wines are barrelled in racks, the oldest at the bottom graduating to the youngest on the top. Each year one-third of the oldest wine is drawn off and the barrels are topped up from those above with new wine being introduced into the top line of casks.

Sweet Reserve: The addition of unfermented grape juice or concentrate prior to bottling to give a balance of sweetness and acidity to white wines.

Tartrates: Harmless crystals known as "wine diamonds" in the trade. They can form a deposit in white wines particularly if the bottle is chilled too much. They might spoil the appearance of the wine but not its flavour or health. Most producers will extract tartrates by chilling their wine before bottling.

Varietal: A wine made from a single grape type which will bear its name on the label. In Ontario, to qualify as a varietal, the wine must contain at least 75% of the variety designated on the label.

Vinifera: The best wine grapes of European varieties, such as Chardonnay, Riesling, Sauvignon Blanc, Gewurztraminer, Gamay, Cabernet Sauvignon, Pinot Noir and Merlot.

Vintage: The wine of a single year as designated on the label or neck label. Under Ontario wine regulations the wine must have at least 85% of the wine originating from the year stated on the bottle.

Viticulture: The science and art of grape growing.

Vitis: The Latin name for vine, usually in conjunction with a particular species—i.e., Vitis vinifera.

Bibliography

Adams, Leon D. *The Wines of America*. Houghton Mifflin. (Boston, 1973).

Bespaloff, Alexis. *The Fireside Book of Wine*. Simon and Schuster. (New York, 1977).

Butler, Frank Hedges. *Wine and the Wine Lands of the World*, T. Fisher Unwin. (London, 1926).

de Courtenay, J.M. *The Culture of the Vine and Emigration*. Joseph Davreau. (Quebec, 1863).

Doxat, John. *The World of Drinks and Drinking*. The Cookery Book Club. (London, 1971).

Forbes, Patrick. *Champagne, The Wine, the Land and the People*, Gollancz. (London, 1967).

Frumkin, Lionel. *The Science and Technique of Wine*. Patrick Stephens. (Cambridge, England, 1974).

Hallowell, G. *Prohibition in Ontario*. Love Printing Service. (Ottawa, 1972).

Johnson, Hugh. *The World Atlas of Wine*, Mitchell Beazley. (London, 1971).

Lichine, Alexis. *Encyclopedia of Wines and Spirits*. Cassell. (London, 1976).

Marrison, L.W. *Wines and Spirits*. Penguin (London, 1973).

Massee, William E. *Wines of America*. McCall Publishing Company. (New York, 1970).

Masson, Georges. *Wine From Ontario Grapes*. G. Masson. (St. Catharines, Ontario, 1979).

Menzies, Mr. *The Beaconsfield Vineyard*. Joseph Nelson Jnr., General Agent. (Montreal, 1880).

Morison, Samuel Eliot. *The European Discovery of America*. Oxford University Press. (New York, 1971).

Newman, Peter. *The Bronfman Dynasty*. McClelland & Stewart. (Toronto, 1978).

Peller, Andrew. *The Winemaker*. Alfin Publishers. (Toronto, 1982).

Penning-Rowsell, Edmund. *The Wines of Bordeaux*. Penguin. (London, 1973).

Prial, Frank J. *Wine Talk*. Times Books. (New York, 1978).

Rannie, William F. *The Wines of Ontario*. W.F. Rannie. (Lincoln, Ontario, 1978).

Reid, John. *LCBO Wines and Spirits Guidebook*. Greey de Pencier. (Toronto, 1978).

_____. *ALCB Wines and Spirits Guidebook*. Greey de Pencier. (Toronto, 1976).

Rowe, Percy. *Red, White and Rosé*. Musson/General. (Toronto, 1978).

_____. *The Wines of Canada*. McGraw-Hill. (Toronto, 1970).

Saintsbury, George. *Notes On a Cellarbook*. Macmillan. (London, 1920).

Schoonmaker, Frank. *Encyclopedia of Wine*. A & C Black. (London, 1975).

_____. *The Wines of Germany*. (Revised by Peter Sichel.) Hastings House. (New York, 1980).

Sharp, Andrew. *Vineland 1000*. Andrew Sharp Publications. (Toronto, 1977).

_____. *Winetaster's Secrets*. Horizon. (Toronto, 1981).

Sichel, Peter and Allen, Judy Ley. *Which Wine?*. A & W Visual Library. (New York, 1977).

Simon, André. *The Commonsense of Wine*. Bonanza Books. (New York, 1964).

Wagner, Phillip M. *Grapes Into Wine*, Alfred A. Knopf. (New York, 1976).

_____. *American Wines and How to Make Them*, Alfred A. Knopf. (New York, 1936).

Younger, William. *Gods, Men and Wine*, The Wine & Food Society. (London, 1966).

Yoxall, H.W. *The Wines of Burgundy*. Penguin. (London, 1974).

Varietal Index

(wines of a single grape type listed by winery)

ALIGOTÉ:
Chateau des Charmes (Ont.) pp. 143-44.

AUXERROIS:
Andres (BC) p. 169.
Chateau des Charmes p. 144.
Gray Monk (BC) p. 179.

BACO NOIR:
Brights (Ont.) p. 136.
Charal (Ont.) p. 140.
London (Ont.). p. 164.

CABERNET SAUVIGNON:
Andres (BC) p. 169.
Chateau des Charmes (Ont.) p. 142.
Jordan Ste-Michelle (BC)—not tasted.
Mission Hill (BC) p. 182.

CHAMBURCIN:
Inniskillin (Ont.) p. 156.

CHANCELLOR:
Sumac Ridge (BC) p. 185.

CHARDONNAY (Pinot):
Andres (Ont.) p. 131.
Andrew Wolf (Alberta) p. 202.
Brights (Ont.) p. 138.
Casabello (BC) p. 177.
Charal (Ont.) p. 141.
Chateau des Charmes (3) (Ont.) p. 144.
Chateau-Gai (Ont.) p. 149.
Inniskillin (2) (Ont.) p. 157.
Jordan (Ont.) p. 162.
Newark (Hillebrand Estates) (Ont.) p. 154.

CHASSELAS:
Andrew Wolf (Alberta) p. 201.
Uniacke (BC) p. 186.

CHELOIS:
Inniskillin (Ont.) p. 156.

CHENIN BLANC:
Calona (BC) p. 173.
Casabello (BC) p. 176.
Jordan Ste-Michelle (BC) p. 180.
Mission Hill (BC) p. 183.
Sumac Ridge (BC) p. 185.
Uniacke (BC) p. 186.

DE CHAUNAC:
(Red)
Grand Pré (N.S.) p. 203.
London (Ont.) p. 165.
Mission Hill (BC) p. 184.
Montravin (Podamer) (Ont.) p. 168.

(White)
Andres (Ont.) p. 130.

(Rosé)
Colio ("Rosato") (Ont.) p. 152.

LEON MILLOT:
Inniskillin (Ont.) p. 156.

MARÉCHAL FOCH:
Brights (Ont.) p. 136.
Calona (BC) p. 172.
Charal (Ont.) p. 140.
Chateau-Gai (Ont.) p. 147.
Claremont (BC) p. 178.
Colio (Ont.) p. 152.
Grand Pré (N.S.) p. 203.
Inniskillin (Ont.) p. 152.

g